The Only Hope of the World

George Bernard Shaw and Russia

Olga Soboleva and Angus Wrenn

PETER LANG

Oxford • Bern • Berlin • Bruxelles • Frankfurt am Main • New York • Wien

Bibliographic information published by Die Deutsche Nationalbibliothek
Die Deutsche Nationalbibliothek lists this publication in the Deutsche Nationalbibliografie;
detailed bibliographic data is available on the Internet at http://dnb.d-nb.de.

A catalogue record for this book is available from the British Library.

Library of Congress Cataloging-in-Publication Data:

Soboleva, Olga, 1959-
 The only hope of the world : George Bernard Shaw and Russia / Olga
Soboleva and Angus Wrenn.
    p. cm.
 Includes bibliographical references and index.
 ISBN 978-3-0343-0745-1 (alk. paper)
 1. Shaw, Bernard, 1856-1950--Knowledge--Russia. 2. Shaw, Bernard,
1856-1950--Appreciation--Russia. 3. English literature--Irish
authors--Russian influences. I. Wrenn, Angus James. II. Title.
 PR5368.R87S63 2012
 822'.912--dc23

                    2012020026

Cover image: A photograph of George Bernard Shaw taken shortly after his trip to the
USSR (1932). LSE Archives (with the permission of the Society of Authors).

ISBN 978-3-0343-0745-1

Peter Lang AG, International Academic Publishers, Bern 2012
Hochfeldstrasse 32, CH-3012 Bern, Switzerland
info@peterlang.com, www.peterlang.com, www.peterlang.net

The Only Hope of the World

Contents

List of Figures   vii

Preface by Professor Leonee Ormond   ix

Acknowledgements   xi

Introduction   1

CHAPTER ONE

Admirals and Amiable Gentlemen: Shaw and the Russian Anarchists   11

CHAPTER TWO

'All Art at the Fountainhead Is Didactic': Shaw and Lev Tolstoy   41

CHAPTER THREE

'A Fantasia in the Russian Manner': Shaw and Maxim Gorky   73

CHAPTER FOUR

'Mr Shaw Has Always Had a Weakness for Shrews':
Shaw and *Annajanska, the Bolshevik Empress*   101

CHAPTER FIVE

'Russia Is All Right and We Are All Wrong':
Shaw's Trip to the USSR   135

CHAPTER SIX
'Dear Liar': Shaw's Last Plays   175

Bibliography   213

Index   227

List of Figures

Figure 1 'Old revolutionists in England' – prominent members of 'The
Friends of Russian Freedom' (1890), on whose committee
Shaw served for some twenty years (Stepniak-Kravchinskii,
Tchaikovskii, Lazarov, Volkhovskii, Shishkov and Mrs Stepniak).
LSE Archives.   16

Figure 2 A drawing of Sergius Stepniak-Kravchinskii by Bernard Shaw
himself (c. 1890).   18

Figure 3 Catherine the Great portrayed in the costume of the Preobrazhenskii Guard by Vigilius Erichsen (c. 1762). The State
Hermitage Museum, St Petersburg.   106

Figure 4 Prince Peter Kropotkin, prominent émigré Russian anarchist and
a friend of Shaw for over thirty years, with his daughter Sasha.   109

Figure 5 Bernard Shaw given a highly orchestrated mass greeting upon
his arrival by train in Moscow, July 1931. LSE Archives.   148

Figure 6 Bernard Shaw with Lady Nancy Astor and Russian communists,
Moscow 1931 (from left to right: Karl Radek, Anatolii Luna-
charskii, Lady Nancy Astor, Bernard Shaw, Artemii Khalatov).
LSE Archives.   150

Figure 7 Bernard Shaw on his Moscow trip 1931, meeting Anatolii Lunacharskii and Konstantin Stanislavskii. LSE Archives.   150

Figure 8 Sergei F. Sokolov and George Bernard Shaw visiting a Moscow
factory (1937, oil on canvas).   151

Figure 9 'Bernard Shaw on the USSR: the English bourgeoisie is extremely
shawcked', Moscow News, 8 August 1931.   160

Figure 10 A Soviet postal stamp, issued for the centenary of Bernard Shaw
(1956).   177

Figure 11 A scene from Jerome Kilty's play Dear Liar (based on Shaw's
letters to Mrs Patrick Campbell), which has run on the Russian
stage for half a century (Mossovet Theatre production, 1963, Shaw
– Rostislav Pliatt, Mrs Patrick Campbell – Liubov' Orlova).   210

Preface

George Bernard Shaw was the leading British playwright in the first decades of the twentieth century. His plays were often revived, well into the mid-century and later, and, at the time of his death in 1950, he was a famous, if eccentric, figure. His belief in social change was well known, but his exact political stance has baffled many. How could a leading writer, the question is, admire a ruthless dictator like Stalin? This book sets out to answer some of the questions by giving a full account of Shaw's long love-affair with Russia.

Shaw was not, of course, alone in this fascination. Virginia Woolf, with whom he had little else in common, was much influenced by Russian literature, reading Tolstoy and Chekhov in translations by Shaw's friend, Constance Garnett. Among Woolf's fellow members of the Bloomsbury Group were devotees of Serge Diaghilev's Ballets Russes which took London by storm in 1909–1911. Shaw read widely in Tolstoy and Chekhov, and also in the works of Maxim Gorky. The influence of Chekhov on Shaw's *Heartbreak House* of 1919 has often been discussed, but the central issue under discussion here is less one of literary associations than of political effect. How did Shaw's reaction to events in Russia affect his work? There are full discussions here of Shaw's response to the work of Tolstoy and Gorky, with special reference to the effect of Gorky's play *Summerfolk*, another work with marked similarities to *Heartbreak House*. Shaw never met Tolstoy, who felt that Shaw's satirical style was ill chosen for serious issues, and who also sought a religious solution, something alien to the Irish writer. Shaw *did* meet Gorky, during one of the Russian writer's visits to England, and the two men continued to correspond.

Shaw was among those who greeted the Russian revolution of 1917 with enthusiasm, an enthusiasm which, in his case, never died. He believed that Russia had set an example for the rest of the world, and neither the savage treatment of opponents, nor of the Tsar and his family, changed his mind.

The response is clear in some of his later plays, although it has to be said that these are among his less popular works. One chapter of this book looks closely at *Annajanska, the Bolshevik Empress*, first performed in January 1918. In this little-known short drama, a daughter of the house of Romanov takes up arms with revolutionaries and becomes a leader. The authors show how the play relates to Shaw's earlier drama, *Great Catherine* of 1913, where the subject is Catherine the Great. They also relate *Annajanska* to the far better known *St Joan* of 1923, comparing these three studies of strong female personalities. The case is not straightforward, however, as the book shows. Shaw is, as so often, making it clear that he admires a strong leader. He may have been a pacifist and a believer in social reform, but he was certainly not a believer in democracy.

The central event under discussion here is Shaw's visit to Russia in 1931. This has always been regarded as an extraordinary expedition, but in fact, Shaw had been delaying for years. The usual reaction is to believe that a clever and independent man was hoodwinked by the Soviet authorities. From the analysis of the events given here, it would seem that the episode was, once again, rather more complex than has been supposed. The authors have gathered together all available information, including the striking facts that Stalin spent two hours with Shaw, when most audiences were no more than twenty minutes, and that the Russians paid him substantial royalties, something which rarely happened to foreign authors. This book also introduces the play, *Fourteen Little Red Huts* of 1932, by Andrei Platonov, which parodies the enthusiastic reception of Shaw, and which the authors of this volume have themselves staged with considerable success.

One of the strengths of this book lies in bringing together Olga Soboleva's knowledge of Russian history and writing and Angus Wrenn's expertise in the study of the literature of the late nineteenth and early twentieth centuries. Both writers are on the staff of the London School of Economics, which has a special relationship with Shaw, one of its founders. They have written a highly entertaining and informative book, which leaves the reader to struggle with the unanswerable question. Was Shaw simply being obstinate, or did he really believe that Stalin was a liberator?

— PROFESSOR LEONEE ORMOND

Acknowledgements

We are particularly grateful to Graham Camfield at the London School of Economics (LSE) Library for his erudition in this field and continuous support of our research over a number of years, as well as to Imogene Mackay, who provided crucial expertise with archival materials. We are extremely grateful to the Director of the LSE Language Centre Nick Byrne for enabling this project to come to fruition and to Professor Leonee Ormond, an authority on Shaw, who has kindly written the preface and supported us at all stages. In working on the manuscript, we owe many debts to Professor Robin Milner-Gulland and Alex Sobolev for taking time to read the drafts and for the most useful suggestions that they made. We are also grateful for the opportunity we have had to discuss the project with Professor Patrick Wright, doyen of Iron Curtain scholars.

We also offer thanks to the following people and institutions for assisting us while we were at work on this project: the British Library, the London Library, the State Archive of the Russian Federation (in particular to Nina Abdulaeva and Alexei Trefakhin), LSE Archives, Professor Julian Graffy, Richard Ormond, Natalia Abozina, Dr Caroline Corbeau-Parsons, and the late Dr Frank Lappin. Finally, we would like to express our appreciation to Jack Blumenau, Russell Banfi, Rahim Rahemtulla and Cameron Paige, who played an instrumental role in our rediscovery of Shaw's *Annajanska, the Bolshevik Empress*.

Introduction

This book grew out of a small exhibition on Shaw's trip to the USSR, which we curated at the London School of Economics, an institution founded in 1895 by his fellow Fabians Beatrice and Sidney Webb, who also shared his enthusiasm for the Soviet Union. Research on the separate trips which Shaw and the Webbs made there in the 1930s led in turn to the realization that Shaw's continued interest in Russia in fact went back several decades into the nineteenth century, and it soon became clear that the Russian and Soviet dimension had an important bearing upon the development of Shaw's career, which was ripe for retelling in a post-Soviet era.

At the time of writing, in the early twenty-first century, George Bernard Shaw enjoys a positive reputation, even if he is generally regarded as being a little too remote in period – he was after all born as long ago as 1856 – to be considered an altogether twentieth-century figure and a major influence upon the drama of the present day. A generation older than his fellow Dubliner, James Joyce, Shaw was nearing seventy when *Ulysses* was published and modernism the order of the day. Shaw may be as didactic and politically engaged as Bertolt Brecht, who indeed responded to *Saint Joan* with a play of his own, *Saint Joan of the Stockyards*, yet Shaw's drama seems to belong more to the nineteenth than the twentieth century. His most celebrated work remains that which was – save for the vital element of his own inimitable wit, which is capable of rivalling Oscar Wilde's – closest in essence to the 'debate play' or 'discussion play' inaugurated by Ibsen as long ago as the 1870s. *Mrs Warren's Profession*, *Arms and the Man*, *Major Barbara* and above all *Pygmalion* remain the plays most frequently revived, with only altogether less frequent productions of *Heartbreak House* and *Saint Joan* to reveal that Shaw was capable of a wider range of forms and moods. If most of his work (he wrote more plays than Shakespeare) is now unperformed Shaw nevertheless enjoys continuing fame, probably in large measure thanks to the film of *Pygmalion* and the play's adaptation as a hit musical *My Fair Lady*, the latter a development since the playwright's death, and one which he blocked during his lifetime.

Author of the work which inspired one of the most successful musicals since World War II, Shaw is not today commonly regarded as in any way 'dangerous'. The tendency to romanticize the biting social satire in this work began with its first London production by Beerbohm Tree in 1914 (and provoked the playwright's ire). The re-branding of Shaw as a playwright safe for use in mainstream musicals and operettas, initiated by Oscar Straus's *Der tapfere Soldat* (*The Chocolate Soldier*, 1908), which so disappointed Shaw that he banned further such adaptations during his lifetime, would seem to have been accomplished.

The fact that Shaw in the above plays either celebrates the unheroic male (Bluntschli in *Arms and the Man*) or satirizes the traditional man of action (Sergius in the same play) is easily elided with Shaw's vaunted pacifism. Here, after all, is a playwright who bravely insisted upon pacifism in his pamphlet 'Commonsense about the War', published in 1915, when other writers such as Rudyard Kipling were active in the recruitment drive which led to the debacle in the trenches on the Western Front. Here too is a writer, himself an Irish immigrant who had left school at fifteen and had never fitted easily into polite London society (Henry James referred to him as 'that unspeakable Irishman'[1]), who seemed ready to take the side of the New Woman seeking emancipation (Vivie in *Mrs Warren's Profession*) and by the same token appreciated the social exclusion experienced by a lowly Covent Garden flower-seller. Shaw, it is perhaps popularly assumed, must have been on the side of the common man or common woman, against the repressive forces of privilege. Surely a play which demonstrates that a girl from the street can be passed off as a polite lady of impeccable pedigree at an ambassadorial reception must be based upon a sense of the universal worth of ordinary people.

Concentration upon the canonical, frequently revived plays, all written by the early 1920s, however masks major developments which took place in the 1920s and 1930s. Even before this, Shaw gave evidence of his

---

1   Quoted in Christopher Fitz-Simon, 'Shaw, George Bernard', in Colin Chambers, ed., *Continuum Companion to Twentieth Century Theatre* (New York: Continuum Press, 2002), 685.

growing interest in Russian history, with his short play *Great Catherine*, written in 1913, which presents, in the guise of a supposedly historical setting and involving figures from history such as Prince Potemkin, another opportunity to return to the idea of the powerful, assertive female figure, this time by reference to Catherine the Great. The outbreak of the First World War initially filled Shaw with a horror which he was rare in daring to express at the time. He was to be vilified for his views by the popular press, being caricatured in cartoons wearing the Iron Cross, and even his lifelong friends and closest political allies, Beatrice and Sidney Webb, declined to publish his proposed sequel to the 1915 pamphlet intended to be called 'More Commonsense about the War'. Within theatrical circles, Shaw, by far the most successful playwright in English by this date, found himself shunned. The playwright Henry Arthur Jones, hitherto an ally, saw fit to declare Shaw 'an enemy within our walls' on the strength of his pacifist views as well as his support for Irish self-determination.

The aftermath of the war which Shaw had done so much to oppose brought about a profound change in the public stance taken by this most politically engaged of playwrights. Although the statements which he made in the later 1920s do not relate to Shaw's greatest work (*Saint Joan* had already been written by 1923) they nonetheless have implications which demand a re-examination of the stance Shaw is on record as having actually taken at various junctures earlier in his career, in some cases as far back as the 1880s. From the end of the First World War Shaw had been frequently voicing his grave disappointment with the compromises which were, in his view, fatally to mar the Treaty of Versailles and also, from the mid 1920s, expressing enthusiasm for the dictators beginning to emerge in European politics. In many ways the culmination of these statements in favour of totalitarianism rather than the established order of western European democratic regimes was Shaw's controversial 1931 trip to the Soviet Union, when as recipient of the 1925 Nobel Prize for Literature he was feted as an internationally celebrated engagé socialist writer, and given an audience with Joseph Stalin himself. Yet the visit is only the most tangible and obvious sign of an interest in Russian culture which by then went back half a century. Shaw on arrival in London in 1876 had proceeded to mix with circles frequented by Russian and other Slav émigrés, and his own engagement in their political cause, as radical revolutionaries in exile from repressive tsarism, is shown by his regular membership of the Friends of Russian Freedom, set up by his friend Annie Besant, and activities on their behalf over a period of more than twenty years.

Foreign interest in Russia was at this time by no means confined to a small clique of political activists. From the 1890s, Dostoevskii's work, often in English translation by Shaw's friends the Garnetts, as well as the works of Tolstoy (with whom Shaw had a significant correspondence in his final years), had begun to exert a hold upon the imagination of literary circles in western Europe. Aylmer Maude, Tolstoy's English translator, served on Fabian committees with Shaw, and in this period experimental 'Tolstoyan' communities, based on Tolstoy's own collectivist principles, British counterparts of the Russian Dukhobors, were established in Britain, often among the same social circles with whom Shaw mixed in the Fabian Society. From the turn of the century, too, Chekhov's plays, and still more so his short stories, became influential on prominent practitioners of the form, such as Katherine Mansfield. Russia was perceived by those like Mansfield's friend D.H. Lawrence, who railed against the excessive urban sophistication of Western culture, as a refreshing breath of the authentically natural and even primeval. Rupert Brooke's comment to Edward Marsh, on viewing Diaghilev's Ballets Russes in 1912: 'They, if anything, can redeem our civilization. I'd give everything to be a ballet designer,'[2] is representative of a view which became pervasive. Stravinskii's ballets *The Firebird*, *Petrushka* and *The Rite of Spring*, all drawing upon Russian folklore, revolutionized music, while the influence of a comparable primitivism is to be found in Matisse's monumental painting, *La Danse*, which was immediately bought up by the Russian collector Shchukin, recognizing the common culture. Shaw's friend J.M. Barrie wrote *The Truth about the Russian Dancers*. Shaw echoes Brooke's comment when he himself remarks: 'this strange intensive culture of the Russian soul, which makes all our Western souls seem vulgar in comparison.'[3]

2   Quoted in Modris Eksteins, *Rites of Spring: The Great War and the Birth of the Modern Age* (New York: Mariner Books, 1989), 26.
3   Bernard Shaw, Letter to Maxim Gorky, 28 December 1915, *Bernard Shaw Collected Letters*, Dan H. Laurence, ed. (London: Max Reinhardt, 1965–1988), vol. 3, 343.

While it is important to appreciate that Shaw's interest in Russia was by no means a solitary fixation but developing in an era of what might at its height even be termed a widespread 'Russia mania', the same can also in a considerable degree be said of Shaw's interest in the fledgling Soviet Union. His visit there in 1931 was far from the first to be made by a British intellectual, but had a number of important precedents. It might even be argued that the fact that Shaw took over a dozen years before setting foot on Russian soil suggests a certain reluctance on his part. Meanwhile other writers had preceded him. Somerset Maugham had visited in the early days, while the Civil War was still raging, but his motives were perhaps more connected with espionage activities than with ideological solidarity. Shaw's erstwhile fellow Fabian H.G. Wells had also visited at a comparably early date and had written up his experiences in *Russia in the Shadows*. Like Shaw, Wells was to meet Stalin himself. The journalist, travel writer and novelist Arthur Ransome had spent an important period there, his second wife, a Russian, being Trotskii's secretary at the time of the Revolution. The mathematician turned philosopher Bertrand Russell had visited in 1922, as also had the sculptress Clare Sheridan, who sculpted Lenin and Trotskii from life and knew Shaw personally.

It is interesting to note that Shaw's references to Stalin prior to the 1931 visit, though generally complimentary, were far fewer than they became afterwards. Significantly, *The Intelligent Woman's Guide to Capitalism and Fascism*, as it was titled on its first appearance in 1928, did not become *The Intelligent Woman's Guide to Socialism, Capitalism, Fascism and Sovietism* until it was revised and reissued in 1937.

What distinguishes Shaw from many of these figures is that his own work came consistently to reflect a response to the emerging position in Soviet Russia. This is true both at the literal level, for example in the figure of the Russian commissar in *Geneva*, and in the provision of an alternative ending for *The Millionairess*, 'for Soviet countries' and also in the sense in which his plays, together with their lengthy prefaces, may be seen as a 'dialogue' with Russia and the idea of a soviet society. And the word dialogue is justified because this was not simply a question of Shaw as man of letters responding to Stalin the man of action. Clearly it was even possible for Shaw to have an influence upon the soviet leader, as exemplified by the following exchange. In the *New Statesman* Shaw outlined his position on the invasion of Poland in 1939:

> As Poland's cause is lost, we have no further excuse for continuing the war. Where-upon we threw off the mask of knight errantry and avowed flatly that we did not care about Poland and were out on old balance-of-power lines to disable Germany which we now called abolishing Hitlerism. If we won it would be Versailles over again, only worse, with another war even less than twenty years off. Apologies for war won't do, however thickly we butter them with bunk and balderdash about liberty and democracy, and everything we have just abolished at home. Our business now is to make peace with Hitler and with all the world instead of making more mischief and ruining our people in the process.[4]

And this position was immediately taken up by the official soviet media, who quoted Shaw as an authority: 'One should admit that Bernard Shaw is right in many respects,' maintained *Izvestiia*, 'for the criticism should be directed not at the Nazi Germany, but at the hypocrisy of the western governments, pursuing their imperialistic goals in the world conflict.'[5]

Clearly in the late 1930s Shaw remained a name, at least among soviet readers, whose authority could be used to present a convincing conclusion to an argument. It is this sense of a reciprocal dialogue between Shaw and Russia, and perhaps especially the emerging soviet regime, which our study hopes to demonstrate above all, filling a major gap in the scholarly literature on Shaw to date. In this context, there are two points that should be specifically highlighted. In general, our approach works from the premise that Shaw always prized personalities above theories and movements: 'Russia is the country of Pushkin and Gogol, of Turgeniev and Tolstoy, of Tchekov and Gorky, of Stepniak and Kropotkin,'[6] he wrote. And although ideas were at all times essential, what made all the difference for him were the individuals involved: 'to talk about the production of a play to the Moscow people, is not only a means of making three hours pass like twenty minutes,

---

4   Quoted in 'Soviet Editorial on Hitler Peace', *The New York Times* (10 October 1939).
5   'Peace or War', *Izvestiia* (9 October 1939).
6   Shaw, Letter to Maxim Gorky, 28 December 1915, in *Collected Letters*, vol. 3, 343.

but to make it impossible to believe that it is the same play which was produced at His Majesty's Theatre.'[7] He remarked to H.G. Wells, 'I myself am as strongly susceptible as anyone to the fascination of the Russian character as expressed by its art and personally by its artists.'[8] The latter remark leads us to the second major feature of this study: an attempt to delineate this dialogue of personalities by focusing on textual analysis of Shaw's dramatic work, rather than upon the more purely political writings, covered in key monographs such as Gareth Griffith's *Socialism and Superior Brains*.[9]

Our survey of Shaw's engagement with Russia will begin with an examination of his earliest encounters, when he was still new to London, and before he became a playwright, in the 1880s and will demonstrate the important common ground he found with Russian émigré activists. In an era when the Russian radicals were often forced into exile in western Europe, Shaw was himself finding his feet politically (and, for that matter, the political left in Britain was still in its embryonic stage, not yet represented in parliament). The Russian anarchists and other revolutionary radicals were to have a profound and lasting effect upon Shaw's political and social thinking, which very often manifests itself in works written several decades later.

The following chapter will explore in detail the extensive correspondence upon which Shaw embarked with no less a figure than Leo Tolstoy, perhaps the preeminent writer in nineteenth-century Russian literature. Shaw's contact with Tolstoy will be placed in the context of the latter's reception in the west; and the two authors' shared belief in the didactic value of literature as well as their often comparably radical views on the organization of society will be analyzed.

It should be stressed from the outset that this survey will not include a consideration of Shaw and Anton Chekhov. As already mentioned, Shaw was always more susceptible to personalities than to movements and trends, and he was never to enjoy any personal meetings or correspondence with

---

7 Shaw, Letter to Maxim Gorky, 7 December 1916, in *Collected Letters*, vol. 3, 439.
8 Shaw, Letter to Maxim Gorky, 28 December 1915, in *Collected Letters*, vol. 3, 343.
9 Gareth Griffith, *Socialism and Superior Brains* (London: Routledge, 1993).

this greatest of Russian dramatists. To this extent our approach departs from that of Anna Obraztsova in her pioneering work in this field (at present unavailable other than to Russian-speaking scholars),[10] which aims at establishing some common ground with the major Russian writers of the turn of the twentieth century. While Chekhov is alluded to prominently by name along with Tolstoy in the preface to *Heartbreak House*, where the play is described as a 'Fantasia in the Russian Manner on English Themes', the Russian dramatist can hardly be regarded as a proponent of ideologically charged didactic drama, which was one of the features of Shaw's work at the time. In this light, his *Heartbreak House* will be examined within the framework of the plays of Maxim Gorky, who like Shaw was to find favour with the Bolshevik regime and had already impressed Shaw since the beginning of the twentieth century. The strong parallels with Gorky's *Summerfolk* of 1904 are explored.

A subsequent chapter will focus on a one-act play, *Annajanska, The Bolshevik Empress*, first performed in 1918 and rarely revived since. It will be argued that this play, although short, is however pivotal in the development of Shaw's response to the Russian Revolution (he wrote it a matter of days after the Bolshevik revolution of 1917). It will be shown that the play is both inspired by personal friends of Shaw's from the Russian émigré community in London, with whom he had enjoyed a friendship over many years, and a response to the emerging political picture in Russia at the end of the First World War.

Shaw responded to the Bolshevik Revolution with alacrity and later developed links with the emerging Bolshevik regime (he sent his longest theatrical work, the 'metabiological Pentateuch' *Back to Methuselah* to Lenin, who inscribed his copy) but it was a number of years before Shaw sampled in person the Soviet experiment. An analysis of the controversial and high profile trip which Shaw eventually made to the USSR in 1931 is given in the penultimate chapter.

---

10   A.G. Obraztsova, *Bernard Shou i russkaia khudozhestvennaia kultura na rubezhe IX–XX vekov* (Moscow: Nauka, 1992).

A final chapter evaluates the influence of Russian factors upon the plays of Shaw's late period from the 1920s and 1930s and also considers their reception in the USSR, both before and after World War II. This chapter will show that, having made his 1931 trip there, Shaw even subsequently tailored some of his late work specifically with a Russian, and Soviet, audience in mind, and proved conformist as regards Soviet ideology, alluding to the USSR as the utopian 'land of the future'.

The sheer extent of Shaw's career is immediately striking. Born in 1856, when Shaw left school in 1871, at the age of fifteen, the ill-fated Paris Commune had fallen only months before. In London Shaw became a close friend of Karl Marx's daughter Eleanor, indeed her common-law husband Edward Aveling inspired Shaw's play *The Doctor's Dilemma*. As early as the mid-1880s Shaw met Russian nihilists and anarchists, such as Prince Peter Kropotkin and Sergius Stepniak, who predated and deviated from the emerging Marxist hegemony of the Bolsheviks in the First World War. Later, though nominally a Fabian reform socialist, Shaw came to an accommodation with Bolshevist Marxism, especially following the establishment of the New Economic Policy in the mid-1920s, and the abandonment of communist internationalism and permanent revolution in favour of communism in one nation and the setting up, under Stalin, of the Five-Year Plans. The latter clearly appealed strongly to the Fabian mind. His nine-day trip to the USSR in 1931 was long enough to persuade Shaw of the efficacy of the Soviet system, if he had needed any persuading, but not long enough to allow him to find fault with it. Beatrice Webb, who with her husband Sidney very much represented the heart of Fabianism, was to pay a visit of several months to the USSR a year later, and commented on Shaw's report on his trip for the Fabian Summer School of 1931: 'It is odd that it is [Russia's] domination by a creed that seems so attractive to GBS; he being that great destroyer of existing codes, creeds and conventions, seems in his old age, to hanker for some credo to be enforced from birth onwards on the whole population.'[11] In the 1930s Shaw repeatedly

---

11   *The Diary of Beatrice Webb*, 8 August 1931, Norman and Jeanne MacKenzie, eds (London: Virago Press Limited, 1985), vol. 4, 249–50.

took to task the democratic governments of Western Europe and the USA, and he compared them unfavourably to the dictatorial regimes established in the era: Mussolini's in Italy, Stalin's in the USSR and even (with some caveats) Hitler's in Germany. Even after World War II Shaw, having pointedly failed to criticize the Soviet show trials of the mid-1930s, remained loyal to Stalin as the preeminent political leader of his age. The last piece of journalism to appear before his death, 'G.B.S. on the A-Bomb', included an attack on western aggression against the Russians in the Korean War, and when he died three months later a photograph of Stalin, looking down like Big Brother in Orwell's *Nineteen Eighty-Four*, published just the previous year, still adorned Shaw's home at Ayot St Lawrence. Russia accompanied Shaw to the very end.

CHAPTER ONE

Admirals and Amiable Gentlemen: Shaw and the Russian Anarchists

The high profile nature of Shaw's eventual trip in person to the Soviet Union in 1931, when he was widely feted as a great socialist playwright, recently awarded the Nobel Prize, and when he was given an audience with Stalin himself, has perhaps tended to obscure links between Shaw and Russia which go back much further. In fact they can be traced to his earliest period, in the late 1870s and through the 1880s, before he became a successful playwright. During the first twenty years of his residence in London, after moving there from Dublin in 1876, Shaw came frequently into contact with Russian émigré political dissidents who in several cases were to exert a lasting influence upon him. Shaw may even be viewed as something of an émigré himself, albeit from no further afield than Ireland, which was at that date, and was to remain until the First World War, part of the United Kingdom. It is indeed possible to detect some note of dissent if not quite political dissidence in Shaw's own background, to the extent that he, his sisters and his mother ceased attending church (they came from a Protestant family) even before they had left Ireland, still a country dominated by religion, and Shaw's earliest words in print (a letter to a newspaper) voice religious radicalism.[1]

Once resident in London Shaw's dissent rapidly took on a specifically political character. He began to mix in emergent socialist groups, in what was a period of marked political unrest during the 1880s. The second Reform Act of 1867 had come only ten years prior to Shaw's move to England. The Elementary Education Act of 1870, under which, for the first time, all parents were obliged to send their children to school, was very recent history.

---

1   Bernard Shaw, Letter in *Public Opinion*, 3 April 1875, quoted in A.M. Gibbs, *A Bernard Shaw Chronology* (New York: Palgrave, 2001), 33.

The London which Shaw entered was in the ferment of agitation, seeking a meaningful shift of political power towards the working class following these constitutional and legislative developments. Such features as the secret ballot and limits on campaigning budgets, today taken for granted in British politics, were introduced into the electoral system only in 1884. It was widely perceived that the working class could and should now aspire to power, though a Labour Party with elected representatives in parliament still lay a good decade and more away. The mood of social unrest in the 1880s was widespread. Even a figure not normally associated with political engagement, the American novelist Henry James, also resident in London since 1876, published a novel *The Princess Casamassima* in 1886 which exchanged his normal upper-class, drawing-room milieu for a working-class cast centred on the book-binding trade, who are sucked into revolutionary activity and an attempted assassination of a visiting foreign prince. This is by no means far removed from the real-life circles in which Shaw started moving in London during the same years. Friendships he developed included those with Annie Besant and Eleanor Marx, daughter of Karl Marx. Marx himself died before Shaw had any opportunity to get to know him, but Shaw is depicted by William Archer in the British Museum Reading Room, habitually consulting both a score of Wagner's *Tristan und Isolde* and the French translation of *Das Kapital*, which had as yet to be translated into English.[2] The Reading Room was where Marx himself had worked for years on *Das Kapital* and it was in this environment that Shaw met on a daily basis many figures who shared similar radical social and political concerns.

In his earliest years in London Shaw was still taking conventional paid employment (amongst others for the nascent Edison Telephone Company) but increasingly he gravitated towards living by his pen, ghosting musical articles for his mother's singing teacher and lover George Vandeleur Lee (the motive for his mother's and sisters' removal to London in the first instance). In due course Shaw became engaged in his own right as a reviewer of music, art, literature and drama for a number of journals, among which the most prominent was *The Pall Mall Gazette*. In the same period Shaw was introduced to the circle of William Morris, known to posterity for his impact on interior design and printing, but in his lifetime a

2   Gibbs, *A Bernard Shaw Chronology*, 49.

highly politically engaged figure, whose views verged toward revolutionary communism. Through Morris Shaw came into close contact with radical figures such as Edward Aveling, partner of Eleanor Marx, as well as Robert Cunninghame Graham, nominally a Liberal MP but with strong left wing leanings, who favoured land nationalization among other progressive policies. Shaw himself spent the 1880s making a name for espousing socialist views and attempting (with hardly any success) to establish himself as a novelist. (He produced no fewer than five novels during the decade, none of which made any significant mark.) He was, however, becoming a highly effective lecturer on the circuit of radical and left-wing clubs and associations. Here Shaw found himself reacting to the major political issues of the day. Besides the purely domestic (the attempt to secure genuine representation for the working class in the House of Commons) foreign policy questions also featured in discussion. The 1880s saw Britain (at the time under the Liberal prime minister Gladstone) called upon to take (or taking upon itself) the role of broker in the Balkans. Here, since the middle of the century, there had been a growing power vacuum, given the decline of the Ottoman Empire, which had formerly colonized much of the Balkans for several centuries. Bulgaria was granted nationhood in 1878 and became an international bone of contention between Russia (Britain's enemy back in the Crimea in the 1850s) and the Western Powers. At this date Austria-Hungary was nominally linked with Russia and Germany in the League of the Three Emperors, but in practice feared Russian expansionism, while the British were anxious that Russia should not obtain naval access to the Mediterranean, and were also coming separately into conflict with Russia in Afghanistan. This sense of wariness regarding tsarist Russia is evidenced in an 1887 letter from Shaw to the journalist W.T. Stead: 'But the word put in for Russia, and so brilliantly seconded by Madam Novikoff, compelled an assent that was at its best a sullen one, for were the tsar personally another Angel Gabriel, we should none the less be mad to build upon the stability or good faith of a despotic bureaucracy.'[3] Shaw shows here the conflict of interests which arose, with the left broadly in support of Gladstone (at least as far as parliamentary reform and Home Rule were concerned) yet wary of becoming linked with despotic tsarism.

---

3   Shaw, Letter to W.T. Stead, 8 June 1887, in *Collected Letters*, vol. 1, 172.

By the 1880s a significant émigré community of politically engaged Russians and Slavs was gathered in London and it was in precisely these circles that Shaw began to move. Important figures whom he encountered included Olga Novikoff, Prince Peter Kropotkin, Sergius Kravchinskii (known in the west as Sergius Stepniak) and Esper Serebriakov, as well as the political agitator Nikolai Tchaikovskii.

The process of Russian political emigration had started as early as the 1850s, after the failed revolutions across many European countries which brought figures such as Karl Marx and Friedrich Engels, as well as the Russian Aleksandr Herzen, to Britain as political refugees. Although the 1860s and 1870s appear on the surface to be a time of political liberalization, denoted most of all by the emancipation of the serfs in 1861, there was also growing dissent. The emancipated serfs were not given any land ownership and were thus economically still dependent upon their former masters, while the tsar (Alexander II) responded to various failed assassination attempts by Nihilist terrorists by becoming increasingly repressive of rights of assembly and freedom of expression of political views. Differing visions regarding the correct strategy to follow developed within revolutionary groups. The 'narodniki' movement, essentially drawn from the middle and upper classes, although it sought to empower the peasants was often viewed by them with suspicion. The middle class revolutionaries, of urban origin, came to despair of what they viewed as the peasants' perverse loyalty to the figure of the tsar, and their refusal to support the revolutionaries when they embarked upon a terrorist campaign directly targeting the tsar from the mid-1870s. This led to a dispute between Tchaikovskii and Sergei Nechaev concerning the importance of terrorism within revolutionary strategy. Following the falling-out Tchaikovskii left Russia, in the first instance for the USA. However, after the failure of a utopian community he had attempted to set up in Kansas, Tchaikovskii moved to London by the 1880s. Although Tchaikovskii returned to Russia to support the 1905 attempted revolution he disagreed strongly with the Bolsheviks, after the split with the Mensheviks in 1912, and following the revolutions of 1917 he in fact became a prominent White Russian and once again fled Russia for Britain after their defeat in the Civil War. During a period of three decades, Tchaikovskii was prominent in Russian émigré activism in London and as such came regularly into contact with Shaw.

The years in which Shaw settled in London were a period in which immigration to Britain from continental Europe was more or less untroubled by any formal moves to keep political refugees out. As John Slatter says:

> This formal toleration was almost unlimited. Between 1826 and 1905, as is well-known, no immigrant or visitor to Britain, whatever he came for, could be prevented from landing, apart from the two years after 1848 when aliens could theoretically be excluded but in fact were not [...] Until 1890, when another long-defunct Act was revived to require it at certain ports, immigrants did not even have to notify anyone of their arrival. Nor could any alien be expelled from Britain, except under extradition treaties, of which there were few before 1870 and none at all even after 1870 which included political crimes. Where exactly the line was to be drawn between political and non-political crimes was uncertain – deliberately left so by the framers of the 1870 Extradition Act, who thought it was best left to the courts.[4]

Tchaikovskii had been one of the leaders of the 'narodniki' populist socialist movement in the 1870s, indeed it was one of his erstwhile associates, Andrei Zheliabov who was to be responsible for the 1881 assassination of the tsar.[5] Shaw mentions meeting Tchaikovskii at the initial meeting of a London pressure group called The Friends of Russian Freedom in 1885, and in 1887, at the instigation of Charlotte Wilson, he interceded with Henry Norman about an article on Tchaikovskii in the *Pall Mall Gazette*. Mentioned in the above letter to Stead, another Russian émigrée, Olga Novikoff had known Thomas Carlyle (who died in 1881) and was also a friend of Gladstone. She was active as a journalist in London and devoted to fostering better relations between Britain and Russia. Disraeli nicknamed her the MP for Russia. Yet her background is not at all that of a typical political dissident in exile. Born Olga Kireeva, she was the goddaughter, and even, it has been claimed, the illegitimate child of Nicolas I. Her family were attached to the court and she grew up in court circles in St Petersburg. While promoting closer relations between her country of residence, Britain, and her homeland she was very far from being a radical political exile. On the contrary, she actively opposed the admission of some radical Russian political exiles to Britain.

---

4   John Slatter, *Russian Political Emigrants in Britain, 1880–1917* (London: Frank Cass, 1984), 24.
5   Slatter, *Russian Political Emigrants in Britain, 1880–1917*, 68.

Figure 1 'Old revolutionists in England' – prominent members of
'The Friends of Russian Freedom' (1890), on whose committee Shaw
served for some twenty years (Stepniak-Kravchinskii, Tchaikovskii,
Lazarov, Volkhovskii, Shishkov and Mrs Stepniak). LSE Archives.

These included both Peter Kropotkin and Sergius Stepniak, to whom Shaw was first introduced in 1884 through William Morris. Stepniak was the adoptive name (signifying 'man of the steppe') of Sergei Mikhailovich Kravchinskii (1852–1895). Stepniak, known familiarly as 'Steppy' by Shaw and others, was perhaps the quintessential émigré Russian revolutionary of the late nineteenth century. From a middle-class military background he had been trained for, and initially served in, the Russian army but became radicalized among Nihilist circles while he was receiving his officer training. By the early 1870s Stepniak had, in common with many of his generation and class, become disillusioned with the failure of the emancipation of the serfs in 1861 to lead to genuine social change. Stepniak's precise revolutionary views were always subject to frequent reorientation, but in this period he rapidly came to the view that tsarism must be overthrown if there was to be a real chance of the development and modernization of Russian society towards anything akin to that in Europe. It is important to understand that Stepniak and his fellow revolutionaries from the officer classes did not consistently trust in a proletarian, peasant revolt against the existing order. More precisely, they did not think that the largely uneducated, indeed illiterate population were in any position to set up an adequate replacement system of government, should any uprising succeed. One of Stepniak's fellow revolutionaries, Leonid Shishko, gives the following account of his views in the early 1870s, by which time the tsarist government had turned repressive and reactionary:

> Studying the French Revolution, he came more and more to the conviction that the personal energy of its heroes played the chief role in it; that, in essence, the revolution was controlled by a small group of men. From this he drew the conclusion that even for Russia a revolutionary coup was not impossible: it would take only the appearance of strong and energetic leaders.[6]

This view of the importance of strong leaders both puts Stepniak in line with the earlier Russian Nihilist revolutionary movement of the 1850s, which arose among the middle and upper classes rather than among the workers,

---

6   Donald Senese, *Stepniak-Kravchinskii* (Newtonville, MA: Oriental Research Partners, 1987), 2.

and also makes him an important possible influence upon Shaw's own later political thinking from the 1920s and beyond. The emphasis in Russian revolutionary activity in this period was upon the sheer need to remove tsarist absolutism, rather than immediately to empower the working class.

Figure 2 A drawing of Sergius Stepniak-Kravchinskii by Bernard Shaw himself
(c. 1890).

By the 1870s Russian revolutionary circles were increasingly calling for the violent removal of the tsar and other members of the regime. Stepniak was at the forefront of such efforts. Resigning from the army in 1871, he gave lectures on economics and history in radical circles in St Petersburg, as it was among the workers in an industrial city rather than among the peasants that it was thought that the best hope for revolutionary success lay. However, forced to devote most of his energies to avoiding arrest by the tsarist secret police, Stepniak became disillusioned and went abroad, where he became engaged in nationalist uprisings against Turkish rule in the Balkans, in 1875, before moving on to Italy. Here he came under the anarchist influence of Mikhail Bakunin and his followers and was also imprisoned for nine months.

By this point, revolutionary activity back in Russia had taken on a more overtly terrorist character, with Vera Zasulich's attempted assassination of General Trepov in 1878. This spurred Stepniak both to return to Russia and to attempt to follow her example. Despite the contrary advice of fellow revolutionaries Stepniak insisted on carrying out a daring stabbing of General Mezentsov, St Petersburg Chief of Police. Still more remarkable than the sheer daring of the attack was Stepniak's success in eluding subsequent capture. Stepniak even published an article *A Death For A Death* in 1882 (translated into English 1888) but in due course again became disillusioned with the lack of revolutionary progress in Russia and also forced for his own safety to flee abroad as a wanted man. He reached London by way of Geneva and Milan in 1884 and there met Shaw at the Hyde Park demonstration on 21 July, which protested against the House of Lords resistance to a Third Reform Act.[7]

Stepniak exerted an important influence upon William Morris and Sidney Webb during the 1880s and 1890s. According to Morris's fellow artist Burne Jones, the depiction of the repression of socialists in Russia in Stepniak's *Underground Russia* (1882) was 'one of the inciting causes of his Socialism.

---

7   'Sergey Kravchinsky', *Oxford Dictionary of National Biography*, <http://www.oxforddnb.com/view/article/62226>.

Marx he read later, to enable him to meet arguments.'[8] Stepniak met Shaw shortly after his arrival in London. Shaw, at this point in the process of throwing his allegiances behind the reform gradualist Fabian society, rather than Hyndman's revolutionary Marxist Social Democratic Federation, was astonished at Stepniak's reasonableness and moderation. They were to remain friends throughout Stepniak's life, and indeed Shaw was one of those involved in efforts on behalf of Stepniak's widow after his death in an accident while crossing a railway line in West London in 1895. Among others who took up Stepniak in England were Annie Besant, a renowned socialist activist and particularly close to Shaw during the 1880s, as well as the Fabians Hubert Bland and his wife (the children's novelist E Nesbit), and Edward Aveling and Eleanor Marx. Shaw's correspondence makes it clear that he and Stepniak were on very close, friendly terms, taking part together in socialist activities, such as the Trafalgar Square demonstration in 1885 which led to the arrest of William Morris and Henry Hyndman.[9] At precisely the time when Shaw was coming to know Stepniak personally, and also through the Friends of Russian Freedom Peter Kropotkin, these two exiles were the subject of direct and indirect efforts by the Russian tsarist regime to get them extradited from their refuge in Britain. Two terrorist bombs were exploded in London, in the Haymarket and Piccadilly, only a matter of days after the Russians, via Madame Novikov, had appealed for these activists to be expelled from Britain. This struck Friedrich Engels, writing in *Der Sozialdemokrat*, as altogether too much of a coincidence:

> I do not hesitate, for the time being to lay the blame for the explosions in London on January 24, 1885 at the door of the Russians. Irish hands may have laid the dynamite, but it is more than probable that a Russian brain and Russian money were behind it.
>
> The means of struggle employed by the Russian revolutionaries are dictated to them by necessity, by the actions of their opponents themselves. They must answer to their people and to history for the means they employ. But the gentlemen who

8   Quoted in Senese, *Stepniak-Kravchinskii*, 38.
9   Shaw, Letter to Mrs Pakenham Beatty, 22 September 1885, in *Collected Letters*, vol. I, 140.

are needlessly parodying this struggle in Western Europe in schoolboy fashion, who are attempting to bring the revolution down to the level of Schinderhannes, who do not even direct their weapons against real enemies but against the public in general, these gentlemen are in no way successors or allies of the Russian revolutionaries, but rather their worst enemies. Since it has become clear that nobody apart from Russian officialdom has any interest in the success of these heroic deeds, the only question that remains to be asked is which of them were coerced and which of them volunteered to become the paid agents of Russian tsarism.[10]

In September of the same year Shaw wrote canvassing support from friends for the newly convened Friends of Russian Freedom, which also enjoyed support from several of the more radical Liberal MPs and even one Tory, to express solidarity with Russian dissidents in exile in the West. He saw fit to reassure friends that they would find that in person Stepniak belied his reputation as a dangerous erstwhile terrorist revolutionary:

> The enclosed prospectus may interest Paquito. Stepniak, who received it coldly at first, has taken it up with some enthusiasm. A society with the object of diffusing information about Russia cannot be expected to feel very grateful to the diffuser of Marcia, which is a gross and wanton misrepresentation of facts from beginning to end; but if the poet will give his name and half a crown, his offence may possibly be condoned. I perceived last Sunday that your imagination drew a hideous picture of Stepniak. But you need not be apprehensive. I assure you I shall never connive at the infliction upon you of any socialist of the plentiful 'scallawag' type. Stepniak is an amiable middle aged gentleman who will probably be rather afraid of you, but who will make you feel that he is worthy of your friendly and distinguished consideration. But you are not likely to see him at Teviotdale just yet. If I were in his place, and a stranger living a selfish, lonely, and luxuriously idle life, were to send for me to entertain him at his dinner, and shew myself to him as a curiosity, I would accept the invitation, but I would bring a heavy club along and lay that stranger out.[11]

10 Frederick Engels, 'Real Imperial Russian Privy Dynamiters', *Der Sozialdemokrat* (29 January 1885), quoted in Karl Marx, Frederick Engels, *Collected Works* (New York: International Publishers, 1990), 292–4.

11 Shaw, Letter to Mrs Pakenham Beatty, 4 September 1885, in *Collected Letters*, vol. 1, 138–9.

When Stepniak published his novel *The Career of a Nihilist* in 1889 and sent a copy to Shaw the latter revealed that he had already obtained a copy for himself, although he had not yet managed to read much of it: 'Scott has just sent me a copy of "The Career of a Nihilist" [...] I have not had time to read further than p. 59, which is too soon for any opinion worth delivering.'[12] This reference is tantalizing. On the one hand Shaw thought highly enough of the novel to obtain a copy; on the other hand his opinion of it is not given. Shaw's diaries from the 1880s and 1890s make it clear that, besides being a founder member of the Friends of Russian Freedom, Shaw attended subsequent meetings of this organization well into the early twentieth century (he spoke at a meeting in 1905) and may have continued to be involved up to its dissolution, in the years before the First World War.

The extent of Shaw's ideological affinity with Stepniak and another émigré erstwhile revolutionary, Esper Serebriakov, is hard to gauge conclusively. Shaw first met Serebriakov through Stepniak in 1884.[13] He had enjoyed high rank in the Russian navy but, from a similar middle-class background to Stepniak's, developed Nihilist sympathies and had jumped ship[14] and eventually settled in England. Shaw met Serebriakov and Stepniak at a time when he was developing his own political stance. In the early 1880s he had described himself as an independent socialist. As late as 1882 Shaw was writing to Charlotte Payne: 'My politics are those of an atheistic radical with no very strong attachments to any established party.'[15] but he was shifting from groups like the Zetetical Society, more purely a debating and discussion group strictly free of a political position (but where he had first met Sidney Webb), towards a more avowedly reform and democratic socialist position. Though he did not join until it was already a year old,

12   Shaw, Letter to Stepniak, 17 November 1889, in *Collected Letters*, vol. 1, 227.
13   *Bernard Shaw: The Diaries, 1885–1897*, Stanley Weintraub, ed. (University Park, PA: Pennsylvania State University Press, 1986), vol. 1, p. 1019. Also covered in an article by Shaw in the *Pall Mall Budget* (19 April 1884).
14   Dan H. Laurence, Editorial comments to *Bernard Shaw Collected Letters*, vol. 1, 424.
15   Shaw, Letter to C Payne, 20 August 1882, quoted in Gibbs, *A Bernard Shaw Chronology*, 47.

Shaw soon came to align himself with the Fabian Society. By early 1885 (just after William Morris split from the Marxist Henry Hyndman) Shaw, now a reformist rather than a revolutionary, was disdaining the application to him of the title 'comrade':

> The Socialist League have circulated a handbill containing two resolutions which I never saw, with a statement that they will be supported by 'Comrade Shaw'. I consider the action of the League in announcing me as 'comrade', as immoral in its way as the Nile expedition. I am G. Bernard Shaw of the Fabian Society, member of an individualist state, and therefore nobody's comrade.[16]

In this light it is interesting to observe Shaw's relationship with these two Russian émigrés in London. It was evidently cordial, for Shaw was later to make use, which he freely acknowledged, of both Stepniak and Serebriakov (whom he refers to as a 'Bulgarian admiral') when he came to write *Arms and the Man* in the 1890s. If his primary aim was to be satirical at their expense it seems inconsistent that he should begin his letter to Charles Helmsley, manager of the Avenue Theatre, with a request to send complimentary tickets for them to Stepniak: 'Among the people who are to add lustre [to] the first night are Stepniak & the Bulgarian admiral who gave me the local color. They will go together.'[17]

Besides the 'local color' gleaned from Serebriakov, thanks to his knowledge of the Balkan setting, Shaw may also have owed a more substantial debt to Stepniak. The borrowing of the name Sergius is obvious, but in more far-reaching terms Stepniak's pessimism with regard to the hopes of achieving a revolution at the level of the common people, without the leadership of a revolutionary elite (jacobinism to its detractors) may well have provided an early stimulus towards Shaw's growing disillusionment with any idea of relying upon the working class to bring about the meaningful development of a socialist state. It needs to be stressed that many of the Russian émigré revolutionaries, although considering themselves socialists, were by no means Marxists. Stepniak had come under the anarchist

16   Shaw, Letter to J.L. Mahon, 13 April 1885, in *Collected Letters*, vol. 1, 131.
17   Shaw, Letter to C.T.H. Helmsley, 17 April 1894, in *Collected Letters*, vol. 1, 424.

influence of Marx's rival Mikhail Bakunin during his time in Italy and he retained, as seen, a sense of belief in the need for enlightened leadership and above all for the rapid overthrow of the existing tsarist regime rather than waiting for the working-class to develop sufficiently of its own accord before taking over power.

Shaw's own thinking in the 1880s displays on the one hand a reluctance to be labelled 'comrade' with all the overtly revolutionary (and anti-individualistic?) connotations of that appellation, and yet elsewhere a readiness to declare an atheist and socialist stance. He does appear to assert at some points the supremacy of the people, for example in a letter at the beginning of 1885 to Edmund Harvey, alluding to his character Smilash in the novel *An Unsocial Socialist*: 'Until people make their own laws it matters little where their laws are made or what the nationality of the capitalists who make them may be.'[18] This gives all the appearance of doctrinaire anti-capitalism and seems to place faith in the common people as those who should hold the reins of power, but within the same decade Shaw was also expressing disillusionment and frustration with the working classes, on the strength of his own electioneering activities, writing to an unidentified correspondent in October 1887:

> We call the working men proles because that is exactly what they are, and exactly what they complain of being. It is not our business to flatter them, but to put out that they are a disunited, faithless, servile crew who have only to unite, keep faith, and renounce all servility to make themselves men and citizens. They are getting to know it too, and to think just as much of the men who tell them so, as of those who try to catch their votes by telling them, that they are the salt of the earth.[19]

This view seemed only to harden as Shaw went through the 1880s, becoming ever more politically active (he was eventually to be elected as a local councillor in St Pancras in 1897). By October 1890 he was writing to Beatrice Potter (soon to marry Sidney Webb): 'I am much discouraged over Lancashire. The men there want a thorough rousing. They are slaves

18   Shaw, Letter to Edmund Harvey, 16 January 1885, in *Collected Letters*, vol. 1, 112.
19   Shaw, Letter to Unidentified Correspondent, 21 October 1887, in *Collected Letters*, vol. 1, 176.

through and through, standing up with a certain sturdiness for their rights as INFERIORS, but accepting the position of inferiors abjectly;'[20] and in the same week to another Fabian, Edward Girdlestone: 'If you go on to say that the working classes are going to take over the land and capital of the country in a spirit of pure self sacrifice, or for any other reason than that it will benefit themselves, then I lacerate the very soul of Wood by my derisive heehaws.'[21]

Shaw's pessimistic attitude towards the working class seems to have hardened as the 1880s went on, partly no doubt as the result of endless political campaigning. Yet he must also have found common ground with the Russian émigrés and their low esteem for the judgement of the Russian people. In that country, the mass of the people were only recently emancipated from serfdom. They were not to become literate and educated on any scale until the Soviet era in the third and fourth decades of the twentieth century, and were additionally hamstrung by servile admiration for the tsar. For all these reasons, in the view of many of the émigrés, they could not be entrusted on their own with the building of a socialist state.

Shaw's pessimism is often accounted for by reference to other, later sources. In the late 1890s Shaw was to encounter for the first time the ideas of Friedrich Nietzsche, who reacted to Darwinism both by rejecting traditional religion and by asserting the idea of the necessity for the emergence of a superman or uebermensch. Shaw himself was no uncritical follower of Darwin and still less of social Darwinism, preferring the ideas of Darwin's French predecessor Lamarck and Samuel Butler's rebuttal of Darwin's ideas of natural selection. However that lay a decade ahead, in the 1890s. (Shaw asserts that he did not have enough German to read Nietzsche in the original and at first assimilated only the idea of 'beyond good and evil', to which he responded after being introduced to it by a reader of his own *Quintessence of Ibsenism*).[22] In the 1880s the figure who seems to resurface in Shaw's thinking is a political philosopher the diametric opposite of any radical left wing

20   Shaw, Letter to Beatrice Potter, 6 October 1890, in *Collected Letters*, vol. 1, 267.
21   Shaw, Letter to E.D. Girdlestone, 13 October 1890, in *Collected Letters*, vol. 1, 269.
22   Shaw, Letter to Archibald Henderson, 5 September 1905, in *Collected Letters*, vol. 2, 553.

tradition, Thomas Carlyle. One prominent element in Carlyle's ideology onto which Shaw latched was the idea of 'work', which Robert Whitman in *Shaw and the Play of Ideas* links to the attack on idleness in Shaw's *The Intelligent Woman's Guide to Socialism and Capitalism* (1928):

> With a passion that may well have owed something to his early reading of Carlyle, Shaw considered idleness the first of the deadly sins because it is counterproductive, a dead weight holding back social progress. 'When every possible qualification of the words Idle Rich has been made, and it is fully understood that idle does not mean doing nothing (which is impossible), but doing nothing useful, and continually consuming without producing, the term applies to the class, numbering at the extreme outside one-tenth of the population, to maintain whom in their idleness the other nine-tenths are kept in a condition of slavery so complete that their slavery is not even legalized as such.'[23]

That Shaw was influenced early on by Carlyle is confirmed by a letter of 1890 to an unidentified correspondent who had evidently contacted Shaw, seeking advice on a political pamphlet he had written. Shaw responds by advocating the author of *Latter-Day Pamphlets* as a model for adoption. Moreover, Shaw's specific comments in this letter seem to recognize Carlyle's anti-democratic tendencies:

> If you examine the cautious, formal, but conscientious wording of Carlyle's early writings, you will see with what hard work he attained to the freedom & directness as well as the force of his mature style. Now, you have tried to jump head over heels into *his* style (not your own) at once; and although you have not made such a desperate bungle of it as your cheek deserved yet you have done nothing but say at second hand what he said at first hand – and said so well, that there is not the least occasion for you to come forward & finish the job, especially as things, bad as they are, are better in your own line than they were in his. The world does not now want to be told that society is rotten: it wants to know how it came to be rotten and what it should do to get sound. There is no use telling it that the sparrows are all fed and that you are Christianity and Democracy & so forth. It knows better [...] and that you have become over excited over Carlyle's tricks & are lashing out in clever imitation of his pamphlets. I worked at literature for nine years without earning a pound; and at present I can do little more than scrape along as a bachelor, vegetarian, teetotaller, non smoker &c.[24]

23   Robert Whitman, *Shaw and the Play of Ideas* (Ithaca, NY and London: Cornell University Press, 1977), 62.
24   Shaw, Letter to an unidentified correspondent, 11 February 1890, in *Collected Letters*, vol. 1, 242–3.

How close Shaw's thinking comes to Carlyle's emerges when comparison is made with the latter's *Chartism*:

> Democracy, we are well aware, what is called 'self-government' of the multitude by the multitude, is in words the thing everywhere passionately clamoured for at present. Democracy makes rapid progress in these latter times, and ever more rapid, in a perilous accelerative ratio; towards democracy, and that only, the progress of things is everywhere tending as to the final goal and winning-post. So think, so clamour the multitudes everywhere. And yet all men may see, whose sight is good for much, that in democracy can be no finality; that with the completest winning of democracy there is nothing yet won, – except emptiness, and the free chance to win! Democracy is, by the nature of it, a self-cancelling business; and gives in the long-run a net result of zero. Where no government is wanted, save that of the parish constable, as in America with its boundless soil, every man being able to find work and recompense for himself, democracy may subsist; not elsewhere, except briefly, as a swift transition towards something other, and farther. Democracy never yet, that we heard of, was able to accomplish much work, beyond that same cancelling of itself.[25]

While Shaw's pessimism is commonly perceived as a development belonging to his late career, and might in a sense be regarded as a response to Darwin and social Darwinism (the crude assumption that the fittest should be allowed to survive within human society at the expense of its weaker elements), it is significant that Carlyle had adopted a pessimistic rhetoric quite independently, even before the Darwinian revolution took place a decade later in the nineteenth century. And of course by the twentieth century Shaw's pessimism concerning the masses did lead him to express enthusiasm for eugenics. Shaw's diary for 23 January 1890 reveals him reading Carlyle, and moreover Carlyle on the subject of universal suffrage: 'I read Carlyle's essays on Chartism until it was time to go to my lecture, at which old Lucraft turned up.'[26]

When Stepniak, perhaps the closest of Shaw's Russian émigré friends in London in the 1880s and 1890s, was killed in the 1895 rail accident, Shaw gives an oddly sardonic account of Stepniak's death, which reveals a fixation with audacity and bravura worthy of Sergius in *Arms and the Man*, as well as recalling his earlier daring assassination of General Mezentsov:

---

25   Thomas Carlyle, *Chartism* (London: James Fraser, 1840), 53–4.
26   *Bernard Shaw: the Diaries 1885–1897*, vol. 1, 58.

'He was slain through pure dare devilry – wanted to perform the feat of bounding across before the train, and being older than he thought, was caught, Achilles-like, by the heel.'[27] Shaw and other Fabians rallied in efforts to provide for his widow (Stepniak was only forty-three at his death). A scheme was devised for a memorial to Stepniak, and Shaw made himself active in writing for contributions, including the following approach to R.B. Haldane, at the time a Liberal MP but who was later to become a Labour politician:

> Did you know Stepniak? He has left his widow without any resources; and we are getting up a Stepniak Memorial which will be, under some pretence or other, a provision for Madame S., if she can be prevailed on to accept it. Spence Watson is treasurer & we have all sorts of respectable people in it besides our own riff raff. May we put your name on the General Committee? We want Liberals especially, as Stepniak was, as far as Russia was concerned, the only Liberal left in England since Bright died.[28]

Shaw's relations with the Russian anarchist Peter Kropotkin developed rather later than those with Stepniak and Serebriakov, and the earliest references in Shaw's correspondence to Kropotkin suggest that Shaw found him annoyingly superior in manner:

> Stepniak contributions should be sent to E.R. Pease, Fabian Society, 276 Strand, W.C. Give him the Rowdy Ove's address, so that we may circularise him. The matter is very troublesome: Steppy left his wife without a cent; but the blood of the Russian aristocracy, when it takes to the cause of the people, boils at a hint of money. Pooh Bah not in it with Kropotkin & Co. We are pretending that we are endowing a translation of his works.[29]

Correspondence between Shaw and Kropotkin through the 1880s and 1890s, at least as far as Laurence's *Collected Letters* is concerned, is confined to these references, although since the opening up of Russian state archives after 1991 there are several more, significant letters not as yet published in the west. It is clear that by virtue of their common support for the Friends

---

27   Shaw, Letter to Pakenham Beatty, 23 January 1896, in *Collected Letters*, vol. 1, 588.
28   Shaw, Letter to R.B. Haldane, 22 January 1896, in *Collected Letters*, vol. 1, 587.
29   Shaw, Letter to Pakenham Beatty, 23 January 1896, in *Collected Letters*, vol. 1, 588.

of Russian Freedom, under the leadership of Shaw's fellow Fabian Edward Pease, they must have been regularly conscious of each other's presence. Shaw became a highly successful playwright from the middle of the 1890s and would in this capacity have been well-known to Kropotkin. At the same time it is evident that Shaw read Kropotkin's work attentively, if not necessarily agreeing with all of his views.

If Shaw detected a certain air of diffident superiority where Kropotkin was concerned this is in some respects not surprising. Peter Kropotkin was by birth a prince, indeed he could trace his aristocratic line back before the Romanovs to the Rurik dynasty. Nevertheless, he had from an early date repudiated his princely title, and, after a scientific training, came under the influence of advanced political thinking while in Europe in 1872. He espoused a form of communist anarchism which represented a hybrid of the mutualist thinking of Proudhon and the collectivist ideas of Bakunin. Having become involved with Nikolai Tchaikovskii in St Petersburg he was arrested in 1874 and managed to escape from captivity in 1876 before his case came to trial. All but the last two years of the remainder of his life were spent in the West, by far the larger part (over three decades) in Britain. He reached Britain by way of Switzerland, where he met his wife Sofia Ananieva-Rabinovich, a Ukrainian exile and fellow biologist, and France, where he was imprisoned in 1883, a victim of reactionary legislation in force since the crushing of the Paris Commune. Kropotkin sought refuge in England in 1886, following an amnesty, and subsequently established himself as an important writer on zoology besides his political work.

A 1902 letter to Kropotkin casts Shaw in a significantly different light from the author of the 1896 letter regarding the recently deceased Stepniak. By this stage Shaw was a man of means, both in his own right (he now had more than a half a dozen major theatrical successes both in Britain and America to his name) and as the husband of the heiress Charlotte Payne-Townshend. Shaw, along with the other Fabians, took a line in support of the British Government in its pursuit of the Second Boer War (1899–1902) which contrasted with Kropotkin's anarchist pacifist attitude. However, he was keen to offer Kropotkin financial support:

I know that you are ill. People who use their head as their instrument should stay in bed for six months once every twelve years [...] Can I help you in any way? [...] If we had more opportunities to meet I wouldn't be put in a position to speak about this, but perhaps you have already forgotten about my existence. I would like to remind you about myself; in spite of my blasphemies against science and my view of the war as a crusade against the Old Testament. I still claim the privilege of a comrade.[30]

Again, in February 1905, solicitous about Kropotkin's poor state of health, Shaw offered the Russian financial assistance.[31] In 1908 Shaw wrote a long letter to Kropotkin which reveals that he had read the latter's recently published account of the French Revolution. Shaw is at odds with Kropotkin's attitude regarding the recent failed attempt at a Revolution in Russia in 1905.

I cannot imagine how anything that we can do here can be of any use in Russia. If Russians were suffering from a foreign despotism, like Poland or Ireland, then European public opinion might do something to restrain the Government. As it is, What can we do? There is a limit to newspaper agitation, because the first necessity of journalism is novelty; and if the Russian Government arranges ten executions per day, the result is that at the end of nine days no human being will read a paragraph about a Russian execution.

I do not believe anything can be done now until the pressure of the Russian autocracy develops some real political and administrative ability in the ranks of the revolution. However infamous the Government of the Czar may be, at all events, it is a Government, and does contrive in some sort of a function to administer public affairs. And it will never be displaced by mere humanitarian indignation. It can only be displaced by a rival administration of some sort. The Russian Revolution is very much worse off than the French one was [Kropotkin was at this time writing a book on the French Revolution], because European democracy was not strong enough in the XVIII century to prevent the monarchs of Europe from making a combined attack on the Revolution and thereby driving the whole French nation into the revolutionary camp in a fever of patriotism. At the present time, the European democracies are strong enough to prevent their Governments from going to the aid of the Czar, but not strong enough

30   Shaw, Letter to Peter Kropotkin, 1 January 1902, GARF (State Archive of the Russian Federation), F. 1129, Op. 2, Ed. hr. 2816. This is also alluded to in A. Henderson, *Bernard Shaw: Playboy and Prophet* (London: D. Appleton and Co, 1932), 673.

31   Shaw, Letter to Peter Kropotkin, 16 February 1905, GARF, F. 1129, Op. 2, Ed. hr. 2816.

to go to the aid of the Revolution; consequently, there is no peril from without suf-ficiently terrifying to consolidate the Russian people in support of the revolution. The present wretched guerrilla warfare of executions and assassinations does not seem to advance matters; and its sensational horrors have long since palled on the newspaper reading public.

I may be wrong in all this, but I think my opinion is fairly representative one. All the socialists I meet have given up talking about Russia: when you mention it they simply shrug their shoulders and give it up as hopeless. The notion that a public meeting in London could do any good would seem to them merely fantastic. You must remember that the Russian Government is fighting desperately for its life; and governments in this position are not influenced by public meetings. When they are shooting and hanging and flogging and imprisoning out of mere class prejudice and spite, an expression of disgust abroad may check them, or at least induce them to proceed more secretly, but when they are exterminating enemies who, if spared, will not hesitate to exterminate them, nothing will stop them, but an adequate resistance on the part of the victims.[32]

The letter is revealing because it shows Shaw indicating the difficulty of stimulating sufficient opposition to the excesses of tsarism, and stress-ing that the Western public will be unable to sustain interest in atrocities for any length of time. This is surely the voice of Shaw the experienced journalist, who had furthermore been involved in continued political cam-paigning in Britain for some twenty years by this date. At the same time Shaw reveals that in his capacity as playwright he was heavily involved with theatrical productions of his plays (in this case the play *Getting Married*) and had conflicting calls upon his time: 'I need hardly say that we should be delighted to see your wife and discuss the matter with her. Just at pre-sent my wife is travelling in France (we have both had influenza badly) for the sake of health, and I am rehearsing a play for production on the 18th of May – a business which, in its trivial way, is almost as absorbing as a revolution. Perhaps, therefore, we had better not make an appointment until after that date.'[33]

32   Shaw, Letter to Peter Kropotkin, 25 April 1908, GARF, F. 1129, Op. 2, Ed. hr. 2816. We give Shaw's text here in its entirety, as, to our knowledge, these letters (1 January 1902, 16 February 1905, and 25 April 1908) have not been hitherto available outside Russia.

33   Shaw, Letter to Peter Kropotkin, 25 April 1908.

There is a distinct sense that Shaw was wary of becoming too closely involved in calls to oppose the Russian tsarist government at this point. Shaw spoke in London in February 1905, at a meeting of the Society of the Friends of Russian Freedom, convened in response to the Bloody Sunday massacre in St Petersburg, where unarmed peasants and workers were fired on by troops outside the tsar's Winter Palace, having gathered there to voice dissent after Russia's ignominious defeat in the Russo-Japanese War of 1904. The meeting featured more outspoken voices than his own, including that of J.B. Cunninghame Graham (Shaw's friend who had given him the line 'I never withdraw', perhaps the best speech from *Arms and the Man*). By comparison, Shaw's comes across as the voice of realism, which led him to put aside any other commitment to pacifism he might have expressed in other contexts, saying 'to oppose the State they must do it with arms in their hands.'[34]

In the ten years before the First World War a conflict of interests arose for British radicals of the kind affiliated with the Friends of Russian Freedom, who were concerned to improve the position regarding repression in tsarist Russia. At least nominally, since the 1850s, Russia had been a state in varying degrees hostile to Britain. It had been the enemy during the Crimean War of 1854 and in this period figures like Charles Urquhart had encouraged the idea that Russia should be looked upon as a bogeyman. According to Urquhart (admittedly an extreme Russophobe) the tsarist Russian regime was bent upon infiltrating and disabling British interests both out in the Empire and closer to home. Urquhart had been influenced by his involvement in Afghanistan in the middle of the century, where Britain and Russia were rival colonial powers in the so-called 'Great Game', and conceived his views before German reunification. By the 1880s, 1890s and the first decade of the twentieth century, the Great Naval Race between Britain and Germany under Kaiser Wilhelm II led to the formation in 1904 of the Entente Cordiale between Britain and France in response to the Triple Alliance between Germany, Austria-Hungary and Italy. Three years later the Entente was extended to include Russia. In terms

---

34   'The Crisis in Russia', *The Times* (2 February 1905).

of geopolitical strategy this extension made eminent sense: the Triple Alliance now found itself opposed on both its western and eastern borders. But for members of the political left in Britain the idea of alliance with tsarist Russia provoked distinct qualms. Since the anti-semitic pogroms following the assassination of tsar Alexander II in 1881 there had been a huge wave of emigration from Russia, much of it to Britain. Organizations such as the Friends of Russian Freedom, found themselves put in a divided position, having spent twenty years opposing tsarist atrocities against Jews and then in 1905 the shooting of unarmed peasants and workers who were simply protesting in favour of political rights, only now to discover that the British Government had entered into an alliance with the tsar's ministers. The conflict must have been akin in many ways to that experienced by the Left in Britain when, following the proxy fighting between the USSR and the Axis Powers in the Spanish Civil War, in 1939 Stalin gave his blessing to the Molotov-Ribbentrop non-aggression pact with Nazi Germany.

Within the sphere of primarily literary, rather than political contacts (though the two categories very frequently overlapped) Shaw continued to enjoy important relationships which connected him with Russia and Russian culture in the years leading up to the First World War. Known to Shaw at least since the time when he married Kropotkin's daughter Sasha (who is to figure in Chapter IV in the discussion of Shaw's one act play *Annajanska, the Bolshevik Empress*), Boris Lebedev (or Lebedeff in the old transcription) (1877–1948) is a significant figure in Anglo-Russian literary relations at the fin-de-siècle. He was one of the translators who were involved in a considerable burgeoning in Shaw's reception in Russia from 1905 onwards. Lebedev's correspondence with Shaw between 1913–1915 shows evidence of his efforts to promote Russian adaptations of Shaw's dramas (*Fanny's First Play*, *Misalliance*, *Androcles and Lion*, and *Pygmalion*), as well as to oppose unauthorized publication and production of his works in pre-revolutionary Russia, where translations of foreign authors were exempt from copyright restrictions. 'When I arrived in Petrograd,' Lebedev wrote to Shaw in October 1915,

I was unpleasantly struck by the news that the Imperial Dramatic Theatre here is presenting 'Pygmalion', but not in my translation. It is evidently done from German, because Higgins is called there by all personages 'Herr Professor'!

I wrote to the Director of Imperial Theatres pointing out that it is very inappropriate when there is a friendship between England and Russia to produce in a State Theatre a translation not authorized by the famed English author. The Director replied me that actors have already learned their parts in this translation and that it is most difficult to re-learn them again. That probably is true, but the question remains why actors began to learn their parts in the unauthorized translation. I think you might write a letter about it in 'The Times' and say that the Director of the State Theatre here were very unkind to you without any reason.[35]

Earlier, Shaw had been far from a success with Russian audiences. *Candida*, the first play, intended to be put on in Moscow and St Petersburg, in the closing years of the nineteenth century, was in the event withdrawn. However, after 1905, the year of the failed revolution which led to the setting up of the first Duma and also considerable liberalizing of limitations upon freedom of speech, a series of successful Russian productions of Shaw's plays ensued, starting with *Arms and the Man*.[36] Within the first decade of the twentieth century *Mrs Warren's Profession* was also staged. A remarkable situation arose concerning the latter play. In Great Britain, a constitutional monarchy, but with extensive suffrage by this date, stage censorship nevertheless persisted, entrusted to an unelected court official, the Lord Chamberlain, who banned Shaw's play on account of its references to prostitution. Things were no better in a democratic republic, the United States, where the theatre showing the play was raided by the New York police. Meanwhile in supposedly repressive tsarist Russia *Mrs Warren's Profession* received a successful St Petersburg run in 1907.[37]

Among Russophiles of British origin active in London literary life, Shaw had known the sisters Grace, Clementina and Constance Black since

35 Boris Lebedev, Letter to Bernard Shaw, 14/27 October 1915, LSE Archives, F. SHAW/15/3, list 21–2.

36 Laurence Senelick, '"More Looked at then Listened to": Shaw on the Prerevolutionary Russian Stage', *SHAW The Annual of Bernard Shaw Studies*, 27 (2007), 101–2.

37 Alexandra Theatre in St Petersburg in 1907–1908, followed by a run at the Korsh Theatre in Moscow in 1908.

the 1880s. The latter married Edward Garnett and besides being politically radical became as Constance Garnett, together with her husband, pivotal in the reception of classic Russian literature in English, translating Tolstoy, Turgenev, Dostoevskii and Chekhov. According to Senese she and Edward Garnett were responsible for giving a politically radical slant to their translations of Turgenev's novels.[38]

A further figure with whom Shaw had contact, through the Society of Friends of Russian Freedom, whose journal *Free Russia* he edited, was another Russian political émigré, Felix Volkhovskii. Born in 1846 and active from the 1860s, when he founded the One Rouble Society, Volkhovskii was imprisoned and on escaping from Siberia sought asylum in Britain in 1890. He attempted to reconcile the divergent factions within the Russian émigré community and was reproached by Tchaikovskii for the excessive overtures which he made towards the English literary elite (as they were perceived within revolutionary circles). Volkhovskii was important because he enabled British readers, through translation, to become acquainted with Russian literature which was not essentially confined to aristocratic life but represented the lives of workers and peasants. Volkhovskii died in August 1914, on the very eve of the First World War.

Another Russian connection Shaw enjoyed was with Alfred Voynich, whose wife Ethel, daughter of the great mathematician George Boole, was fluent in Russian and active as a translator, having been tutored in the language by Stepniak, along with Constance Garnett. As Ethel Voynich she published a novel, *The Gadfly*, which was based on Stepniak's career and, though long forgotten in English, went on to become a cult bestseller in the USSR, adapted as a film boasting a score by Shostakovich.

The early contacts between Shaw and these various Russian émigrés in London are significant because they provide an important background to Shaw's emerging political ideas later in his career. Shaw's turn in the 1920s towards the emerging dictators in Europe: first Mussolini, later Hitler and above all Stalin in the Soviet Union, has conventionally been explained by the manifest failure of the democratic governments of the day to put

38   Senese, *Stepniak-Kravchinskii*, 59.

aside national interests and genuinely pursue enlightened policies, leading
to the failure of the League of Nations in its leader-role. Shaw had started
off as an enthusiast of the League at its founding but rapidly became disillusioned and by the late 1930s was parodying it as a lost cause in the play
Geneva, his last before the outbreak of the Second World War. In 1928 Shaw
had declared in the preface to his play *The Apple Cart*, written in 1928 and
first performed in Germany and Poland before its British premiere at the
Malvern Festival of 1929:

> The first performance of this play at home and abroad provoked several confident
> anticipations that it would be published with an elaborate prefatory treatise on
> Democracy to explain why I, formerly a notorious democrat, have apparently veered
> round to the opposite quarter and become a devoted Royalist. In Dresden the per-
> formance was actually prohibited as a blasphemy against Democracy.[39]

Shaw must surely be accused of a certain disingenuousness here. Not,
however, in regard to his commitment to strong, dictatorial leaders, which
had been in evidence at least since 1927, when, in an article for the *Daily
News* 'Mussolini: a Defence', Shaw had said that for the Italians Mussolini
was 'the right sort of tyrant'.[40] Far from it, Shaw's disingenuousness in
the 1930 preface to *The Apple Cart: A Political Extravaganza*, lies rather
in his description of himself as 'formerly a notorious democrat'. His own
writings consistently give the lie to such a claim. Perhaps because of his
unwavering commitment to the extension of suffrage to women, Shaw
had gained, and probably enjoys to this day, a reputation as a writer whose
allegiances must, logically, be with democracy. In fact the truth was very
different. Already, at the turn of the twentieth century, Shaw had in the
preface to *Man and Superman* inveighed against democracy, at least in its
current form, since the extension of suffrage to all adult males in the late
nineteenth century:

---

39   Bernard Shaw, Preface to *The Apple Cart*, in Bernard Shaw *Collected Plays*, Dan H.
      Laurence, ed. (London: Max Reinhardt, 1971), vol. VI, 249.
40   Quoted in Griffith, *Socialism and Superior Brains*, 252.

Now we have yet to see the man who, having any practical experience of Proletarian Democracy, has any belief in its capacity for solving great political problems, or even for doing ordinary parochial work intelligently and economically. Only under despotisms and oligarchies has the Radical faith in 'universal suffrage' as a political panacea arisen. It withers the moment it is exposed to practical trial, because Democracy cannot rise above the level of the human material of which its voters are made. Switzerland seems happy in comparison with Russia; but if Russia were as small as Switzerland, and had her social fortifications and a population educated by the same variety and intimacy of international intercourse, there might be little to choose between them. At all events Australia and Canada, which are virtually protected democratic republics, and France and the United States, which are avowedly independent democratic republics, are neither healthy, wealthy, nor wise; and they would be worse instead of better if their popular ministers were not experts in the art of dodging popular enthusiasms and duping popular ignorance.[41]

The phrase of interest from the *Apple Cart* preface 'I, formerly a notorious democrat' definitely leads the reader to suppose that Shaw had been a supporter of democracy up to some point in the recent past, in the 1920s, and was beginning to look to alternative political systems of government only at this juncture. This may well be the reputation which Shaw not only in his lifetime but since his death in 1950 has continued to enjoy. However, as indicated above in relation to the early influence of Carlyle, Shaw is far from being unequivocally entitled to any such reputation. That he supported women's suffrage, and wrote plays such as *Mrs Warren's Profession*, *Candida*, *Major Barbara* and *Pygmalion* which showed dynamic, self-reliant female figures (very often far more impressive than their male counterparts) has chiefly served to cloud the issue. In fact Shaw had been inveighing against democracy in his dramatic output at least since this Preface from 1903, and also *The Revolutionist's Handbook* in the same work, with its strongly negative verdict. The pessimism in *Man and Superman* may be explained by Shaw's response to Nietzsche, from whom he takes the idea of the Superman who must evolve to make democracy, a democracy of the genetic elite, worthwhile. Shaw rejects 'blind' classic Darwinism

---

41   Bernard Shaw, 'The Revolutionist's Handbook' (*Man and Superman*), in *Collected Plays*, vol. II, 754.

(so-considered on account of its deterministic features) in favour of his own brand of Bergson-inspired vitalism, with the Life Force seeking out the development of inspired genius, upon whose development would depend the overall survival of the human race.

The negative attitude towards democracy which Shaw had encountered early in the work of Carlyle, within a British context, would have been augmented in the 1880s, as Shaw began to come into contact with the Russian émigrés in London, from middle and upper-class, even aristocratic backgrounds. Although revolutionary in their politics and utopian in terms of the state they hoped eventually to construct, they had developed their views in the Russian context, where the masses were far more illiterate and uneducated than those in Britain and were overwhelmingly rural peasants, still in thrall to religion in the form of the Orthodox Church, in a way that no longer had any real analogue in Britain.

While Shaw might seem to protest at the residual social superiority of Kropotkin, princely by birth, it would appear that the pessimism towards the masses which he and other Russian radical émigrés showed in this era provided an early stimulus for his own later profound scepticism regarding the masses and the wisdom of entrusting them with political power in the form of 'Proletarian Democracy'.

Overall, the 1880s and 1890s need to be seen as a period in which there is evidence of major conflicting currents in Shaw's political thinking. Far from being, as he claimed in the preface to *The Apple Cart* a 'notorious democrat', although a proponent of women's rights and an opponent of the existing political establishment, Shaw was by no means a convinced democrat. Shaw might proclaim his commitment to Fabian gradualist, democratic socialism and insist upon distinguishing himself from inclusion under any umbrella with the Liberal Party, while at the same time rejecting important elements of Marxism (the theory of value). Yet for all his practical engagement in local government Shaw's pronouncements already display a disillusion with what democracy and universal suffrage (then but a decade old) were likely to mean in practice. This led him to reach back to a pessimistic political philosopher of an earlier age. Significantly Carlyle's negative views on democracy, as well as his veneration of the supreme value of work, predate any of Darwin's publications and may be seen as having been reached independently of any impulse from scientific determinism. (Essentially they were a response both to his work as historian of the French Revolution and to the political agitation of the First Reform Act and the Chartist movement). In later chapters we will see Shaw giving full vent to comparable views once major dictators emerged on the European political scene, in the wake of the collapse of the Hapsburg, Hohenzollern and Romanov dynasties in the First World War, and the slide from 1929 into world economic recession.

CHAPTER TWO

'All Art at the Fountainhead Is Didactic':
Shaw and Lev Tolstoy

No other writer in Russia has experienced such unprecedented glory and success in his lifetime as Lev Tolstoy. In 1898, Chekhov wrote to Aleksei Suvorin 'I shall not be at Tolstoy's on the eighth of August. First of all, it is too cold and damp to make the journey, and secondly what for? His life is a permanent celebration anyway, and there is absolutely no reason to single out any particular day.'[1] Towards the end of the nineteenth century Tolstoy was, perhaps, the most famous man in Europe. Photographs made his white beard and austere countenance familiar to people cultured and uncultured the world over. Pilgrims of every rank and class – statesmen, generals, artists, reformers, students and labourers – came to see the sage of Iasnaia Poliana (Tolstoy's family manor in Central Russia where he spent the majority of his life), and for those looking for spiritual enlightenment his words were of much greater importance than those of the Church fathers or state officials. The fundamental significance of the subjects he addressed, his opinions in both his fiction and philosophical tracts, the conviction and power with which the opinions were uttered, the brilliance of his accomplishment as an artist – all combined to invest the man with an import which no thoughtful person could neglect, and which caught the fancy of others.

---

1 M.P. Gromov and A.M. Dolotova, eds, *Perepiska A.P. Chekhova* (Moscow: Khudozhestvennaia literatura, 1984), vol. 1, 261. Here and hereafter all translations unless otherwise indicated are the work of the authors, the original text is given in brackets ('8 августа я не буду у Толстого, во-первых, оттого, что холодно и сыро ехать к нему, и во-вторых – зачем ехать? Жизнь Толстого сплошной юбилей. И нет резона выделять какой-нибудь один день'). Aleksei Suvorin (1834–1912) was an eminent and immensely rich journalist and press magnate, whose publishing empire exerted considerable influence during the last decades of the Russian Empire.

When in 1909 the Russian literary journal *The Herald of Knowledge* carried out a readership survey, Tolstoy was named the most popular author by an overwhelming majority of 295 votes; Darwin came second with 152; while Karl Marx languished in sixteenth position with 52.[2] As a moral thinker and social reformer, Tolstoy had a major impact on the views of the Russian intelligentsia of the time, on those who effectively defined the state of events during these years of the country's social and political unrest. One of the reasons for such an exceptional vogue was the distinct political dimension of his writings – their profound anti-establishment spirit and consistent negation of the existing order which appealed to various layers of the Russian intellectual elite, from the liberal circles of Merezhkovskii and Minskii to defiant anti-monarchist radicals like Lenin and Kropotkin. One might say that the sheer scale of his influence could be rivalled only by that of Voltaire, Goethe and Victor Hugo, who were equally revered by an entire generation of contemporaries.[3] As Suvorin famously put it:

> There are two tsars in Russia: Nicholas II and Lev Tolstoy. Who is the mightier? Nicholas II cannot do anything with Tolstoy, cannot undermine his reign; while Tolstoy is constantly shaking the throne of Nicholas and his dynasty. They curse him; the Synod has an order against him. Tolstoy responds, and his sayings are instantaneously distributed in manuscripts and foreign newspapers. Would one dare touch him?[4]

In England Tolstoy rose to fame on the wave of the Great Eastern Crisis in the aftermath of the Russo-Turkish war of 1877–1878. The conflict brought to a head the rivalry between England and Russia for their

2   Dmitrii Oleinikov, 'Kumiry chitaiushchei publiki nachala stoletiia', *Rodina*, 3 (1998), 72.
3   As Semion Frank put it in his jubilee article (1908) dedicated to the eightieth anniversary of the great writer (S.L. Frank, *Russkoe mirovozzrenie* [St. Petersburg: Nauka, 1996], 440).
4   A. Suvorin, *Dnevnik* (Moscow: Novosti, 1992), 316 ('Два царя у нас: Николай II и Лев Толстой. Кто из них сильнее? Николай II ничего не может сделать с Толстым, не может поколебать его трон, тогда как Толстой, несомненно, колеблет трон Николая и его династии. Его проклинают, Синод имеет против него свое определение. Толстой отвечает, ответ расходится в рукописях и в заграничных газетах. Попробуй кто тронуть Толстого').

dominance in Central Asia. By spring 1885 it was descending into a serious threat of an Anglo-Russian war, when after the clash of interests on the Afghanistan borders, the British press raised a cry of danger to India. By July 1887 the Boundary Commission was still negotiating the frontiers, the Russians were still pursuing their advance into Asian territories, and the closer they came to British India the more attention was given to the study of the threatening northern opponent. A rapid and appreciable interest in Russian culture spread across British society, and people avidly seized at any book that could throw light on the life and customs of the vast Russian empire. Written and published within a week, Charles Marvin's *The Russians at the Gate of Herat* (1885) had sales of 65,000 copies; Smith, Elder, & Co (London) reprinted Armin Vámbéry's *Central Asia and the Anglo-Russian Frontier Question* (1874) as well as his *Travels in Central Asia* (London, John Murray, 1864); other titles during this period included *All the Russians* (1885) by E.C. Phillips; *History of Russia* (1885) by W.K. Kelly, and *The Russian Storm-cloud* (1886) by Sergius Stepniak. It was only natural that at that time, when the interest in Russian affairs ran at a very high pitch, the editors started looking for suitable translations of Russian literature, and in some six years the *Fortnightly Review* declared that 'the Russian novel now has the vogue, and deserves to have it.'[5]

Though the new interest embraced Russian literature as a whole, Tolstoy was one of the main attractions. Up until 1885 his name was barely known to the British audience (familiar mainly with the writings of Turgenev) to the extent that *The Contemporary Review* could refer freely to Dmitrii Tolstoy, the Russian Minister of Home Affairs, simply as Count Tolstoy, without any fear that the identity might be mistaken.[6] Henry James' notable essay on Turgenev's literary legacy as well as his *Art of Fiction*,

---

5   Matthew Arnold, 'Count Leo Tolstoi', *Fortnightly Review*, 42/252 (1887), 783.

6   'Contemporary Life and Thought in Russia', *The Contemporary Review*, 47 (1885), 727–36. At the end of the 70s there appeared a couple of publications that tried to attract attention to Tolstoy's writings, but they were very sparse: see for instance, W.E. Henley, 'New Novels', *The Academy*, 329 (1878), 186–7; W.R.S. Ralston 'Novels of Count Leo Tolstoy', *Nineteenth Century*, 5 (1879), 650–69; or C.E. Turner, *Studies in Russian Literature* (London: Kessinger Publishing Company, 1882).

published in 1884,[7] also make no mention of Tolstoy. His volumes, however, were everywhere by 1887: six translations of his works were published between 1885 and 1888, not to mention nineteen American editions which were on sale in Britain. In a short period in the mid-80s, practically everything Tolstoy had written in the preceding thirty-five years was translated and published in English (including W.S. Gottesberger's edition of *War and Peace*, translated from French by Clara Bell in 1886);[8] he was hailed as incomparably the greatest writer who had ever lived, occupying in fiction the same position that Shakespeare occupies with all drama[9] – a highly ironic statement, as some ten years later Tolstoy (as well as Shaw) would become known for his vociferous Shakespeare-hatred.

One can name a number of reasons (cultural, social and political) that could account for such an unprecedented vogue. Firstly, there appeared three discerning literary studies which pointed distinctly in the direction of Tolstoy's works (he was ranked second only after Turgenev). The first was by Eugène Melchior de Vogué, a critic, a traveller and a scholar of Russian life and letters, who had been writing on Russian literature for the *Revue des Deux Mondes* (by this time *War and Peace* had already become available in French in a St Petersburg edition of 1880 and in a Paris edition of 1885). The series of his essays *Les écrivains russes contemporaines* – Turgenev,

---

7   Henry James, 'Ivan Turgénieff', *Atlantic Monthly*, 53 (1884), 42–55; Walter Besant and Henry James, 'Art of Fiction', *Longman's Magazine*, 4/23 (1884), 502–21.

8   The influx of Tolstoy's translations was partly facilitated by the availability of the general body of his works unprotected by intellectual copyright. In 1884 Tolstoy assigned the rights to all of works published before 1881 to his wife, being very generous with the remaining part of his intellectual property, and in 1891 he publicly renounced the copyrights of all he had written after 1881. Free of copyright restriction and royalties, publishing houses around the world issued impressive runs of Tolstoy's works almost immediately upon their official publication in Russia.

9   W. Sharp, 'New Novels', *The Academy*, 871 (1889), 22. Among the major articles on Tolstoy at the time one can also mention Matthew Arnold's publication 'Count Leo Tolstoi', *Fortnightly Review*, 783–99; W.E. Henley, 'Count Tolstoi's Novels', *Saturday Review* (1 January 1887); 'Count Tolstoi's Life and Works', *Westminster Review*, 130 (1888), 278–93.

Tolstoy, Dostoevskii and Gogol[10] – was published in a collected volume *Le roman russe* (Paris, 1886) and became almost immediately available in English.[11] The second study was Ernst Dupuy's *Les grands maîtres de la littérature russe*, which came out in Paris in 1885 and was reprinted in England two years later.[12] Finally, in 1888 C.E. Turner published his lectures on Tolstoy presented at the Royal Institution, which received high commendations from the review, saying that it was 'a kind of pendant to the excellent work of M. de Vogué.'[13] Both monographs added 'new oil to the recently kindled fire of interest'[14] in the Russian novelist and strongly contributed to the penetration of his works into Western Europe.

Secondly, the writings of Tolstoy were widely promoted by the Russian Anarchists, who settled in England in the mid-80s. Despite his misgivings about violent anarchist revolutionary tactics, Tolstoy was known for his anti-establishment doctrine. As early as 1857, he wrote to his friend Vasilii Botkin: 'The truth is that the State is a conspiracy designed not only to exploit, but above all to corrupt its citizens [...] and I shall never serve any government anywhere.'[15] Over the last twenty years of his life he persistently reiterated an anarchist critique of the state and promoted books

10 Eugène de Vogué, 'Les écrivains russes contemporaines', *Revue des Deux Mondes*, 59 (1883), 786–821; 64 (1884), 264–301; 67 (1885), 312–56 ; 72 (1885), 241–79.

11 E.M. Vogué, *The Russian Novelists*, Jane Loring Edmands, trans. (Boston: D. Lothrop Company, 1887).

12 Ernst Dupuy, *Great Masters of Russian Literature*, Nathan Haskell Dole, trans. (London: J & R Maxwell, 1888). The first English translation of the monograph was published by T.Y. Crowell & Co. of New York in 1886.

13 C.E. Turner, *Count Tolstoi as Novelist and Thinker* (London: Trübner and Co, 1888), reviewed by William Richard Morfill, 'Literature', *The Academy*, 866 (1888), 364.

14 Nathan Haskell Dole, preface to Ernst Dupuy, *Great Masters of Russian Literature*, 1.

15 Lev Tolstoy, Letter to V.P. Botkin, 24–25 March/5–6 April 1857, in Lev Nikolaevich Tolstoy, *Collected Works*, 90. vols, V.G. Chertkov, ed. (Moscow: Khudozhestvennaia literatura, 1928–1958), vol. 60, 158 ('Правда, что государство есть заговор не только для эксплуатации, но главное для развращения граждан [...] Это я почувствовал, понял и сознал нынче. И это сознание хоть немного выкупает для меня тяжесть впечатления [...] с нынешнего дня я не только никогда не пойду смотреть этого, никогда не буду служить нигде и никакому правительству').

by Proudhon, Kropotkin and Stepniak-Kravchinskii to his readers.[16] 'The Anarchists,' he wrote,

> are right in everything, – in their negation of the existing order, and in their asser-
> tion that it will not be worse without the power than, with the existing customs, it
> is with the violence of the power. But they are mistaken in thinking that anarchy can
> be established by means of revolution, – that anarchy can be instituted. Anarchy will
> establish itself; but this will happen because a greater and even greater number of
> people will not need the defence of the governmental power, and a greater and even
> greater number of people will be ashamed to apply this power [...] Everything is so,
> everything is correct which they discuss and do [...] Only one thing must be changed
> by them, – violence and murder by a non-participation in violence and murder.[17]

These affinities were clearly reciprocated by the Russian socialist-anarchist circle, and in 1884, when Stepniak found himself in exile in England he started a strong campaign promoting the writings of Tolstoy, which he believed was the most effective way of acquainting foreign audiences with Russian society.[18] For instance, Thomas Hardy attended one of these lectures in 1893 and had some vivid recollections of this event.[19] Later on, Kropotkin wrote of Tolstoy in the article on anarchism in *The Encyclopae-*

16   It was Tolstoy who edited Kropotkin's manuscript of *Paroles d'un révolté* (*Words of
      a Rebel*), published illegally in St Petersburg in 1906 (G. Woodcock, I. Avakumovic,
      The Anarchist Prince [London: T.V. Boardman & Co, 1950], 367).

17   Lev Tolstoy, Extracts from Unpublished Diaries, in *The Complete Works of Count
      Tolstoy*, Leo Wiener, trans. (Boston: Dana Esters & Company, 1904–1912), vol. 23
      (1905), 521 and 527.

18   S.M. Stepniak-Kravchinskii, *Collected Works* (Moscow: Khudozhestvennaia literatura,
      1958), vol. 1, xxi. In this context it is also worth noting that Constance Garnett, one
      of the most prominent translators of Tolstoy into English (*The Kingdom of God is
      Within You*, 1893 and *Anna Karenina*, 1917), learned the Russian language in the
      Russian anarchist circle: Volkhovskii was her first tutor and later on she took up
      translating Russian literature under the directions of Stepniak-Kravchinskii. This
      explains Garnett's emphasis on social and political undertones that coloured all her
      translations of the time (Edward Garnett, *The Golden Echo* [London: Chatto &
      Windus 1953], 10).

19   F.E. Hardy, *The Later Years of Thomas Hardy, 1892–1928* (London: Macmillan, 1930),
      22.

dia Britannica, naming him one of the prominent representatives of the movement, who based his position on 'the teachings of Jesus and [...] the necessary dictates of reason.'[20]

Finally, it is worth bearing in mind that Tolstoy's almost overwhelming fame was not merely that of an unparalleled novelist. His tracts on religion, social ethics and aesthetics also fed the swelling stream of his reputation. In this respect, the major landmark in establishing Tolstoy's standing in England was the 1885 publication of *My Religion*. Written in 1843 and banned from circulation in Russia, the book was translated by Huntington Smith and published by T.Y. Crowell of New York. The same year it appeared in France, as *Ma réligion*, and in England as *Christ's Christianity* (including also *How I Came to Believe* and *My Confession*). In all three countries the book aroused much controversy, but, as the *Literary World* put it, undoubtedly gave an impulse to the interest in the Russian writer 'which has been excited within a few months.'[21] *My Religion* contained a definitive religious message, centred on the Sermon on the Mount, that was strongly and individually expressed: it pointed out the failure of people to live up to the teachings of Christ, called into question Orthodox doctrine, advocated renunciation, non-violence and non-resistance, and proclaimed the great changes occurring not only in Tolstoy's soul but also in his way of life (he turned to vegetarianism and physical labour and renounced his private and intellectual property). As a result, all over the West there emerged hundreds of Tolstoyans, concerned primarily with his Christian doctrines and theories which, in the opinion of many, were advanced even

20   Without naming himself an anarchist, Leo Tolstoy, like his predecessors in the popular religious movements of the fifteenth and sixteenth centuries, Chojecki, Denk and many others, took the anarchist position as regards the state and property rights, deducing his conclusions from the general spirit of the teachings of Jesus and from the necessary dictates of reason. With all the might of his talent he made (especially in *The Kingdom of God is Within You*) a powerful criticism of the church, the state and law altogether, and especially of the present property laws' [Peter Kropotkin, 'Anarchism', in *Encyclopaedia Britannica* (Cambridge: Cambridge University Press, 1910], 918).

21   'Tolstoi's War and Peace', *The Literary World*, 17 (1886), 348.

more powerfully in the novels than in his didactic essays. For instance, prominent among such followers in England was W.T. Stead, editor of the *Pall-Mall Gazette* from 1883 to 1890 and founder of the *Review of Reviews* in 1890, who initiated the new style of tabloid journalism, and was a strong advocate of peace through arbitration. He was forcefully attracted by the pacifist elements of Tolstoy's doctrine, and was, in general, so enthusiastic, unconventional, and bold that he was accused by the Tory press in particular of being under the intellectual dominance of Russia.[22] In 1896 John Coleman Kenworthy established a community of Tolstoyans at Purleigh, and although this particular colony survived only a few years, its branches (Whiteway Colony in Gloucestershire and Stapleton Colony in Yorkshire) are still active today.[23] In 1901 Tolstoy's international fame grew even stronger when he was excommunicated for his teachings by the Russian Orthodox Church.

Having always been at the front line of literary and social events, Shaw could not stay aloof from this growing attention to the new pre-eminence of Russian literature. A number of his articles and critical essays on the writings of Tolstoy, as well as his personal correspondence with the Russian writer show that he took a great interest in his works and ideas – an interest also enhanced, perhaps, by the strong, unusual and baffling personality of the Russian author that struck a chord with Shaw's own character. Like Tolstoy, he was very prolific and had an unparalleled ability to make 'front page' comments on the current agenda. Like Tolstoy he was often cynical about human institutions and possessed many Tolstoyan traits: shrewdness of observation, irony interrelated with pity but tempered by charity, lucidity and grace of language as well as a profound respect for the sanctity of the written word. In fact, both men had very much in common, but Tolstoy's impact on the creative output of the British dramatist is a question of a slightly different order.

Far-flung literary movements that have their roots in the distinct character of a certain period have a tendency to arise more or less simultaneously in different countries to give colouring to the literature of the era.

---

22   Frederic Whyte, *Life of W.T. Stead* (London: Jonathan Cape, 1925).
23   Charlotte Alston, 'Tolstoy's Guiding Light', *History Today*, 60/10 (2010), 32–8.

One such movement was the 'realism' of the second half of the nineteenth century that had its specific features in France, Russia and England. It is hard to say in what exact proportions the practice of a given artist partakes of the common impulse characteristic of the age, on the one hand, or is patterned on the practice of another artist, who also is subject to the tendencies of the era. In fact Shaw himself strongly objected to the very idea of such influence and said that he thought of other dramatists no more 'than a blacksmith shoeing a horse thinks of the blacksmith in the next county'; he was appalled by those artists who went to books for their inspiration, and called these authors 'both blind and deaf'.[24] Tolstoy offered further complications in this context. The distinctive feature of his writings is the submergence of 'art', at least of the kind that can readily be grasped or imitated. His works can be regarded as a world in itself; and his strength lies rather in his insight into characters, and in his mastery of the scenes which arise. His influence, therefore, can be traced only in a broader sense of the word, not in terms of borrowing themes and reiterating motifs, but rather in terms of common sources of inspiration – a constructive dialogue that shapes the creative energy of the artist.

Shaw's first comment on Tolstoy's writings appeared in 1898, when the English translation of his unorthodox aesthetic treatise *What Is Art?* was published by Aylmer Maude (only a year after the Russian original). The work gave rise to extensive controversy, and the majority of critics immediately belaboured it into oblivion, finding its 'propositions incomprehensible' and its attempt to present peasants as a touchstone of all art ridiculous.[25] Shaw, on the other hand, immediately came to the rescue of Tolstoy's essay.

24　'I never dreamt of Ibsen or De Maupassant any more than a blacksmith shoeing a horse thinks of the blacksmith in the next county [...] If a dramatist living in the world of multifarious interests, duties and experiences in which he lived has to go to books for his ideas and his inspiration, he must be both blind and deaf' (quoted in Archibald Henderson, *George Bernard Shaw: His Life and Works* [London: Stewart and Kidd Co, 1911], 301).

25　For the review of criticism of Tolstoy's essay see Aylmer Maude, *Tolstoy on Art* (Oxford: Humphrey Milford Oxford University Press, 1924), v; Aylmer Maude, *Tolstoy on Art and Its Critics* (Oxford: Humphrey Milford Oxford University Press, 1925), 18–32; or an anonymous article 'Tolstoi's Views of Art', *Quarterly Review*, 191/382 (1900), 359–72.

'This book,' he wrote in an extensive review in the *Daily Chronicle*, 'is a most effective booby trap. It is written with so utter a contempt for the objections which the routine critic is sure to allege against it that many a dilettantist reviewer has already accepted it as a butt set up by Providence [...] Whoever is really conversant with art recognizes in it the voice of the master.'[26] He pointed out that the majority of critics failed to understand Tolstoy's challenging definition of the social function of art as 'a means of union', which consisted of transmitting the best feelings among men, and, consequently, bore a direct relation to humanity as a whole.[27] The emphasis, therefore, was not on the taste of a simple peasant but rather on the value of this experience for every man: 'The assertion that art may be good art, and at the same time incomprehensible to a great number of people, is extremely unjust and its consequences are ruinous to art itself; but at the same time it is so common, and has so eaten into our conceptions, that it is impossible sufficiently to elucidate the whole absurdity of it.'[28]

It is uncanny that only a couple of months earlier the same thoughts were defended by Shaw in a number of his own writings on the subject, such as *The Perfect Wagnerite* (December 1898) and the preface to his *Plays: Pleasant and Unpleasant* (March 1898[29]). In the former he drew attention to life-like and accessible art[30] and the latter highlighted the social importance of drama, claiming that a theatre should be regarded as an educational

---

26 *Daily Chronicle* (10 September 1898), reprinted in Maude, *Tolstoy on Art and Its Critics*, 3.

27 'A means of union among men, joining them together in the same feelings and indispensable for the life and progress towards well-being of individuals and of humanity' (Lev Tolstoy, *What Is Art?*, in *The Novels and Other Works of Lyof N. Tolstoï*, Aylmer and Louise Maude, trans. (New York: Charles Scribner's Sons, 1902), vol. 19, 387).

28 Tolstoy, *What Is Art?*, 431.

29 First published in March 1898, *Plays: Pleasant and Unpleasant*, vol. II (London: Constable and Co Ltd).

30 'There is only one way of dramatizing an idea; and that is by putting on the stage a human being possessed by that idea, yet none the less a human being with all the human impulses which make him akin and therefore interesting to us' (Bernard Shaw, *The Perfect Wagnerite: A Commentary on the Ring of the Niblungs* [London: Grant Richards, 1898], 30).

establishment rather than mere entertainment for a select group of intellectuals: 'The theatre is growing in importance as a social organ. Bad theatres
are as mischievous as bad schools or bad churches; for modern civilization
is rapidly multiplying the numbers to whom the theatre is both school and
church.'[31] In practical terms, Shaw was one of the great supporters of the
Stage Society, founded by the Fabians in 1899. This theatre group was committed to the production of non-commercial plays of artistic merit which
they regarded as a potent force for social change; and the Society's choice
of plays in its opening years were mainly examples of social realism: Ibsen's
The League of Youth and Hauptmann's *The Coming of Peace*.

Likewise, Shaw shared Tolstoy's rejection of the popular contemporary
idea of 'art for art's sake', as well as his firm commitment to the prevalence
of ideological and moral content as a quintessential element of artistic work
(to the extent that Henry James once pointed out that the formlessness of
English and American fiction originated with Tolstoy).[32] In his appraisal of
the creative process, Tolstoy placed prime emphasis on worthy and original
ideas which, in his opinion, constituted the essence of genuine inspiration:
'As thought-product is only then real thought-product when it transmits
new conceptions and thoughts and does not merely repeat what was known
before, so also an art-product is only then a genuine art-product when it
brings a new feeling (however insignificant) into the current of human
life.'[33] One can hardly miss the striking similarity with Shaw's postulations
expressed in his later writings of 1901–1903. 'What is the use of writing
plays or painting frescoes,' he wrote in the preface to his *Three Plays for
Puritans*, 'if you have nothing more to say or shew than what was said and
shewn by Shakespeare, Michael Angelo, and Raphael? [...] If technical
facility were the secret of greatness in art, Mr Swinburne would be greater
than Browning and Byron rolled into one, Stevenson greater than Scott or
Dickens, Mendelssohn than Wagner, Maclise than Madox'[34]; or two years

31   Bernard Shaw, Preface to *Plays Pleasant*, in *Collected Play*, vol. I, 378.
32   Henry James, 'The New Novel', in *Notes on Novelists and Some Other Notes* (New
      York: Charles Scribner's Sons, 1914), 328–9.
33   Lev Tolstoy, *What Is Art?*, 407.
34   Bernard Shaw, Preface to *Three Plays for Puritans*, in *Collected Plays*, vol. II, 42–4.

later in the preface to *Man and Superman*: 'Effectiveness of assertion is the Alpha and Omega of style. He who has nothing to assert has no style and can have none: he who has something to assert will go as far in power of style as its momentousness and his conviction will carry him.'[35]

This is not to say that Shaw simply reiterated the ideas of the Russian novelist, but rather that he found in them an explicit validation of his own thoughts, articulated, for instance, as early as 1893 in his play *The Philanderer* – a severe mockery of those who are nothing but an embodiment of blasting and obliterating words, 'funny without being vulgar', humorous without being of any importance to the masses.[36] Following Tolstoy, who associated the predilection for form with so-called 'counterfeit art',[37] he always strove for originality in discussion or writing and claimed that 'new ideas make their technique as water makes its channel; and the technician without ideas is as useless as the canal constructor without water, though he may do very skilfully what the Mississippi does very rudely.'[38] In this respect, it is worth pointing out that the mastery of artistic techniques was not totally neglected in the writings of the British dramatist – he was greatly interested in precision of expression, as well as in the form of the argument presented in his dramas. The subject matter is of prime importance, he maintained, but the form must be tuned to the content, and the 'changing in techniques must inevitably follow from these changes in the subject matter of the play.'[39]

In fact, it was to be precisely the question of artistic form and appreciation of style that provoked the first falling-out between Tolstoy and Shaw, as well as their first, though indirect, exchange of correspondence. The matter concerned their attitude towards Shakespearean drama, of which they both had a relatively low opinion, believing that as a thinker

35   Bernard Shaw, Epistle Dedicatory to *Man and Superman*, in *Collected Plays*, vol. II, 526.

36   G.K. Chesterton, *George Bernard Shaw* (New York: John Lane Company, 1909), 128.

37   Tolstoy, *What Is Art?*, 444.

38   Shaw, Preface to *Three Plays for Puritans*, in *Collected Plays*, vol. II, 44.

39   Bernard Shaw, *Quintessence of Ibsenism* (New York: Bretano's, 1928), 231.

and philosopher, the Bard of Avon was seriously overrated. As Shaw put it in one of his letters: 'I have striven hard to open English eyes to the emptiness of Shakespeare's philosophy, to the superficiality and second-handedness of his morality, to his weakness and incoherence as a thinker, to his snobbery, his vulgar prejudices, his ignorance, his disqualifications of all sorts for the philosophic eminence claimed for him.'[40] Tolstoy's extreme dislike for Shakespeare had been widely known within his circle. At the age of twenty-seven, during an informal dinner with his friends, among which there were quite a few prominent Shakespeare scholars, he declared that only those 'imbued with verbosity could be impressed by Shakespeare and Homer.'[41] Since then the writing of the great English poet had never escaped his far-reaching attention, and was inevitably portrayed in a negative light. Thus, for instance, in 1856 he made a note in his diary: 'Finished "Henry IV". No!'[42]; and in January 1884 he wrote to his wife, Sofia Tolstaia: 'I was reading "Coriolanus" ... it is, incontrovertibly, nonsense that could only please actors' or 'It was with great attention that I read "Macbeth" this morning – it is a fairground spectacle, written by a clever and quick-minded actor, informed by many clever books.'[43]

40   Shaw, Letter to Vladimir Tchertkoff, August 1905, in *Collected Letters*, vol. 2, 551.

41   N.N. Gusev, *Lev Nikolaevich Tolstoy. Materialy k biografii, 1855–1869* (Moscow: Akademiia Nauk SSSR, 1957), 5. In his memoirs, Tolstoy's friend from Kazan' University, B.N. Nazar'ev, testifies to a similar conversation that occurred in the mid-1850s; he once called on a friend who met him with the following remark: 'How sorry I am that you are late [...] What marvels you would have heard ... you would have learned that Shakespeare is an inexhaustible graphomaniac, and that our amazement and regard for Shakespeare are nothing more than a desire to keep up with others and the habit of repeating foreign opinions.' ('Как жаль, что опоздали [...] Вот бы наслушались всяких чудес ... Узнали бы, что Шекспир – дюжинный писака, и что наше удивление и восхищение Шекспиром – не более, как желание не отстать от других и привычка повторять чужие мнения.') (V. Nazar'ev, 'Zhizn' i liudi bylogo vremeni', *Istoricheskii vestnik*, 11 (1890), 442; also quoted in Gusev, *Lev Nikolaevich Tolstoy. Materialy k biografii, 1855–1869*, 5).

42   *Lev Tolstoy, Diaries*, 16 November 1856, in *Collected Works*, vol. 47, 100.

43   Tolstoy, Letters to Sofia Tolstaia, 28 and 29 January 1884, in A.E. Gruzinskii, ed., *Pis'ma gr. Tolstogo k zhene (1862–1910)* (Moscow: A.A. Evenson, 1915), 214–15 ('Читал Шекспира "Кориолана" ... несомненную чепуху, которая может нравиться только

It was not until 1903, however, that Tolstoy decided to summarize his reflections in an essay on Shakespearean drama that, as he put it, had bewildered him during the entirety of his creative life.

> Calling to mind that struggle between doubt and self-deceit, my efforts to attune myself to Shakespeare, which I went through owing to my complete disagreement with this universal adulation, and, presuming that many have experienced and are experiencing the same, I think that it may not be unprofitable to express definitely and frankly this view of mine, opposed to that of the majority [...] for the last fifty years. In order to test myself, I recommenced reading Shakespeare several times in every possible form, in Russian, in English, in German and in Schlegel's translation, as I was advised. I have read the dramas and the comedies and historical plays a number of times, and I invariably underwent the same feelings: repulsion, weariness, and bewilderment.[44]

For a few years his essay *Shakespeare and Drama* remained on the back burner: initially it was written as a preface for the Russian edition of Ernest Crosby's volume on *Shakespeare's Attitude to the Working Classes*. The project, however, had not been realized; and it was only in the summer of 1905 that Tolstoy agreed to submit his article as a foreword to the new English edition of Crosby's work. The translation was commended to Vladimir Chertkov – Tolstoy's most devoted friend and spiritual executive, who at that time found himself living in exile in England,[45] and could easily proceed with the task.

актерам' or 'Утром прочел "Макбета" с большим вниманием, – балаганную пьесу, писанную умным и памятливым актером, который начитался умных книг').

44   Lev Tolstoy, *Tolstoy on Shakespeare*, Vladimir Tchertkoff, trans. (New York and London: Funk & Wagnalls Company, 1906), 3–5.

45   In 1897, Vladimir Chertkov was forced to leave Russia as a result of his help and support to the Dukhobors (Spirit Fighters) – a Christian sect whose doctrine was very close to that of Tolstoy. 'Spirit Fighters', was originally a derogatory label which the Russian Orthodox authorities used to accuse them of being at war with the Holy Spirit; but they embraced it as conveying that they fought with spiritual rather than temporal weapons. The Dukhobors were persecuted by the Orthodox Church and the government of Nicholas II, before being allowed to leave the country in 1897. Tolstoy arranged for the royalties from his novel *Resurrection* and some other stories to go to the migration fund.

In this context, it is worth mentioning that Tolstoy was not unique in his Shakespeare-heresy – it was a strong and venerable tradition among men of letters and counted among its ranks such eminent figures as Voltaire, Napoleon, Byron and William Morris. Nicholas Rowe, Shakespeare's first editor and biographer, presented 'an apology for him as a writer with obvious and admitted shortcomings'; and Dr Johnson came out with some 'downright hard hitting criticism'[46] in his scholarly research. Tolstoy, nevertheless, was fully aware of the controversial nature of such an outlook, which, in his own words, was 'in direct opposition [...] to that established in the whole European world.'[47] Reasonably enough, he had always been looking for some extra evidence in support of his postulations, dutifully provided by those who were aware of his views. Stasov, for instance, once sent him a volume of Max Nordau's *Französische Zeitmässigkeiten* with an article on Schiller's *Don Carlos*, where the works of Shakespeare had been unfavourably reviewed.[48]

Shaw's negative attitude towards Shakespeare must have been sufficiently well known all around. On many occasions the British dramatist expressed extreme disdain for Stratford's favourite son: one section in Shaw's preface to *Three Plays for Puritans* was symptomatically entitled 'Better than Shakespeare', and a series of his reviews of the English productions of Shakespeare's plays, as well as a number of articles published in the *Saturday Review* in 1895–1898, bore clear witness to his attempts to dissolve the myth surrounding the classic playwright. Although neither of these works featured conspicuously in Tolstoy's essay, he was undoubtedly aware of Shaw's views, which were mentioned directly in their correspondence with Chertkov. Thus, in one of his letters concerning the publication of the article, Chertkov reminded Tolstoy of 'the foremost British critic [Bernard Shaw]' who, as Tolstoy might remember, 'had a similar adverse

---

46   Shaw, Letter to Tchertkoff, August 1905, in *Collected Letters*, vol. 2, 552.

47   Tolstoy, *Tolstoy on Shakespeare*, 3.

48   V.D. Komarova and V.L. Modzalevskii, eds, *Lev Tolstoy i V.V. Stasov. Perepiska, 1878–1906* (Leningrad: Priboi, 1929), 314. Vladimir Stasov (1824–1906) was one of the most eminent Russian art and music critics of the nineteenth century, a long-term friend of Lev Tolstoy and a great supporter of realist art and *The Mighty Five* group of Russian composers that included Borodin, Musorgskii and Rimskii-Korsakov.

attitude towards Shakespeare', and of how Tolstoy, 'had even been taken aback, though only initially, by a certain similarity between his own claims and those that had been elaborated regarding Shakespeare by Shaw.'[49]

Given the circumstances, it was only natural that while working on his translation of Tolstoy's essay, Chertkov decided to approach Shaw, asking for advice and clarification of certain issues, and at the same giving him an outline of Tolstoy's stance. Shaw responded with a long and enthusiastic letter, manifesting his full endorsement of the Russian novelist's views (this letter was even included in the first edition of the volume that contained Tolstoy's preface and Crosby's *Shakespeare's Attitude to the Working Classes*). 'I, for one,' wrote Shaw,

> shall value Tolstoy's criticism all the more because it is the criticism of a foreigner who cannot possibly be enchanted by the mere word music which makes Shakespeare so irresistible in England.
>
> In Tolstoy's estimation, Shakespeare must fall or stand as a thinker, in which capacity I do not think he will stand a moment's examination from so hard-headedly keen a critic and religious realist.[50]

Shaw radically changed his opinion of Tolstoy's essay when he saw the full text published some three months later (November 1905). He hastened to write to Chertkov an extended letter (soon followed by another), which contained a meticulous and rather harsh criticism of Tolstoy's analysis and a straightforward conclusion that 'in general it was a very bad article.'[51]

Without disregarding his other writings, Tolstoy placed the focus of his analysis on *King Lear*, which, as he admitted, was commonly regarded

---

49 Vladimir Chertkov, Letter to Lev Tolstoy, 21 November 1905 (archive of the Tolstoy Museum in Iasnaia Poliana), quoted in S. Breitburg, 'B. Shou v spore s Tolstym o Shekspire', in *Literaturnoe nasledstvo* (Moscow: Akademiia Nauk SSSR, 1939), vol. 37/38, 618 ('о Bernard Shaw, здешнем первом литературном критике, который, помните, высказывался против Шекспира [...] было даже "в первую минуту досадно" на некоторое сходство соответственных своих предположений с тем, "что он [Шоу] пытался выяснить по поводу Шекспира"').

50 Shaw, Letter to Tchertkoff, August 1905, in *Collected Letters*, vol. 2, 552.

51 Shaw, Letter to Tchertkoff, 3 November 1905; quoted (in Russian) in Breitburg, 'B. Shou v spore s Tolstym o Shekspire', 624.

as the pinnacle of Shakespeare's creative output (*"King Lear* may be recognized as the perfect model for the dramatic art of the whole world," says Shelley'[52]). Tolstoy thought highly neither of the intellectual substance nor of the artistic qualities of the play. He claimed that its contents revealed a monstrous and vulgar view of life, which presents the elevation of the powers of this world as a result of their inherent superiority over the common man and refutes not only religious, but even any humanitarian efforts to alter the existing *status quo* of society:

> The subject of Shakespeare's pieces, as is seen from the demonstrations of his greatest admirers, is the lowest, most vulgar view of life, which regards the external elevation of the lords of the world as a genuine distinction, despises the crowd, e.g., the working classes, and repudiates not only all religious, but also all humanitarian strivings directed to the betterment of the existing order.[53]

Furthermore, he believed that the play lacked sincerity of expression, which was detrimental to its artistic value, making it a piece of mechanical and meaningless claptrap: 'sincerity is completely absent from all of Shakespeare's works. In all of them one sees intentional artifice; one sees that he is not in earnest, but that he is playing with words.'[54]

The first point was entirely supported by Shaw, who was 'in fair agreement' with the corresponding chapters (VI–VIII) of Tolstoy's text (and on this subject his opinion remained unchanged from his impressions of the first draft).[55] Shaw affirmed that the intellectual value of Shakespeare's plays was completely overrated; he agreed that Shakespeare had a poor philosophical outlook; that his plays conveyed no religious, moral, or social thought worthy of consideration, and as he mentioned earlier, 'After the criticism of Tolstoy, Shakespeare as a thinker must be discarded, for under the scrutiny of such a gigantic, bold critic and realist as Tolstoy, he will in no sense pass the test.'[56] He also pointed out that he himself had

52 Tolstoy, *Tolstoy on Shakespeare*, 7.
53 Tolstoy, *Tolstoy on Shakespeare*, 93–4.
54 Tolstoy, *Tolstoy on Shakespeare*, 94.
55 Shaw, Letter to Tchertkoff, 3 November 1905, quoted in Breitburg, 'B. Shou v spore s Tolstym o Shekspire', 623.
56 Shaw, Letter to Tchertkoff, August 1905, in *Collected Letters*, vol. 2, 552.

put forward a similar view in the preface to his recently reprinted novel *The Irrational Knot*, where he defined

> the first order in literature as consisting of those works in which the author, instead of accepting the current morality and religion ready-made without any question as to their validity, writes from an original moral standpoint of his own, thereby making his book an original contribution to morals, religion, and sociology, as well as to *belles lettres*. I place Shakespeare with Dickens, Scott, Dumas *père*, etc., in the second order, because, though they are enormously entertaining, their morality is ready-made; and I point out that the one play, 'Hamlet', in which Shakespeare made an attempt to give as a hero one who was dissatisfied with the ready-made morality, is the one which has given the highest impression of his genius, although Hamlet's revolt is unskilfully and inconclusively suggested and not worked out with any philosophic competence.[57]

Unlike Tolstoy, however, Shaw made a strong distinction between Shakespeare as a philosopher and Shakespeare as an artist. While debunking his reputation as a thinker, he had a genuine admiration for Shakespeare as a musician of words. 'It is quite impossible,' he wrote, 'to make them [the English] understand that Shakespeare's extraordinary literary power, his fun, his mimicry, and the endearing qualities that earned him the title of 'the gentle Shakespeare' – all of which, whatever Tolstoy may say, are unquestionable facts – do not stand or fall with his absurd reputation as a thinker.'[58] Shaw believed that as a foreigner, Tolstoy was utterly insensitive to the stylistic nuances and poetic subtlety of Shakespeare's language and exemplified his claim by two incontestable lapses that occurred in Tolstoy's text,[59] and could not be seen as anything other than a failure of perception. The first referred to the last scene of the tragedy, specifically to The Duke of Albany's remark to Regan: 'If you will marry, make your loves to me',

---

57   Shaw, Letter to Tchertkoff, August 1905, in *Collected Letters*, vol. 2, 551.
58   Shaw, Letter to Tchertkoff, August 1905, in *Collected Letters*, vol. 2, 552.
59   According to Shaw's letter, the text that he received also contained a major factual error: when discussing *Othello*, both Othello and Iago were presented by the author as negroes (not even Moors); struck by such an extraordinary 'discovery', Shaw asked Chertkov to verify the translation; and the point about Iago was corrected in the published version of the text (Shaw, Letter to Tchertkoff, 3 November 1905, quoted in Breitburg, 'B. Shou v spore s Tolstym o Shekspire', 624).

which was read literally by the Russian novelist, completely missing the irony of the Duke's offer.[60] Another concerned the second scene of the same act, which contains Edgar's notable words: 'Men must endure / Their going hence, even as their coming hither; / Ripeness is all.' Once again, Tolstoy took the phrase at face value, and by placing the emphasis on its first part, interpreted it as Edgar's cheerful advice not to fall into despair,[61] which, according to Shaw, completely distorted the deeper metaphysical meaning of the quotation, turning it into sheer banality. In the same vein, Shaw denied emphatically Tolstoy's point on the lack of originality in the speeches of Shakespeare's characters, that 'Lear raves exactly as does Edgar when feigning madness' and that 'both Kent and the fool speak alike.'[62] With his intrinsic sense of irony, Shaw concluded that after such a claim Tolstoy may go so far as to say that 'because all the characters in Mozart's opera sing in the same key and in the same artistic style, the aria of Leporello suits Don Giovanni no more than it suits himself.'[63] Shaw affirms that Tolstoy's reading of Shakespeare owes much to the viewpoint of a foreigner, for whom, for instance, the scene of a duel between Edgar and Edmund is nothing but vulgar pomposity and exaggeration, while for the English ear the words 'Draw thy sword that, if my speech offend a noble heart, thine

60   In Tolstoy we read: 'Here everything becomes so confused that it is difficult to follow the action. The Duke of Albany wishes to arrest Edmund, and tells Regan that Edmund has long ago entered into guilty relations with his wife, and that, therefore, Regan must give up her claims to Edmund, and if she wishes to marry, should marry him, the Duke of Albany' (Tolstoy, *Tolstoy on Shakespeare*, 42). Shaw points out that Tolstoy's rendition of the scene is misleading: he overlooks the mocking quality of the Duke's comment, to the effect that 'every English reader will perceive it [the Duke's remark] as a perfectly serious proposal' (Shaw, Letter to Tchertkoff, 3 November 1905, quoted in Breitburg, 'B. Shou v spore s Tolstym o Shekspire', 625).

61   In Tolstoy we read: 'Edgar enters, leading his father Gloucester, seats him by a tree, and goes away himself. The noise of battle is heard, Edgar runs back and says that the battle is lost and Lear and Cordelia are prisoners. Gloucester again falls into despair. Edgar, still without disclosing himself to his father, counsels endurance, and Gloucester immediately agrees with him' (Tolstoy, *Tolstoy on Shakespeare*, 40–1).

62   Tolstoy, *Tolstoy on Shakespeare*, 54.

63   Shaw, Letter to Tchertkoff, 3 November 1905, quoted in Breitburg, 'B. Shou v spore s Tolstym o Shekspire', 629.

arm might do thee justice' sound like a call of a trumpet, they are beautiful in sound, heroic in content and are not associated with anything vulgar in the one who pronounces them.[64]

In general Shaw dismissed the entire approach of the Russian novelist, who attempted to apply the principles of formal logic to the realm of imagination and creative fantasy. 'If Tolstoy will start arguing [...] as if he tries to examine the validity of a proven fact, instead of criticising the value of artistic imagination,' wrote Shaw, 'the readers will lose their patience.'[65] Even more emphatically he denied Tolstoy's claims regarding the unmotivated behaviour and illogical reactions of Shakespearean characters. As an example he took the last scene of *King Lear*, which found the following rendition in Tolstoy's article:

> After this enters Lear with the dead Cordelia in his arms, although he is more than eighty years old and ill. Again Lear begins his awful ravings, during which one feels as embarrassed as after an unsuccessful joke. Lear demands that all should howl, and, alternately, believes that Cordelia is dead and that she is alive [...] Then he says that he killed the slave who hanged Cordelia. Next he says that his eyes see badly, but at the same time he recognises Kent, whom all along he had not recognised.[66]

Shaw maintains that such a trivialized rendition of the original can be called nothing but 'childish': not only does it obliterate the remarkable euphony of Shakespeare's language, but it also destroys the emotional poetic power of the text: 'I am not blinded by Shakespeare's glory,' writes Shaw, 'but I try to avoid reading the last scene of "King Lear", because it makes me cry and upsets me [...] Life is not logical [...] and it is not for Tolstoy, writing his productions as a poet, to condemn Shakespeare for not writing his as a jurist.'[67] All of the above led him to conclude that 'in this way one can

---

64   Shaw, Letter to Tchertkoff, 3 November 1905, quoted in Breitburg, 'B. Shou v spore s Tolstym o Shekspire', 629.
65   Shaw, Letter to Tchertkoff, 3 November 1905, quoted in Breitburg, 'B. Shou v spore s Tolstym o Shekspire', 625.
66   Tolstoy, *Tolstoy on Shakespeare*, 44–5.
67   Shaw, Letter to Tchertkoff, 3 November 1905, quoted in Breitburg, 'B. Shou v spore s Tolstym o Shekspire', 625–6.

disparage any literary work of the classical rhetorical school'[68] and that 'to his genuine criticism of Shakespeare, Tolstoy added a pointless accusation worthy of that made by English Quakers regarding the "Resurrection."'[69] Such a harsh verdict, however, did not prevent Shaw from accepting Chert-kov's request to publish the first letter as an afterword to Tolstoy's essay; he only asked for an assurance that there would be a note (dutifully placed by Chertkov) to the effect that he did not identify himself with the lapses in Tolstoy's text mentioned above.[70]

Chertkov, for whom Tolstoy, as his teacher, could do no wrong, promptly sent both letters to Iasnaia Poliana, saying that 'the harshness of the first one would not upset you, and indeed you may find certain points useful.'[71] He also expressed the opinion that Shaw was simply jealous of the remarkable originality of Tolstoy's views that 'as the English say, have taken all the wind out of his sails.'[72] Tolstoy, indeed, did not seem to be troubled by the letter and in his answer to Chertkov simply pointed out: 'Got your Shaw letter. Do not send me the Shakespeare, but print it as it is. If it does

68   Shaw, Letter to Tchertkoff, 3 November 1905, quoted in Breitburg, 'B. Shou v spore s Tolstym o Shekspire', 626.

69   Shaw, Letter to Tchertkoff, 3 November 1905, quoted in Breitburg, 'B. Shou v spore s Tolstym o Shekspire', 630. A full Russian version of *Resurrection* was published by the London Quaker firm Headley Bros in 1901, and translated into many languages with the proceeds going to the Quakers' Dukhobor Committee (see note 6). But the subject matter of the novel proved an embarrassment to the community of Quakers. The Committee decided that they ought not to accept proceeds from 'a smutty book' and the clerk, John Bellows, refunded the money out of his own pocket (Rosemary Edmonds, Translator's Introduction, in Leo Tolstoy, *Resurrection* [London: Penguin, 1966], 6–7).

70   Shaw, Letter to Tchertkoff, 19 November 1905, quoted in Breitburg, 'B. Shou v spore s Tolstym o Shekspire', 630.

71   Chertkov, Letter to Tolstoy, 21 November 1905, quoted in Breitburg, 'B. Shou v spore s Tolstym o Shekspire', 631 ('резкость первого вас не расстроит, а, может быть, в каких-либо его замечаниях вы и найдете что-либо для себя производительное').

72   Chertkov, Letter to Tolstoy, 21 November 1905, quoted in Breitburg, 'B. Shou v spore s Tolstym o Shekspire', 631 ('как говорят англичане, have taken all the wind out of his sails').

contain those blunders Shaw mentions, correct them yourself.'[73] In fairness to Shaw, it should be said that his regard for Tolstoy was generally quite high and in his last letter he even pointed out that he placed great importance on any opinion the Russian novelist expounded, and thought of him 'as one of the greatest prophets of the time (in the correct biblical sense of the word).'[74] This episode, therefore, did not leave any bitterness, and did not prevent both writers from engaging in further correspondence.

Further rapprochement between Tolstoy and Shaw was undoubtedly facilitated by Aylmer Maude, who was a fellow Fabian and a close friend of the British dramatist. Aylmer Maude received his higher education in Russia and stayed there until 1897. He was an admirer and a frequent guest of Tolstoy at Iasnaia Poliana, where he used to play chess and tennis with the great writer and enjoyed long discussions with members of his circle. Tolstoy made return visits to Maude's house in Moscow, getting to know his wife Louise and their boys, and even teaching them 'to make paper cockerels – the art they never lost.'[75] After the Maudes returned to England, they became the most devoted translators of Tolstoy's works and maintained a regular correspondence until the end of his life. Aylmer Maude was the author of the first English biography of Tolstoy, approved and authorized by the writer himself. In his review of Maude's *The Life of Tolstoy: Later Years* (1911), Shaw claimed that this work had a special significance for the Fabian Society: 'being written by a Fabian, it instinctively answers the particular questions about Tolstoy's life a Fabian would ask' and casts light on facets of Tolstoy's creative output that were particularly important for the Fabians' ethos.[76]

73   Tolstoy, Letter to Vladimir Chertkov, 19 December 1905, in *Collected Works*, vol. 89, 29; also quoted in Breitburg, 'B. Shou v spore s Tolstym o Shekspire', 631 (Получил сейчас ваше письмо Shaw. Шекспира мне не присылайте, а печатайте как он есть. Если есть те blunders, о к[оторых] говорит Shaw, исправьте их сами).

74   Shaw, Letter to Tchertkoff, 19 November, 1905, quoted in Breitburg, 'B. Shou v spore s Tolstym o Shekspire', 631.

75   Harvey J. Pitcher, *The Smiths of Moscow* (Cramer: The Swallow House Books, 1984), 29.

76   Bernard Shaw, 'Our Bookshelf: The Life of Tolstoy: Later Years', 1 May 1911 (first published in *Fabian News* [22 May 1911], 45–6), in Brian Tyson, ed., *Bernard Shaw's Book Reviews* (University Park: Pennsylvania State University, 1996), vol. 2, 254.

It is, perhaps, as a direct result of this influence that Shaw decided to initiate a correspondence with the Russian writer; and it was through Maude that Shaw became aware that Tolstoy paid close attention to his works: in one of her letters to Aylmer Maude (May 1907), Tatiana Sukhotina, Tolstoy's eldest daughter, wrote that Lev Nikolaevich read Shaw's plays with great interest, especially his *Major Barbara* – a message that Maude immediately communicated to Shaw.[77] Aligning himself with Tolstoy's views on culture as a reflection of social concerns, toward the end of 1906 Shaw decided to send him a copy of his play *Man and Superman* (1902–3), to which Tolstoy made a note in his diary (12 January 1907): 'Finished Shaw. He has more brains than is good for him. The article "Progress" is very good; he is very witty.'[78]

In a letter dated 17 August 1908, the Russian writer acknowledged receipt of the play. Tolstoy declared himself delighted with the author's outlook on modern civilization and progress, but made two reproaches. Firstly, Shaw was not sufficiently serious; the second was that the questions raised by Shaw had such importance that people understanding the evils of life so well, and possessing such literary talent as he, did more harm than good by making them subjects for satire. Tolstoy also profoundly disagreed with Shaw on the ways in which social conditions could be improved, placing emphasis on religion and spiritual elevation rather than on the formation of 'supermen', for which, in his words, 'there should be some special conditions that are as unlikely to be achieved as perfecting mankind by means of progress and civilization.'[79] In conclusion, Tolstoy remarked regretfully that, in his opinion, Shaw's views in the play did not come across in a clear and accessible form and required some further elucidation: 'In your book I see a desire to strike the reader with your talent and your wit. Not only is this unnecessary for the issues you raise, but quite often it distracts the reader from the essence of the subject matter, drawing his attention to the

---

77   Aylmer Maud, *The Life of Tolstoy. Later Years* (New York: Dodd, Mead and Company, 1911), vol. 2, 682.

78   L.N. Tolstoy, *O literature. Stat'i. Pis'ma. Dnevniki* (Moscow: Khudozhestvennaia literatura, 1955), 586.

79   Tolstoy, Letter to Bernard Shaw, 17 August 1908, in *Collected Works*, vol. 78, 201–2.

brilliance of expression.'[80] Tolstoy's opinion was also affirmed in the memoirs of Aylmer Maude, who gives the following account of his conversation with Tolstoy during his visit in Iasnaia Poliana in September 1909:

> He had been reading Bernard Shaw's plays, and said that Shaw is original, and many of his sayings are quite admirable and deserve to become quotations; but that he has the defect of wishing to be original and to take his readers by surprise. That is a pity. One desires to merge into the mind of an author one likes, and to do so is impossible if he is bent on saying unexpected things. Tolstoy was much interested to hear of the plot of Blanco Posnet (then not yet published), which he thought very promising – and he wished to read the play, because, as he said, to many people the working of man's conscience is the only proof of the existence of a God.[81]

On his return to England, Maude hastened to pass the message to Shaw, who in reply sent a copy of his *The Shewing-up of Blanco Posnet* (1909) to the Russian novelist, with a letter in which he elucidated its debt to Tolstoy's *Power of Darkness* (written in 1889, and performed by the London Stage Society in 1904). He also mentioned a strong link with his own *Man and Superman*, which, in his words, was based on the same idea, 'but expressed in another way – not in the way that an uneducated man can understand.'[82] Clearly Tolstoy's criticism had not passed unnoticed, and in his letter Shaw specifically mentioned his attempt to follow Tolstoy's example in clarity and simplicity, which would make the play accessible even for an unsophisticated audience: 'In form it is a very crude melodrama, which might

---

80   Tolstoy, *O literature*, 595–6.
81   Maude, *The Life of Tolstoy. Later Years*, 641.
82   Shaw, Letter to Lev Tolstoy, 14 February 1910, in *Collected Letters*, vol. 2, 900. Tolstoy–Shaw correspondence was first mentioned in April 1912, in one of the French leading literary journals *La Grand Revue* (*New York Times* [7 April 1912]). The Russian publishers reacted much quicker: in a letter signed by N.W. Tchaykowsky (c.1911), Shaw was asked for consent regarding the Russian translation of *Blanco Posnet* (LSE Archives, F. SHAW/15/3, list 1). The edition appeared in 1911 and was supplemented by the scene in Hell from *Man and Superman*, as well as by Shaw's correspondence with Tolstoy (Bernard Shou, *Razoblachenie Blanko Pozneta. Stsena v adu*, L.P. Nikiforov and V.M. Shuliatikov, trans. [Moscow: Izd. S. Dorovatovskogo i A. Charushnikova, 1911], 5–13).

be played in a mining camp to the roughest audience. It is, if I may say so, the sort of play that you do extraordinarily well.'[83]

Shaw emphasized that the entire concept of the play was borrowed from Tolstoy's *Power of Darkness*, as he put it in the letter:

> I remember nothing in the whole range of drama that fascinated me more than the old soldier in your 'Power of Darkness' (I do not know the Russian title: that is what we call it in England) [...] and in 'Blanco Posnet' I have exploited in my own fashion this mine of dramatic material which you were the first to open up to modern playwrights.[84]

and although at first glance a comparison between Shaw's *Blanco Posnet* and the *Power of Darkness* does not reveal any close parallels either in setting or in the structure of the plot, there is an intimate connection between these two, apparently different, dramas. Blanco Posnet is a disreputable individual, who challenges and upsets the life of a provincial American town. He is an outcast, but returns the hatred of his neighbours with scorn. Nothing is sacred for Blanco. He ridicules the moralizing rhetoric of his brother Elder Daniel, a priest in the local church; he is a drunk and a philanderer, and is finally chased by townsmen for stealing a horse. On his way out of the town he meets a mother who needs to get her sick son to a doctor. Blanco is deeply touched by her grief. He surrenders the horse, knowing that he will thereby forfeit any chance of escape, and that this merciful deed could cost him his life. It seems that Blanco suddenly has a divine revelation of the path to righteousness; he finds his inner light and his way to God: 'He's a sly one,' says Blanco, 'He's a mean one. He lies low for you. He plays cat and mouse with you. He lets you run loose until you think you're shut of Him; and then, when you least expect it, He's got you.'[85] And although the subject matter of the play is not remotely close to Tolstoy's account of the life of Russian peasants, the general idea is clearly the same – spiritual enlightenment elicited not by the rhapsodies of unworthy prayers, but by

---

83   Shaw, Letter to Tolstoy, 14 February 1910, in *Collected Letters*, vol. 2, 900.
84   Shaw, Letter to Tolstoy, 14 February 1910, in *Collected Letters*, vol. 2, 900.
85   Bernard Shaw, *The Shewing-up of Blanco Posnet*, in *Collected Plays*, vol. III, 774.

a simple act of human kindness. In this context it is worth recalling that it was exactly this aspect of Tolstoy's *Power of Darkness* that Shaw found most penetrating and moving:

> One of the things that struck me in that play was that the preaching of the pious old father, right as he was, could never be of any use – that it could only anger his son and rub the last grains of self-respect out of him. But what the pious and good father could not do, the old rascal of a soldier did as if he was the voice of God. To me that scene where the two drunkards are wallowing in the straw, and the older rascal lifts the younger one above his cowardice and his selfishness, has an intensity of effect that no merely romantic scene could possibly attain.[86]

The major difference between Blanco Posnet and Tolstoy's *Power of Darkness* was in the religious attitudes of the authors (later on, Shaw elaborated on these matters in his article 'Mr Shaw's Clash with Tolstoy'[87]). Shaw disagreed with the idea of Akim's Christian repentance – the proponent of the spirit of Tolstoy's play. In *Blanco Posnet* he is recast into the contemptible Elder Daniels – the mouthpiece of a rotten religious establishment incapable of creating a sustainable morality. Tolstoy, on the other hand, found Shaw's mockery unacceptable and upsetting, as he put it in his response to the British dramatist: 'the problem about God and evil is too important to be spoken of in jest. And therefore I will tell you frankly that I received a very painful impression from the concluding words of your letter: "Suppose the world were only one of God's jokes, would you strive any less to make it a good joke instead of a bad one."'[88]

It is slightly surprising, therefore, that Shaw with his sardonic atheism should have come up with a straightforward drama of flagrant redemption, which in all its seriousness does not sound Shavian enough. On closer consideration, however, one can see that it had been a while that these issues

---

86   Shaw, Letter to Tolstoy, 14 February 1910, in *Collected Letters*, vol. 2, 900.
87   'Mr Shaw's Clash with Tolstoy', *Evening Standard* (6 February 1928). See also David Matual, 'Shaw's The Shewing-up of Blanco Posnet and Tolstoy's The Power of Darkness', in Charles A. Berst, ed., *Shaw and Religion* (University Park: Pennsylvania State University Press, 1981), 129–40.
88   Tolstoy, Letter to Bernard Shaw, 15–26 April 1910, in *Collected Works*, vol. 81, 255.

stayed on his horizon and that he touched upon the questions of acquired consciousness in such works as *Saint Joan* and *Androcles and the Lion* as well as in *The Devil's Disciple*. Leaving aside the rightness of Tolstoy's views on Christianity, it is true that both Shaw and Tolstoy were highly critical of organized religion, and both examined the development of the divine spark within human beings. Not unlike Tolstoy, Shaw was aware of a 'moral passion' (the 'inner light', to use the terminology of Aylmer Maude, who was brought up in a Quaker family) and believed in a divine force that must be recognized, though not necessarily idolized or worshipped. Presumably, this is what Blanco becomes aware of, and what makes him do the right thing – not dissimilar to some of Shaw's other characters, such as Dick Dudgeon in *The Devil's Disciple* or John Tanner in *Man and Superman*, who also find themselves at the mercy of their own moral passion or 'life force' in perpetual progress, as Shaw calls it in one of his perhaps most 'scientific' dramas, *Back to Methuselah*.[89]

The illuminating power of a simple act or an artless viewpoint, so characteristic of Tolstoy's writings, was praised by Shaw as one of the most effective devices in modern drama. In Tolstoy's plays (and prose works) social critique is often expressed through techniques that might be termed 'the outlook of a naïve observer'. This means that the situation is conveyed through the eyes of a character who has neither the knowledge nor the experience to give a competent rendition of the events, and therefore is capable of brushing aside conventional and socially accepted generalities. Being free of habitual perception, he is struck by the incongruity of human behaviour, thus revealing to the audience its complete absurdity. To give only a few examples, one can mention *The Fruits of Enlightenment*, when the peasants bear witness to the peculiar comportment of their masters during a spiritualist séance or an attempt to disinfect the house after the visitors. Similarly, in *Power of Darkness*, the vices of usury are exposed though the peasants' inability to comprehend the concept of the banking system and interest rates:

89   Bernard Shaw, *Back to Methuselah*, in *Collected Plays*, vol. V, 290.

MITRICH Why, brother, that's what they like to do better than anything else. Just mark my word, anyone who's rather stupid, or a woman, for instance, who can't use their money in business, why, they take it to the bank, and, as it were, barley pirogs fall into their mouths all cooked with that money; but it cheats the people. It's a clever trick.

AKIM (sighing) Eh! I see how it is! Why, don't you know, when you haven't any money, it's woe and tribulation; but when you have, it's twice as bad, don't you know? Anyhow, God commanded us to work. But, don't you see, you put your money in the bank and go to sleep, and expect it to feed you, don't you know. Why! It's rascally business, don't you know, and contrary to the law![90]

Shaw's esteem for the effectiveness of Tolstoy's critique was based on similar affinities, for time and again he resorted to comparable devices in his plays. For instance, in *Arms and the Man*, Shaw's antimilitary stance is put across not through a professionally informed serviceman, but through Bluntschli, a Swiss hotel-keeper. The latter has a good grasp of the commercial implications of warfare, and his business-like approach exposes the absurdity of Major Saranoff's patriotic aspirations. Likewise, in *Augustus Does His Bit*, Lord Augustus Highcastle is incapable of grasping the true meaning of war only because he is so keenly interested in it. The unraveller appears to be a simple clerk, who has a poor understanding of military matters, but feels that they bring nothing but suffering to the common people: 'What are they dying for?', he says, 'To keep me alive, ain't it? Well, what's the good of that if I'm dead of hunger by the time they come back?'[91] In the same vein, a servant in *Fanny's First Play* teaches *etiquette* to his master, and a waiter in *You Never Can Tell* becomes the leading authority on issues of polite society. This was Shaw's answer to the established attitude of his contemporaries which, in his own words, 'let light into some dark places and fresh air into some unwholesome sanctuaries,'[92] and which, as one can see, has a curious parallel with the writings of Tolstoy.

90 Lev Tolstoy, *Power of Darkness*, in *The Novels and Other Works of Lyof N. Tolstoï*, vol. 16, 285.

91 Bernard Shaw, *Augustus Does His Bit*, in *Collected Plays*, vol. V, 210.

92 Quoted in Dan H. Laurence, 'Approaching the Challenge', *SHAW: the Annual of Bernard Shaw Studies*, 16 (1996), vol. 16, 31.

In May 1921 Shaw published an article in *The London Mercury*, in which, when analysing the works of Tolstoy, Ibsen, and Strindberg, he defined a new dramatic genre of tragi-comedy, to which he ascribed the majority of his own plays: 'It begins with tragedy with scraps of fun in it, like Macbeth, and ends as comedy without mirth in it, the place of mirth being taken by a more or less bitter and sarcastic irony.'[93] Shaw comes to the conclusion that, as a result of its development, twentieth-century comedy surpassed tragedy in its dramatic power. The latter, in his view, had not evolved much since the time of Antiquity; it had always been 'simple, sublime and overwhelming from the first: it either failed and was not tragedy at all, or else it got there so utterly that no need was felt of going any further.'[94] Comedy, on the other hand, was constantly developing into some new, more effective, form, employing black humour and sardonic farce, which resulted in the so-called hybrid genre of tragi-comedy, where 'the heroes are dying without hope or honour [...] and their existence and their downfall are not soul-purifying convulsions of pity and horror, but reproaches, challenges, criticisms addressed to society and to the spectator as a voting constituent of society.'[95]

Shaw names Tolstoy as one of the greatest masters of this new tragi-comedy genre, mainly for his 'most withering touch when he wants to destroy [...] He touches with his pen the drawing room, the kitchen, the doormat in the entrance-hall, and the toilet-tables upstairs. They wither like the garden of Klingsor at the sign of Parsifal.'[96] As an example, Shaw recalls an episode from Tolstoy's novella *The Death of Ivan Il'ich* (1886), where the visitor who came to console the widow of the deceased had to deal with a couple of practicalities before he was able to turn to his solemn mission: a fight with a revolting squeaking pouffe and the widow's black shawl that was caught on the edge of the dinner table:

93   Bernard Shaw, 'Tolstoy: Tragedian or Comedian?', *The London Mercury*, 4 (1921), 31.
94   Shaw, 'Tolstoy: Tragedian or Comedian?', 32.
95   Shaw, 'Tolstoy: Tragedian or Comedian?', 33.
96   Shaw, 'Tolstoy: Tragedian or Comedian?', 33–4.

Piotr Ivanovitch got up, in order to detach it; and the ottoman, freed from his weight, began to shake and jostle him. The widow her-self was busy disengaging her lace; and Piotr Ivanovitch sat down again, flattening out the ottoman which had rebelled under him. But still the widow could not get free, and Piotr Ivanovitch again arose; and again the ottoman rebelled, and even creaked.

When all this was arranged, she took out a clean cambric handkerchief, and began to weep.[97]

There is no moralizing, no overt irony, wrote Shaw, but 'instantly the mockery and folly of our funeral pomps and cemetery sentimentalities laugh in our faces.'[98] Not unlike Tolstoy, Shaw used similar devices in his own dramas, where a melodramatic stunt was turned into a successful means of social criticism. In this context one can recall cross-dressing in *The Man of Destiny*, which is employed in order to disparage the image of Napoleon or adultery (a man in a woman's bedroom) which contributes to the anti-military stance of *Arms and the Man*.

Social criticism was always at the centre of Shaw's literary agenda. He started his career in strong opposition to the classic melodrama which dominated the Victorian English stage and, in his opinion, was completely extraneous to the fundamental concerns of the day. It is in this spirit that he published a set of his *Plays Unpleasant*, where in the preface to *Widowers' Houses* he mocks commercially viable melodramas, as well as the conservative taste of his contemporaries receptive to this kind of sentimental entertainment:

> the hero was to propose to the sentimental heroine, believing her to be the poor niece instead of the rich daughter of the sweater, or slum-landlord, or whatever he may have been; and I know he was to carry on in the most heroic fashion, and was ultimately to succeed in throwing the tainted treasure of his father-in-law, metaphorically speaking, into the Rhine.[99]

---

97 Lev Tolstoy, *The Death of Ivan Ilyitch*, in *The Novels and Other Works of Lyof N. Tolstoï*, vol. 14, 7.
98 Shaw, 'Tolstoy: Comedian or Tragedian?', 33.
99 Bernard Shaw, Preface to *Widowers' Houses*, in *Collected Plays*, vol. I, 38.

Starting by focusing on the specific social issues of his time (marriage and prostitution in *Mrs Warren*; pacifism and armaments production in *Major Barbara*; the position of women in *Pygmalion*), he moved to a higher level of generalization in his later plays after World War I: evolution in *Back to Methuselah*, the institution of the English middle-class in *Heartbreak House*, and the questions of time and religion in *St Joan*; in his development as a dramatist Shaw was informed by the writing practice of Tolstoy, whom he called a forerunner to his *Heartbreak House*.[100] Following the growing complexity of the content, Shaw felt the need to expand the generic framework of the 'well made play' that had become too narrow to reflect the new spectrum of the human condition. He praised Tolstoy for his contribution to the hybrid genre of tragi-comedy that, in his opinion, was more suitable for the complex reality of modern times. In the same vein, he himself also tried to stretch the limits of dramatic text by infusing it with prose, by supplying long prefaces and extensive prologues to his plays (for instance, Ra's address to the audience in *Caesar and Cleopatra*), and providing detailed scenic directions for the performers, such as, for instance, his remarks for each act of *The Devil's Disciple*, which contain not only instructions for the setting, but also historical references and biographical notes on the characters.

The series of parallels between Shaw and Tolstoy can be extended even further. Both writers believed in the countervailing force of their art, both assumed a distinct anti-military stance in their writings, and both rejected the idea of science as a progressive and non-political force. The track of their thinking was so alike that when Shaw's attention was drawn to Tolstoy's article claiming that 'if a small number of people have power over the majority and oppress it, every victory over nature will inevitably serve only to increase that power and that oppression', he responded that 'it was

---

100 'His *Fruits of Culture*, coming long before Granville Barker's *Marrying of Ann Leete* or the plays of Tchekov, is the first of the *Heartbreak Houses*, and the most blighting [...] The Living Corpse is as alive as most fine gentlemen are. But gentry as an institution crumbles to dust at his casual remark that unless a gentleman gets a berth under Government as a soldier or diplomatist, there is nothing left for him to do but to kill himself with wine and women' (Shaw, 'Tolstoy: Tragedian or Comedian?', 33–4).

so true that it might have been made by himself',[101] or one can compare the following statements, which sound as if they were written by the same hand: 'The most sophisticated technological inventions, such as guns, torpedoes, solitary confinement, excise duty measuring equipment, the telegraph etc., are nothing but harmful for ordinary people'[102] and

> In the arts of life man invents nothing; but in the arts of death he outdoes Nature herself, and produces by chemistry and machinery all the slaughter of plague, pestilence and famine [...] In the arts of peace Man is a bungler [...] his clumsy typewriters and bungling locomotives and tedious bicycles: they are toys compared to the Maxim gun.[103]

Nevertheless, the first proposition is from Tolstoy's article *What Is to Be Done?* of 1882–1886 and the second belongs to one of Shaw's characters. As we have seen, the examples are manifold; and it is not the creative dependence of disciple upon a master, but a kinship of thinking of two of the most influential men of their time, who had a strong impact on its social and cultural agenda, who had an extreme candour of thought and were never afraid to upset the applecart. As Shaw put it in one of his conversations with Stephen Winsten: 'You talked of the age into which I was born as a great age. I regard it as the most villainous page of recorded history, redeemed only by men like Morris and Tolstoy, Ibsen and Gorki.'[104]

101   Stephen Winsten, *Days with Bernard Shaw* (London: Hutchinson and Co, London, 1949), 170.
102   Lev Tolstoy, *Tak chto zhe nam delat'?* (*What Is to be Done?*), in *Collected Works*, vol. 25, 356.
('Самые хитрые изобретения техники направлены прямо [...] на вред народа, как пушки, торпеды, одиночные тюрьмы, приборы для акциза, телеграфы и т.п.'); in his edition of *The Novels and Other Works of Lyof N. Tolstoï* [vol. 18, 216], Aylmer Maude, suggested a freer translation of this quote 'His [man's] most skilful inventions are [...] directly harmful to the people, as guns, torpedoes, solitary prisons, and so on').
103   Bernard Shaw, *Man and Superman*, in *Collected Plays*, vol. II, 653–4.
104   Winsten, *Days with Bernard Shaw*, 195–6.

CHAPTER THREE

'A Fantasia in the Russian Manner': Shaw and Maxim Gorky

On 8 May 1903 Shaw wrote in his letter to Janet Achurch:[1] 'I objected to *Candida* for Mayday because it was the wrong play for it. *Dolls House* is much better, though no doubt a Gorki would have been better still.'[2] On the one hand, these words show how highly the British dramatist thought of the new rising star of Russian realism; on the other, this phrase presents a bit of a mystery to those familiar with the reception of Russian literature at the beginning of the Edwardian era, as at this date Gorky's dramatic works still languished in relative obscurity even among the most progressive representatives of the English cultural elite.

Gorky's name in the West rested much less on his dramas than on his prose fiction. In the early years of the twentieth century he had made his reputation as a graphic and original prose-writer. His fiction was fashionable in Europe as well as across the Channel, and by 1901 Gorky's works were so much in demand that, according to *The New York Times*, several people were fighting over the honour of having introduced him to the English reading public. The paper attributed this privilege to Arthur Hornblow, who was the first to publish a translation of Gorky's short story 'Malva' in 1900.[3] By 1905 there were no fewer than ten translations of Gorky's fiction, including one of his major novels, *Foma Gorgeev* (translated by I.F. Hapgood and

---

1   Janet Achurch (1864–1916) was an English stage actress and theatre manager (she took over the management of The Novelty Theatre in London in 1893). From 1883 onwards, she played many Shakespearean roles, but is, perhaps, best known for interpretations of Ibsen; her most notable performance was Nora in *A Doll's House*.

2   Shaw, Letter to Janet Achurch, 8 May 1903, in *Collected Letters*, vol. 2, 323.

3   Eugene Limedorfer, 'The First Translation of Gorky's work', *The New York Times* (27 July 1901).

published by Fisher Unwin in 1901). These editions were supplemented by two extended studies of his life and writings (one by E.J. Dillon, which makes no mention of Gorky's dramatic pursuits, and another by Hans Ostwald)[4] which gave quite a laudatory rendition of Gorky's fiction and contributed to the rise of his name in England. As the *Westminster Review* put it, 'Few men in the history of literature have risen with such swiftness, none perhaps from such depth.'[5]

The start of Gorky's career saw a prolonged baptism of fire for the author. Born Aleksei Maksimovich Peshkov, he was orphaned at the age of nine and was raised by his grandmother. Deeply affected by her death, he travelled across the Russian Empire for several years, picking a precarious living and mixing with the outcasts and underclasses of society. His literary debut was rapid, unpredictable, and, according to the *Westminster Review*, tinted with the lucky touch of Providence that surrounded the mystery of his exotic talent and excited the popular imagination:

> In the autumn of 1892 there appeared at the office of *Kavkaz*, the leading newspaper in Tiflis, a young man dressed in workman's garb, offering a manuscript for publication. The editor glanced over it, accepted it, and promised to publish it in the following issue of his paper. 'But you have not signed it,' he observed. 'No, but you can sign it for me – Gorky – Maxim Gorky.' (Gorky – bitter, in Russian.) The MS, was entitled 'Makar Chudra,' and was duly published. Gorky had emerged! From this time his rise into fame was by leaps and bounds. In less than five years he was heralded in Russia as a star of the first magnitude, in less than ten his works were translated into every European language.[6]

Gorky was keenly involved in politics, different social movements and antimonarchist revolutionary activities, for which he was regularly expelled from a number of major Russian cities and subjected to periodical (though

---

4   E.J. Dillon, *Maxim Gorky, His Life and Writings* (London: Isbister and Company, 1902); Hans Ostwald, *Maxim Gorki* (London: William Heinemann, 1905). The latter came out two years later than Shaw's letter to Janet Achurch, and had a reference to Gorky's drama *The Lower Depths*.

5   James Burns, 'Maxim Gorky: A Voice from the Depths', *Westminster Review*, 160 (1903), 151.

6   Burns, 'Maxim Gorky: A Voice from the Depths', 150–1.

reasonably brief) arrests. One of these incidents provoked a violent public riot when in February 1905, during a performance of his play *Summerfolk* at The Solovtsov Theatre in Kiev, the audience used this opportunity to express their support for the banned author and demanded his immediate release.[7] Gorky became a member of the Russian Social Democratic Labour Party, and in 1906, using his legendary status, undertook a fundraising trip to the USA, where he met Mark Twain, Upton Sinclair and other literary figures of the time.

As a prolific author and public figure, Gorky was immensely popular in Russia. His works were circulated in an unprecedented print run of 100,000 copies, quickly consumed by various circles of the Russian liberal intelligentsia, as well as the educated members of the merchant and working classes. Literary critics, on the other hand, remained largely unconvinced by the artistic merits of his writings, placing emphasis on the crude realism of his works and on their naturalistic and didactic qualities. 'Maksim Gorky is whatever you want him to be – a preacher, a thinker, – but certainly not an artist,' claimed the reviewer of the *Theatre and Art* journal.[8] Similarly, Dmitrii Merezhkovskii, a prominent writer and one of the leading cultural figures of the time, maintained that although 'there is no art in Gorky's writings, there is something which is hardly less valuable than the highest possible form of art – life, the most genuine archetype of life.'[9]

This opinion was shared by the majority of foreign reviewers, who suggested that the English reader might examine Gorky's fiction either

---

7   *Revoliutsionnyi put' Gorkogo* (Moscow-Leningrad: Khudozhestvennaia literatura, 1933), 100–1.

8   A review of Gorky's *Philistines*, *Teatr i iskusstvo*, 45 (1902), 826 ('Максим Горький является всем, чем угодно, проповедником, мыслителем, только не художником').

9   D.S. Merezhkovskii, 'Gorky i Chekhov' (1906), in *Maksim Gorky: Pro et contra: Lichnost' i tvorchestvo Maksima Gorkogo v otsenke russkikh myslitelei i issledovatelei. 1890–1910-e gody* (St Petersburg: Izdatel'stvo Russkogo Khristianskogo gumanitarnogo instituta, 1997), 645 ('в произведениях Горького нет искусства, но в них есть то, что едва ли не менее ценно, чем самое высокое искусство: жизнь, правдивейший подлинник жизни, кусок, вырванный из жизни с телом и кровью').

as a narrative or as an illumination of 'the mysterious Russian soul'[10] (the critic himself was definitely inclined to pursue the second option). One of the most convinced Russophiles, Edward Garnett, cautioned that Gorky was first of all a man of action, and only secondly a writer;[11] and R. Nisbet Bain believed that he certainly could not be seen as an artist in the same sense as Tolstoy:

> We are wearied to death by endless philosophising, and dogmatising about all things in heaven and earth and under earth. The feeble, impossible hero is a persistent drag upon the narrative; second-hand Nietzschianism is rampant throughout, and, oddly enough, the religious influences which play so large a part in Russian middle-class life are represented as practically non-existent.[12]

The *Westminster Review*, on the other hand, found nothing wrong with the moralizing outpouring of Gorky's fiction. While praising his simmering anger about life in Russia and his determination to speak the bitter truth, it nevertheless pointed out that:

> his wrath against society played havoc with the truthfulness of his picture and the sincerity of his art [...] He has not yet entered into possession of himself and so has not patience enough to think out his characters, he cannot stand aloof from them, and look at them from without in the patient tutored way of the true artist [...] They speak his language and think his thoughts, and so become unnatural and too big for the canvas [...] All Maxim Gorky's little fishes talk like whales; he puts into the lips of his gypsies the most entrancing descriptions of nature, and his tramps are all philosophers engaged in the discussion of the most abstract theories.[13]

All this controversy, however, hardly made any impact on Gorky's standing, and the most important aspect of these critical writings was not the quality of their examination, but the frequency with which they appeared in the English press, sustaining public attention to the author and asserting his popularity among western readers. As a result, by 1910 Gorky was much better known among the English public than Chekhov (the situation has since been reversed), and surveys of British (and French) magazines put

10   Arthur Symons, 'The Russian Soul', *Saturday Review* (3 May 1902).
11   Edward Garnett, 'Maxim Gorky', *The Academy*, 60 (1901), 497.
12   R. Nisbet Bian, 'Maxim Gorky, *Monthly Review*, 5 (1901), 172.
13   Burns, 'Maxim Gorky: A Voice from the Depths', 152–3.

him first in their list of Tolstoy's younger successors, followed by Korolenko, Potapenko and only then, in fourth position, by Chekhov.[14]

Gorky's theatre work remained largely unknown among the British public, and it was not until December 1911 that a play of his enjoyed its first public performance in England. It was a highly successful production, mounted on the stage of the Kingsway Theatre in London, after which a number of British literary figures sent their warmest wishes to the Russian author: 'We the undersigned beg to offer you our sincere congratulations on the serious attention and favourable reception given to your drama *The Lower Depths* by a full and representative audience on the occasion of its performance at the Kingsway Theatre, being the first public performance in England on the second December 1911.'[15] The signatories included Henry James, Arthur Pinero, John Galsworthy, Edmund Gosse, Granville Barker, and Bernard Shaw. Shaw's esteem for Gorky's drama was hardly surprising. One of his favourite hypostases was that of a thinker, pontificating in the theatre which he saw as 'a combination of artistic ritual, profession of faith and sermon,'[16] and one dramatist with a similar spectrum of ideas was Maxim Gorky.

Gorky was encouraged to become a playwright by Chekhov, who also introduced him to the founders of the Moscow Art Theatre. It was with this theatre in mind that he wrote the first two of his seventeen dramatic works – *The Philistines* (1901) and *The Lower Depths* (1902) – which became a key-note in the Art Theatre's repertoire of these years. The former was a powerful depiction of the generational conflict in Russian society, and the latter offered a naturalistic portrait of a destitute, lower-class lodging house with a strong unredemptive vision of the human condition.[17]

---

14   Simon Karlinsky, ed., *Anton Chekhov's Life and Thought: Selected Letters and Commentary* (Evanston, IL: Northwestern University Press, 1997), 334. The same spectrum of interest was displayed by the German audience: according to *Das literarische Echo* from October 1901 to May 1902 the German Press published 24 articles about Gorky; 17 about Tolstoy; 8 about Gogol and only 2 about Chekhov (S. Dinamov, 'M. Gorky i Zapad', *Krasnaia Nov'*, 10–11 [1931], 225).

15   Shaw, Letter to Maxim Gorky, 12 December 1911, in *Collected Letters*, vol. 3, 64–5.

16   Quoted in Judith S. Calvin, 'The GBSsence', *Shaw Review*, 5/1 (1962), 22.

17   For the detailed analysis of the plays see (respectively) Cynthia Marsh, *Maxim Gorky Russian Dramatist* (Bern: Peter Lang, 2006), 69–88 and 89–120.

Max Reinhardt made Gorky famous in Berlin, staging *The Lower Depths* before a German audience for the first time on 23 January 1903 at the Kleines Theater under the title *Nachtasyl* (*The Night Hostel* or *The Doss-House*). The play was directed jointly by Richard Vallentin and Max Reinhardt himself and they both also acted in the principal roles: Max Reinhardt as Luka and Vallentin as Satin. The production was thoroughly rehearsed and carefully researched. August Scholz, the translator of the text,[18] a modest school teacher who made a rapid career for himself after this highly acclaimed performance, went on a special trip to Moscow in order to sign a contract with the author and to familiarize himself with the Art Theatre's production. He returned with a full album of photographs, sketches and recordings of Russian folk music that the actors found extremely helpful for their daily rehearsals and preparatory work.[19] The production was well received by the German public, and in the following years enjoyed over 500 completely sold out performances.[20] In the words of Ostwald, who referred to this event in his monograph on Gorky's works:

> 'The Doss-house' had an unparalleled success when it was performed at the Klein Theater in Berlin. The splendid staging made a magnificent achievement of the 'Scenes from the Abysses,' which thrilled and held the audience like some colossal work of music. And the human value of the work entitles it to rank with the best that has been produced in recent years on the farther side of the Vistula.[21]

---

18   Due to constraints of the tsarist censorship, the first publication of *The Lower Depths* (St Petersburg: Znanie) appeared in an abridged version on 31 January 1903; the first edition of the full text came out in Munich in December 1902 and was entitled *The Lower Depths of Life* (München: F. Marchlewski); the first German translation was circulated within a year: *Nachtasyl, Szenen aus der Tiefe in vier Akten, Deutsch von August Scholz.* (München: F. Marchlewski, 1903). There was a great demand for the St Petersburg edition of the play: the entire print-run of 40,000 copies was sold out in two weeks (Maxim Gorky, *Collected Works (with portraits and facsimiles)*, 30 vols [Moscow: Khudozhestvennaia literatura, 1949–1955], vol. 6, 549.

19   I. Berzak, 'Pervye piesy Gorkogo na zapadnoi stsene', *Teatr*, 3 (1937), 65.

20   F.M. Borras, 'Maxim Gorky the Writer', in Chambers, ed., *Continuum Companion to Twentieth Century Theatre*, 325.

21   Ostwald, *Maxim Gorki*, 72.

The book also included a facsimile of Gorky's letter (1 August 1903) to Max Reinhardt and the cast, where the author expressed his profound gratitude for their kind attention to his work:

> To you, dear Sir, and to your Company, I send my portrait. I must apologize for not doing it before, but I had no time. With it I send an album of sketches of 'The Doss-house' as performed at the Art Theatre in Moscow. I do this in the hope of simultaneously expressing my gratitude to you for your performance of my piece, and of showing how closely you and your ensemble succeeded in reproducing Russia proper, in your presentation of the types and scenes in my play. Allow me to offer my most cordial thanks to you and to your collaborators for your energetic accept-ance of my work. Nothing binds men together so truly as Art – let us join in a toast to Art, and to all who serve her truly, and have courage to portray the crude reality of Life as it is.[22]

German critics, once again, were ambivalent and restrained in their opinions. While praising the director's work and the acting, they remained unconvinced by the artistic excellence of Gorky's drama. Paul Goldman from *Neue Freie Presse* expressed his complete astonishment that the play made such a strong impression on the audience, since, in his words, it had 'neither drama, nor integrity.'[23] 'Gorky is not a playwright,' claimed *Berlin Neueste Nachrichten*, and his 'set of scenes cannot be regarded as a dramatic work in its commonly accepted sense' (*Magdeburg Zeit*).[24] Even Ostwald's monograph in its generally praising summary maintained that: '"The Doss-house" [...] has no serious pretensions to be a drama. It is almost entirely lacking in construction and in development, in crises or catastro-phes resulting from character.'[25]

Notwithstanding all these hesitant remarks and cautious comments, the play was a triumphant success all over Europe: it was staged in Munich

---

22   Ostwald, *Maxim Gorki*, 75.

23   Quoted in '"Na dne" M. Gorkogo na stsene berlinskogo Malogo teatra', *Vestnik inostrannoi literatury*, 3 (1903), 282.

24   Quoted in '"Na dne" M. Gorkogo v berlinskom teatre', *Mir Bozhii*, 3/2 (1903), 81. For a more detailed account see Irina Antonova and Jörn Merkert, *Berlin – Moskau. 1900–1950* (Moscow-Berlin-Munich: Prestel, 1995), 76.

25   Ostwald, *Maxim Gorki*, 71.

and in Vienna, and in 1905 it was performed in Paris with Eleonora Duse.[26] In England, *The Lower Depths* was presented to the selective audience of the London Stage Society on 23 November 1903 (at the Court Theatre). It was a cutting edge production, attended by those who were at the forefront of current theatre life. As an active member and a great supporter of the Society, Shaw was likely to be among the spectators; this, however, casts little light on the mystery of him recommending the play to Janet Achurch (May 1903), which happened some six month earlier than the date of the performance. In this context, it is worth mentioning that the French (*Dans les bas-fonds*) and German (*Nachtasyl*) editions of the play both came out in 1903,[27] and were immediately followed by the English translation (from French), published as *In the Depth*, in Alfred Bates' series *The Drama: Its History, Literature and Influence on Civilisation*.[28] Although it is difficult to say whether Shaw had a chance to familiarize himself with the play prior to his letter to Janet Achurch, he evidently knew about its existence and displayed a keen interest in the works of the young Russian author.

In May 1907 Shaw made a special trip to a soirée at Thomas Hardy's to meet the rising star of Russian drama.[29] The timing could not have been better. Gorky had just returned from his scandalous trip to the United States, where he was attacked by the newspapers for the immorality of his

---

26   The Italian-born actress Eleonora Duse (1858–1924) was one of the biggest stars of the late nineteenth-century theatre. She was known for wearing very little make-up and for her attempts to emphasize the inner compulsions of her characters. Shaw praised her acting over that of Sarah Bernhardt's when he saw them both in London within a couple of days (Bernard Shaw, 'Our Theatres in the Nineties: Duse and Bernhardt', in Diarmuid Russell, ed., *Selected Prose* [New York: Dodd, Mead & Company, 1952], 426–32).

27   Maxime Gorki, *Dans les bas-fonds*, trad. E. Séménoff (Paris: Société du 'Mercure de France', 1903); *Maxim Gorki, Nachtasyl, Scenen aus der Tiefe in vier Akten, Deutsch von August Scholz.* (München: F. Marchlewski, 1903).

28   Maxim Gorki, *In the Depths*, W.H.H. Chambers, trans., in Alfred Bates, ed., *The Drama: Its History, Literature and Influence on Civilisation* (London: The Athenian Society, 1903), vol. 18, 279–352.

29   Martin Ray, *Thomas Hardy Remembered* (Aldershot: Ashgate Publishing, 2007), 360.

common-law marriage with the actress Maria Andreeva (with whom he had been living since his separation from his wife a few years before).[30] Having expressed his contempt for the hypocrisy of the 'bourgeois soul' and his fascination with the boldness of the American spirit, with determination and self-confidence – which Shaw himself may have identified with – he came to London to join the fifth Congress of the Russian Social Democratic Labour Party. And although Hardy's dinner was attended by a number of his illustrious supporters, including Conrad and H.G. Wells, it was Shaw who left the most vivid impression on Gorky's memories of the evening: 'I remember Bernard Shaw – a caustic, though amiable old man. He wore an eccentric jacket to the evening, whereas everyone else wore a tailcoat; this jacket was of an impossible colour, some kind of tobacco, and it was strangely bulky [...] and his shoes were enormous and squeaky.'[31] This brief encounter marked the beginning of a long-term friendship between the two writers that ended only with the death of the Russian author in June 1936.

Shaw regarded Gorky as one of the founders of a new twentieth-century drama that was composed for a popular audience and empowered the notion of social transformation. At this point it is worth mentioning that Shaw always championed those whom he felt were most like himself. He felt intellectual affinities with Tolstoy, praised Zola and Chekhov, and claimed Bergson as a philosophical soul mate. Gorky, perhaps, can be regarded as one of the most typical examples of this kind of ideological kinship – a fervent social realist, who, like Zola, advanced naturalistic fiction towards its ultimate goal of 'Realism *in excelsis*'.[32] Shaw continued to align himself

30   The campaign was led by the conservative newspaper *New York World*, after which President Theodore Roosevelt withdrew Gorky's invitation to the reception at the White House.
31   Anastasiia Mein [Tsvetaeva], 'Iz knigi o Gorkom', in Anastasiia Tsvetaeva, *Collected Works* (Moscow: Izograf, 1996), vol. 1, 64 ('Помню еще: Бернард Шоу – ядовитый старик, но любезный. Явился на званый вечер, где все были во фраках, в каком-то эдаком пиджаке невозможного какого-то цвета, табачного, все у него висит, вот эдак [...] И в скрипучих огромных башмаках').
32   Bernard Shaw, 'That Realism is the Goal of Fiction', a lecture to the Blackheath Essay and Debating Society, 18 January 1888, *SHAW: The Annual of Bernard Shaw Studies*, 16 (1996), 118.

with this tradition of realism *à thèse* for the entire decade preceding World War I. These years were marked by his close correspondence with Gorky, to whom he wrote in 1915 when just starting work on *Heartbreak House* and after he had written *Great Catherine*: 'The Russians are the only people in Europe whose conversation about theatre is intensely interesting to me.'[33]

The influence of the Russian tradition on Shaw's *Heartbreak House* is incontestable. The play bears the subtitle *A Fantasia in the Russian Manner on English Themes* and contains direct references to Tolstoy and Chekhov in its preface. Shaw's engagement with Gorky, in this context, is far less obvious and hardly acknowledged, but pervasive enough to necessitate a further and more painstaking examination. There is certainly neither borrowing from nor direct imitation of the Russian author that are traceable in Shaw's composition of *Heartbreak House* – we are talking about an original elaboration of motifs, of subtle reverberation of thematic issues and a surprising understanding of the Russian idiom (namely the notion of superfluous men typical of the Russian literary tradition) that contributed so palpably to the realistic touch of his *Fantasia*. And while speaking of this kind of reflective influence, the most striking parallels can be seen with Gorky's *Summerfolk* (*Dachniki* in the original)[34] – the third of his dramatic works, completed in November 1904.

In fact, both *Heartbreak House* and *Summerfolk* were written with reference to and in polemics with *The Cherry Orchard* (premiered at the Aldwych Theatre in London on 29 May 1911), and contained remarkable similarities in their creative dialogue with Chekhov's dramas. Both plays are based on the extended metaphor of a house party, oblivious in its cultured leisureliness and drifting towards its inevitable destruction. Both are primarily focused on the position of an intellectual elite that fails to perform its duty of political navigation in the lead-up to First Russian Revolution (1905) in *Summerfolk* and the First World War in *Heartbreak House*.

---

33   Shaw, Letter to Maxim Gorky, 28 December 1915, in *Collected Letters*, vol. 3, 343.
34   *Dachniki*, the Russian title of Gorky's play, can be literally translated as 'summer dwellers' – the people who rent a summer cottage (*dacha*) for holiday and leisure, who are nothing but temporary users devoid of any sense of responsibility or emotional connection to the place.

By the time Shaw started working on the idea of *Heartbreak House* (4 March 1916[35]) the text of *Summerfolk* was available to western audiences in its English (American edition), French (*Les Estivants*) and German (*Die Sommergäste*) translations.[36] Whether Shaw might have read it is debatable, but not unlikely, given how keen he was on the new works of the Russian author. Shaw, after all, was not a hopeless linguist, as he often claimed, and by his own admission had an adequate knowledge of foreign languages: 'I can read French as easily as English,' he wrote, 'and under pressure of necessity I can turn to account some scraps of German and a little operatic Italian.'[37] Supposedly, he could have also heard about the play from Max Reinhardt, who received the newly written manuscript of *Summerfolk* directly from Gorky,[38] and was known to have maintained contacts with both playwrights, producing both of their plays in Berlin: 'Have you had any of my plays at Reinhardt's theatre?' Shaw wrote to Archibald Henderson, 'Dash it, you ought to be full of Berlin's news for me, and you give me none.'[39]

After the unprecedented success of *The Lower Depths* at the Moscow Art Theatre, Gorky anticipated that *Summerfolk* would be performed by the same cast. The production, however, did not run as smoothly as initially intended. After reading the first draft of the play in April 1904, Nemirovich-Danchenko, one of the artistic directors of the theatre, gave a negative response to the author, claiming that *Summerfolk*, 'as it stands, is unsuccessful – and this, unfortunately, is undisputable,' the reasons lie

---

35   Laurence, Editorial comments to *Bernard Shaw Collected Letters*, vol. 3, 408.

36   Maxim Gorky, 'Summer Folk', A. Delano, trans., in *Poet Lore* (Boston), XVI/3 (1905), quoted in Cynthia Marsh, *The File on Gorky* (London: Methuen Drama, 1993), 28; Maxime Gorki, *Les Estivants* (Paris, 1905); Maxim Gorki, *Sommergäste*, August Scholz, trans. (Berlin: J. Ladyschnikow, 1906).

37   Bernard Shaw, 'Parent and Children' (Preface to *Misalliance*), in *Collected Plays*, vol. IV, 39.

38   Maxim Gorky, Letter to Max Reinhardt, c. 22 December 1904, in Maxim Gorky, *Pis'ma*, F.F. Kuznetsov, ed. (Moscow: Nauka, 1998), vol. 4, 204 ('Dear Mr Reinhardt! In a few days Konstantin Petrovich Piatnitskii will send you my play "Summerfolk"' ['Уважаемый г. Рейнгардт! Через несколько дней Константин Петрович Пятницкий пришлёт Вам мою пьесу – "Дачники"']).

39   Shaw, Letter to Archibald Henderson, 21 March 1911, in *Collected Letters*, vol. 3, 21.

in 'the lack of clarity in the author's own beliefs [...], for it seems that he believes in things he is inclined to condemn, and he tends to love what he is attacking with indignation.'[40] Offended by such a profound misunderstanding, Gorky hastened to affirm the differences in their interpretations: 'Having carefully read your review of the play,' he wrote, 'I felt from your attitude to questions which I have already firmly and irrevocably decided that there is a major difference of opinion between us. The difference is insurmountable, and so I find it impossible to give my play to a theatre run by you.'[41] This incident marked the termination of his engagement with the Art Theatre and the premiere took place in St Petersburg instead, at the Komissarzhevskii Theatre, on 10 November 1904.

In *Summerfolk*, the action takes place at a summer cottage rented by Bassov, a successful lawyer, and his wife Varvara. The Bassovs have numerous guests of various social status and occupation, including a famous writer, Shalimov, who has been invited to stay with them. All members of the company idle away their time in longsome conversations, unhappy romantic alliances and family scandals until Marina, a thirty-seven-year-old doctor, challenges the gathering, drawing their attention to the duty of the educated elite to devote their energy to the cause of social transformation, defending in this way the interests of the deprived. The guests remain largely unmoved, apart from Varvara Bassova, who, appalled by the pettiness of their outlook, walks out on the gathering in search of a

40   Vladimir Nemirovich-Danchenko, Letter to Maxim Gorky, 19 April 1904, in V. Nemirovich-Danchenko, *Izbrannye pis'ma* (Moscow: Iskusstvo, 1954), vol. 1, 360–9; Gorky, *Pis'ma*, vol. 4, 282–3 ('пьеса, как она была прочитана, неудачная – это, к сожалению, не подлежит спору [...] причина [...] – неясность веры самого автора [...] начинает казаться, что автор верит в то, что он сам склонен порицать, и он склонен любить то, против чего с негодованием сам восстает'). Stanislavskii, however, was less negative about Gorky's new work 'the play', he wrote, 'did make a strong impression on us – perhaps, we were not sufficiently attentive during the reading, I shall read it on my own' ('пьеса не произвела на нас сильного впечатления – может быть, мы невнимательно прослушали, буду читать ее один'), quoted in Gorky, *Pis'ma*, vol. 4, 282.
41   Gorky, Letter to Vladimir Nemirovich-Danchenko, 20 April 1904, in Gorky, *Pis'ma*, vol. 4, 74; also quoted (in English) in Marsh, *The File on Gorky*, 29.

more purposeful existence. 'The Intelligentsia!', she says in her key-note soliloquy, 'We are not the intelligentsia. We're something quite different. We're just the summer folk of this country – people who've just dropped by from somewhere else. We bustle about looking for comfortable little nests for ourselves [...] and do nothing else but talk a ridiculous amount.'[42]

The fact that *Summerfolk* contained numerous allusions to Chekhov (who died in July of the same year) was picked up on by Russian critics straight after its first performance.[43] Trigorin from *The Seagull* resurfaced in the literary figure of Shalimov, who, like his Chekhovian counterpart, had no idea why and for whom he kept writing and spent most of his time fishing in the local pond. In the same vein, the younger generation of *The Cherry Orchard* was mirrored in Sonia, Marina's daughter, and her studious friend Zimin. Memories of this, the last of Chekhov's plays, which was presented to the audience only ten months earlier (17 January 1904), were still fresh and were echoed in the setting, in the social focus and the general atmosphere of Gorky's drama. On the whole, the play was read as a postscript to *The Cherry Orchard*, in which Lopakhin's dream had found its most wicked and cynical realization. Some critics even saw it as a caustic parody of Chekhov, which partly explained their initial rejection of Gorky's drama. The ancestral estate with its vast orchard and magnificent house was subdivided into summer colonies and rented out to newly emerging businessmen. The latter, however, had no intention of cultivating the land, as Lopakhin hoped for. Educated and settled in society, they became lawyers and engineers, doctors and writers; they began complaining about life, falling into the same old habits of idleness and procrastination, and producing another generation of useless 'summer visitors': 'Ah. Summer

---

42   Maxim Gorky, *Five plays: The Lower Depths, Summerfolk, Children of the sun, Barbarians, Enemies*, Kitty Hunter-Blair and Jeremy Brooks, trans. (London: Methuen, 1988), 193.

43   F. Batiushkov, 'Teatral'nye zametki. 'Dachniki' – stseny M. Gorkogo v dramaticheskom teatre im. Komissarzhevskoi', *Mir bozhii*, 12/2 (1904), 14–23; A. Kugel, 'Dachniki', *Teatr i iskusstvo*, 46 (1904), 814; D. Filosofov, 'Zavtrashnee meshchanstvo', *Novyi put'*, 11 (1904), 328–32 (also quoted in Maxim Gorky, *Collected Works*, L.M. Leonov, ed. [Moscow: Nauka, 1968–70], vol. 7, p. 642).

folk. Villa people,' maintains the villa's watchman in Gorky's drama, 'All
the same. Past five years I seen more of '-em '-n you could count up of stars.
Like bubbles on a puddle in wet weather they are. Up she pops. Bust. Up
she pops. Bust. At's it.'[44]

The resemblances between *Summerfolk* and *The Cherry Orchard* were
so unambiguous that it was even claimed that the authors, who apparently
knew each other well enough, were considerably aware of each other's
works and had been discussing them in their conversations.[45] The first is
somewhat doubtful, and the second debatable; it is, however, difficult
to miss that the two plays were indeed united through a general atmosphere of 'nothing happening' that acquired an expressive and tangible
quality in Gorky's drama and epitomized the life of an obsolete generation devoid of any worries and social concerns. It was a picture of life in
terminal waning, with its wasted talents and disoriented souls, but in this
seamless intertwining of the inconsequential and the dramatic – so characteristic of Chekhov's works – the former was non-existent and the latter
was bold. Chekhov's lingering and delicately refined style was replaced by
the powerful and awkward crudeness of Gorky's writing. *Summerfolk* left
no doubt that the generation of educated and self-righteous demagogues
did not and should not have any input in devising the future. During the
performance the message was so vividly articulated that the middle-class
audience in the stalls took it somewhat personally; and after Varvara's pas-
sionate condemnation in the third act:

> We live like aliens on the earth, strangers [...] We don't know how to make ourselves
> necessary, useful [...] and it seems to me that soon, perhaps even tomorrow, some
> quite different kind of people, strong, bold people, will come and sweep us off the
> earth like so much litter. Yes, I'm growing hostile to all our lies and deception.[46]

the front rows began to hiss and the gallery began to applaud, leading to a
real 'duel' between those who were enthused and those who were outraged.
'During my long years of sitting in the theatre,' recalls a contemporary

44   Gorky, *Summerfolk*, 121.
45   V. Botsianovskii, 'Kriticheskie nabroski', *Rus'* (5 February 1905).
46   Gorky, *Summerfolk*, 162.

critic, 'I have never had the occasion to observe such changes in mood in the audience [...] and such a split in the audience in general.'[47] Later on, recollects Smirnova-Sazonova, a popular writer at the time:

> the Gallery began to call for the author more than before. At first he did not come, then he came out and stood near the footlights. He stared, not bowing to the audience and looked at them with scorn. I expected him to stick his tongue out at us. But the audience was overjoyed and clapped furiously. And the actors let by Komissarzhevskaia also clapped.[48]

Not unlike Gorky, Shaw assumed an active stance in his dialogue with Chekhov, and although *Heartbreak House*, which portrayed a decadent, self-absorbed British society, can also be regarded as yet another tale of false hopes and unfulfilled promises, it did not call to mind the Chekhovian notion of passive loss. Shaw's characters are rather full of vital (even indestructible) energy that is, nonetheless, entirely detached from reality – hence the working title of the play that for a while went under the name of *The Studio in the Clouds*.[49] The characters of Chekhov's dramas, with their pointless aspirations, their sufferings and pathetic resolutions, are entirely incapable of changing their own lives – let alone the fate of Russia. From here comes the bitter irony that permeates his writings, the irony that turns the commotions of the characters into a farce or vaudeville. Shaw's irony comes from a slightly different perspective: the 'life force' of all these people of 'exceptional vitality and sensibility' is completely misspent: 'What makes it puzzling,' he wrote, 'is that the people seem to be so interesting and attractive and novel at first sight that one is led to expect great things from them; and when they are all reduced to absurdity, and even the solution of blowing them to bits misses fire, the spectator feels baffled and disappointed, as if something very promising had been wantonly spoilt.'[50]

47   A.R. Kugel, *Rus'* (11 November 1904), quoted (in English) in Marsh, *The File on Gorky*, 29.
48   Quoted in Marsh, *The File on Gorky*, 30.
49   Laurence, Editorial comments to *Bernard Shaw Collected Letters*, vol. 3, 408.
50   Shaw, Letter to Hugo Vallentin, 27 October 1917, in *Collected Letters*, vol. 3, 513.

The story follows a large house party, hosted by Hesione Hushabye in the surreal *Heartbreak House in north Sussex* – a ship-shaped residence belonging to her father, old Captain Shotover. Arguably, it could be regarded as a metaphorical reference to a ship, which must be guided capably, not only by its crew, but also by its passengers (using the Platonic concept of 'ship of state'). The range of guests (all entangled in romantic relationships not unlike Gorky's *Summerfolk*) represents the various facets of the social and political climate of the time: from the bohemian Hushabyes and aristocratic Utterwords to the *nouveaux riches* businessmen, modern women and burglars. It embraces three generations of English society with a clear message that the future and the power of navigation belongs to none of them.

The older group is represented by the 88-year-old Captain Shotover – one of Shaw's most brilliant creations. The entire play was inspired by this character, introduced to Shaw by Lena Ashwell, who in 1913 told him some stories of her seafaring father, Captain Pocock.[51] A witty and wise killjoy, he stands for the heyday of Victorian England and has no illusions about the future of his country, wrecked by a generation of superfluous 'visitors': 'The captain is in his bunk, drinking bottled ditch-water, and the crew is gambling in the forecastle. She will strike and sink and split. Do you think the laws of God will be suspended in favour of England because you were born in it?'[52]

The major part of Shaw's caustic irony and sarcastic remarks is directed towards the cultured, leisured and completely impotent middle generation of the gathering. Hesione Hushabye, Shotover's stunningly beautiful elder daughter, is an emblem of unrealized femininity; in this respect she refers back to Shaw's Candida (from his earlier eponymous play), though with a negative slant: being unable to fulfil herself in a marriage that has run out of steam, she hides her emptiness and despair under the mask of cold and bitter laughter. Her dashing, mustachioed husband Hector is a

---

51   *Lena's Father* was the first working title of the play (Laurence, Editorial comments to *Bernard Shaw Collected Letters*, vol. 3, 408).
52   Bernard Shaw, *Heartbreak House*, in *Collected Plays*, vol. V, 177.

bit of a dandy, a lady-killer, and an inveterate liar. To fill in the void of his non-existent present, he makes up stories of his former adventures, partly in the hope of impressing Hesione's long-lost sister Ariadne, Lady Utterword. The latter has made her prodigal return to the house pursued by her brother-in-law, the overgrown aristocratic cry-baby Randall Utterword, who exemplifies superfluous aristocratic pride.

The practical thinking men also have a feeble grasp on the present, not to mention their input into the future. Mazzini Dunn, a liberal democrat, lost his business to Alfred (Boss) Mangan, who was successful in his asset-stripping activities, but having acquired the enterprise appeared incapable of keeping it. Even Mangan's 'lower class counterpart' Billy Dunn – the specialist in 'barter operations', who is caught when he tries to rob the house – also finds himself in a crisis and admits his failure to obtain enough 'income' from his crafty occupation. A capitalist without capital and a thief who is offered a job as a property keeper (he turns out to be a former member of the Captain's crew) – this is the paradoxical present of Shavian England.

As an acting agent of plutocracy, Mangan assumes that only men of a practical cast of mind have hands-on knowledge of administration, and to the question: 'Do you expect to save the country, Mr Mangan?' his response is: 'Well, who else will?'[53] In one of his letters, Shaw identified this character with a real political figure of the time – Lord Devonport.[54] The latter was the son of a grocer and made his way to the highest echelons of politics through energy and managerial grip. He was appointed Chairman of the Port of London Authority and was ruthless in his response to the dockers' strike of 1911, refusing to negotiate and publicly declaring that he would starve the men back to work.[55] In December 1916 Lord Devonport was appointed Food Controller to regulate the supply and consumption of food during the First World War. In this position, which required a more

53 Shaw, *Heartbreak House*, 164.
54 Shaw, Letter to Hugo Vallentin, 27 October 1917, in *Collected Letters*, vol. 3, 513.
55 'Britain's Food Dictator Made Fortune as Grocer', *The New York Times* (17 December 1916).

subtle and flexible approach, he proved to be a failure (he was dilatory, fussy and a poor delegator), and had to resign roughly six months later (June 1917). Not unlike Lord Devonport, Boss Mangan seems to have a certain influence in politics, but this influence is shown to produce rather perilous consequences for the others:

> I don't know what you call achievements; but I've jolly well put a stop to the games of the other fellows in the other departments. Every man of them thought he was going to save the country all by himself, and do me out of the credit and out of my chance of a title. I took good care that if they wouldn't let me do it they shouldn't do it themselves either. I may not know anything about my own machinery; but I know how to stick a ramrod into the other fellow's.[56]

'There is no unambiguous political conclusion to be drawn from *Heartbreak House*,' says Gareth Griffith in his insightful analysis of the political implications of the play, 'Neither plutocracy nor the reactionary violence of the colonialists [Sir Hastings Utterword] offer any hope; nor does liberalism [Mazzini Dunn].' What does emerge from 'this chorus of denials and recriminations [...] is a sense of crisis and imminent collapse.'[57]

The younger generation finds its embodiment in Ellie Dunn, a protégé of Hesione, who is struggling to find her place in society. Disillusioned in her romantic pursuits (Marcus Darnley, her lover, turns out to be Hesione's husband), she is quite happy to marry a middle-aged millionaire, Boss Mangan, and is persuaded that: 'Old-fashioned people think you can have a soul without money. They think the less money you have, the more soul you have. Young people nowadays know better. A soul is a very expensive thing to keep: much more so than a motor car.'[58] In the course of the play, Ellie contrives to develop an intimate friendship with the Captain. In Shaw's own words: 'I took the greatest care that [...] she should be in the sharpest contrast with all the heart breakers, and when she is lured into it she should walk over Hector and Hesione straight to the Captain.'[59] With irony and inimitable sympathy the captain reflects on Ellie's practical considerations

---

56   Shaw, *Heartbreak House*, 164.
57   Griffith, *Socialism and Superior Brains*, 242.
58   Shaw, *Heartbreak House*, 143.
59   Shaw, Letter to St John Ervine, 29 October 1928, in *Collected Letters*, vol. 3, 744.

and they have long and amiable conversations together. 'It's prudent to gain the whole world and lose your own soul,' says Shotover, 'But don't forget that your soul sticks to you if you stick to it; but the world has a way of slipping through your fingers.'[60] This link between Ellie and the old Captain can be seen as a symbolic reversal of the time-vector of the play: the younger generation is clinging to the past, and there is very little hope of commanding the future.

Hence the ending suggested by the author – a German air raid misses the house, but the reverberations shake its foundations, and a massive explosion of dynamite hidden in the cellar brings the entire dwelling to self-destruction: the burglar and Mangan are killed, leaving the others to wait eagerly for the next blast. And although Gorky wrote his play as a wake-up call for the Russian educated elite, and Shaw disparaged a different kind of culture, the implication is still the same – the country is inhabited by superfluous 'summer dwellers', living foolish lives of romance, sentiment and snobbery: 'There is no sense in us. We are useless, dangerous, and ought to be abolished,'[61] says Hector in Shaw's *Heartbreak House*, as if echoing the very essence of Gorky's thoughts, who, in conversation with his first wife, described summer visitors as 'the most useless and even harmful people in the world [...] who arrive at the dacha, stuff it with their rubbish and leave.'[62]

Curiously enough, the evil of 'summer-dwelling' is presented in both plays through almost the same spectrum of social archetypes. The childish naivety and self-indulgence of Randall Utterword is mirrored in the hedonistic outlook of Zamislov, who thinks that the essence of life is in 'the art of finding beauty and joy in everything, in eating, in drinking ...'[63] Likewise, the practical cynicism of Boss Mangan calls to mind the calculated attitude of Bassov. The latter is a positivist and accepts only the language of facts (his catch-phrase: 'It's a fact, you know', runs as his hall-mark throughout the play). Bassov's scrupulousness, however, is foregrounded only when the

---

60   Shaw, *Heartbreak House*, 143.
61   Shaw, *Heartbreak House*, 159.
62   Gorky, *Collected Works*, vol. 7, 630 ('самого бесполезного и даже вредного человека на земле [...]: приедет на дачу, нахламит и уедет').
63   Gorky, *Summerfolk*, 111.

matter concerns his own well-being and he is not against compromising his consciousness as long as his services are well paid ('you've got a rich husband, haven't you? – yes, and not all that scrupulous in his affaires either, everybody says this about him'[64]). Finally, the self-deceptive escapism of Hector Hushabye refers to the theories of Riumin, who is convinced that if evil is inexterminable then mankind has a right not to see it: 'I am talking about the person's right to look for a little deception,' he says, 'He can't get away from life's contradictions and he hasn't the strength to purge it of all its evil and filth – so don't rob him of his right not to see all things that poison the soul. Allow him to turn aside from what offends him! He wants to rest, he wants to forget.'[65]

In general, the notion of false pretence and the opposition of appearance versus reality becomes an overarching theme that unites *Heartbreak House* and *Summerfolk*. It is not co-incidental that in *Heartbreak House*, by the end of the play, each one of the characters is revealed to be nothing like they appeared to be at the beginning. A burglar turns out to be the Captain's old fellow; Nurse Guinness happens to be his wife; and Marcus Darnley, Ellie's lover, is in fact Hesione's husband Hector. Randall Utterword, who looks like a gentleman and is apparently well-mannered, turns out to be untalented, peevish, and remarkably idiosyncratic. Lady Ariadne Utterword, on the other hand, is nonchalant and disorganized on the outside, but happens to be quite competent and has 'so much good sense'.[66] Similarly, her sister, Hesione Hushabye, seems to represent the stability of homely virtues, but suddenly rebels against the role of domestic hostess she had been forced to play for many years and exults in the excitement when the bombs start falling, hoping they will continue to come ('But what a glorious experience! I hope they'll come again tomorrow night'[67]). In this respect her rebellion is not unlike that of Varvara, who walks out on her marriage at the end of Gorky's *Summerfolk*.

64   Gorky, *Summerfolk*, 136.
65   Gorky, *Summerfolk*, 113.
66   Shaw, *Heartbreak House*, 162.
67   Shaw, *Heartbreak House*, 181.

The most interesting revelation, however, concerns Boss Mangan, who at the end of the play is revealed to be 'virtually penniless', and Mazzini Dunn, who in fact runs the business. Mangan is a fraud in every sense, and has no qualms about affirming it as a general principle of social philosophy:

> Shame! What shame is there in this house? Let's all strip stark naked. We may as well do the thing thoroughly when we're about it. We've stripped ourselves morally naked: well, let us strip ourselves physically naked as well, and see how we like it. I tell you I can't bear this. I was brought up to be respectable. I don't mind the women dyeing their hair and the men drinking: it's human nature. But it's not human nature to tell everybody about it. Every time one of you opens your mouth I go like this [he cowers as if to avoid a missile], afraid of what will come next. How are we to have any self-respect if we don't keep it up that we're better than we really are?[68]

His words on the virtues of hypocrisy are replicated almost directly by one of Gorky's characters, Riumin, who shares exactly the same philosophy of institutionalized deceit: 'I am against all this laying bare of the truth, all these silly unnecessary attempts to strip life of its poetry, of the beautiful clothes that cover its crude and often unattractive body.'[69]

In *Summerfolk*, the rift between appearance and reality is foregrounded in the very first scene of the play when Bassov, who does not find their summer cottage particularly attractive, asks his wife to drape it in something prettier to create a more presentable exterior: 'You ought to hang something on the walls, you know, some sort of frame ... or a little picture or something ...'[70] Later on, this motif of theatricality is further accentuated through a number of so-called speaking details associated with various characters. For instance, Bassov casually suggests to his friend Shalimov that he puts on the role of lady-killer: 'you know, spread your tail a bit, show off your feathers ... in front of my wife.'[71] In the same way, a number of stage directions related to Vlas, Varvara's brother, outline his acquired pose of

---

68   Shaw, *Heartbreak House*, 166.
69   Gorky, *Summerfolk*, 113.
70   Gorky, *Summerfolk*, 97.
71   Gorky, *Summerfolk*, 129.

house-jester: 'clowning, in a mock-threatening voice' or 'striking a comic pose', 'with mock tenderness'.[72] In fact, almost every episode in the play proves to be deceptive and should not be taken at its face value. Thus, the endeavour to rescue a drowning villager ends in fishing out Dvoetochie's hat; and Riumin's suicide attempt turns out to be a flop: 'A bullet wound? In the shoulder, eh? Now who on earth would want to shoot himself in the shoulder? You got to do it through the heart or the head, if you're really serious about it.'[73] The idea of false pretence finds its utmost expression in the theatrical shows put on regularly by the summer-dwellers. These spectacles, seen as a metaphor for their actual existence, are given a revealing interpretation in the words of the dachas' watchman Pustobaika:

> Dress themselves up in all different kinds of clothes. Say all different sorts of words whatever each one likes to say, at's what he say, Shout, fuss about, as if they was up to something, angry or something. And then they play-act at each other. One play-acts 'Me, I'm clever' or again, 'Me, now, I'm unhappy' … Just whatever one of '-em feels is right, that's what is play-acts.[74]

The concept of life as a game, as an inherently theatrical show where people prefer to play out their roles, acquires an existential quality in the works of Shaw and Gorky; and in response to the question 'how can you love a liar?', the answer is simply: 'But you can, fortunately. Otherwise there wouldn't be much love in the world.'[75] According to the encyclopaedic dictionary, a play is an activity for enjoyment and recreation rather than having a serious or practical purpose.[76] Evidently, this definition is perfectly in line with Gorky's concept of the superfluous 'summer dwellers', which he, incidentally, regarded as a specifically Russian phenomenon. In the letter to Max Reinhardt, he presented it as typical of 'our' intelligentsia, with its exposed ignorance, selfishness and urban disregard for the Russian people, which, perhaps, would not move foreign viewers:

72   Gorky, *Summerfolk*, 98, 102, 104.
73   Gorky, *Summerfolk*, 209.
74   Gorky, *Summerfolk*, 122.
75   Shaw, *Heartbreak House*, 84.
76   *The Chambers Dictionary* (Edinburgh: Chambers, 1998), 1255.

Dear Mr Reinhardt! In a few days Konstantin Petrovich Piatnitskii will send you my play 'Summerfolk'. I think that you will find it neither to your liking nor interesting for the German public: it is excessively 'ours' – merely Russian 'family matters', and I will not be surprised if you find it shallow and dull.

I wanted to depict that part of the Russian intelligentsia which originated from the pro-democratic social layers, and which, having reached a certain elevated social position, lost touch with the common people, [...] forgetting about ordinary people's concerns and about the necessity to improve their opportunities in life.[77]

Gorky was proven wrong in this respect; not only had Shaw managed to present superfluous men as a pervading characteristic of British and European society (drawing attention to their failure to prevent the crisis of the First World War), he also gave an extra dimension to this phenomenon by projecting it onto the dichotomy of humanity and destiny, realism and idealism.

When writing *Summerfolk*, Gorky was inspired by the romantic myth of the inexhaustibility of human power, of a new man and his potential to transform the world. It was at that time that he wrote the philosophical and rhapsodic poem *Man* (1903), where he celebrated the grandeur of mankind and its creative intellect, and endowed Satin (one of the characters in *The Lower Depths*) with the proverbial phrase: 'Ma-a-a-n! It's magnificent! Sounds superb! Ma-a-a-n! He should be respected, not pitied.'[78] His thoughts at the time were also dominated by Giuseppe Mazzini's theories on popular democracy, and more precisely by his treatise *The*

77   Gorky, Letter to Max Reinhardt, c. 22 December 1904, in Gorky, *Pis'ma*, vol. 4, 204.
('Уважаемый г. Рейнгардт, Через несколько дней Константин Петрович Пятницкий пришлёт Вам мою пьесу – "Дачники". Не думаю, что она понравится Вам и заинтересует немецкую публику: это слишком наше, чисто русское "семейное дело", и меня не удивит, если пьеса покажется Вам скучной и пустой.

Я хотел изобразить ту часть русской интеллигенции, которая вышла из демократических слоёв и, достигнув известной высоты социального положения, потеряла связь с народом [...] забыла о его интересах, о необходимости расширить жизнь для него').

78   Gorki, *In the Depths*, in *The Drama: Its History, Literature and Influence on Civilisation*, 347.

Duties of Man (1860). On 24 June 1902, when Gorky was just about to start working on *Summerfolk*, he wrote to Piatnitskii about his reflections on Mazzini's work:

> The priest [F.I. Vladimirskii] came to see me today, we read Mazzini together; the priest enthused tremendously: he was winking and telling me: 'Ah? This is your man, isn't it? What is better than a man? Nothing, my dear! And you should know this – simply nothing! And you should tell the others – nothing is better than a man in this world!'[79]

The reference to Mazzini is indicative in this context, as it suggests yet another link between Gorky's play and *Heartbreak House*. It is uncanny (though totally co-incidental) that almost a decade later Shaw would refer to this same paragon of free thinking by using it as a name for one of his characters:

MRS HUSHABYE [to Lady Utterword] – Her father is a very remarkable man, Addy. His name is Mazzini Dunn. Mazzini was a celebrity of some kind who knew Ellie's grandparents. They were both poets, like the Brownings; and when her father came into the world Mazzini said, 'Another soldier born for freedom!' So they christened him Mazzini; and he has been fighting for freedom in his quiet way ever since. That's why he is so poor.[80]

As a true representative of literary naturalism, Gorky, however, had difficulties in deriving such defiant idealists from Russian reality. From the very beginning he was reproached for the weakness of the positive characters in *Summerfolk*, who appeared either 'plain' or unconvincing even in the eyes of contemporary critics. Marina, for instance, was called 'a directive on legs, who could kindle nothing but the utmost aversion to any goodness

---

79   Gorky, Letter to Piatnitskii, 24 June, 1902, in Gorky, *Pis'ma*, vol. 3, 80 ('Сидел он, поп, у меня сегодня, читали мы с ним книжку Мадзини, восторгался поп и говорил мне, подмигивая: "А? Человек-то? Что есть лучше человека? Ничего нет, государь мой! Так и знайте – ничего нет! И другим поведайте – нет ничего, что было бы лучше человека в мире сем!"').

80   Shaw, *Heartbreak House*, 71.

in the soul of the viewer.'[81] The play did not provide any context for the humanistic prospects of such characters and did not contain any plausible references to their appealing traits. 'Marina L'vovna, Bassova [Varvara] and Vlas prove to the dead they are dead,' wrote Filosofov, when reviewing the premiere of *Summerfolk*, 'They leave in triumph, supported by the capitalist, and celebrate a cheap victory with the applauding audience [...] Surely it is clear that these petty, pitiable people, abandoning the old banality, must inevitably find a new one.'[82]

In *Heartbreak House*, Shaw finds more subtle ways of rendering the conflict. Part of the problem was that Gorky's positive characters were seen as somewhat pre-ordained by the author's imperative, whereas Shaw's were forced to act in a certain way (either good or bad) by the pressures of reality itself. His Mazzini and Mangan were much more than two forgers of capitalist greed and liberal idealism, but drew attention to the innate flaws of modern civilization. Mangan represents the 'so-called realists who know that money is power, power that enables them to turn into profit for themselves the thoughts and ideas of the idealist.'[83] Mazzini is allowed to succeed in business by Mangan, who then bankrupts him and eventually takes over the business, once it becomes robust. The ideas and enthusiasm start with Mazzini, but he lacks the knowledge and ability to apply them towards growing the enterprise. Mazzini appears kind hearted and munificent, but ineffectual. Mangan behaves in an egotistical and unscrupulous, yet influential manner. Shaw maintains, in one of his letters, that modern

81   S. Krechetov, '"Dachniki" Gorkogo', *Vesy*, 3 (1905), 94 ('прописью на ходулях, способной поселить в душе зрителя совершенное отвращение к добру').

82   D. Filosofov, 'Zavtrashnee meshchanstvo', *Novyi put'*, 11 (1904), 328–32, quoted in Gorky, *Collected Works*, vol. 7, 642 ('Марья Львовна, Басова и Влас все время доказывают мертвецам, что они мертвецы, и, победив этих мертвецов, торжественно уходят, опершись на капиталиста, и вместе с аплодирующей публикой празднуют дешевую победу [...] Неужели же неясно, что эти мелкие, жалкие людишки, ушедшие из старой пошлости, неминуемо должны прийти к новой').

83   A.C. Ward, 'Introduction', in G.B. Shaw, *Heartbreak House* (London: Penguin Books, 1961), 156.

civilization does not favour 'the man who is poor because he is honest and has no push, meaning no greed or vulgar ambition' and renders the money-grabbing Mangans powerful.[84]

Can one say that the author's direct sympathies lie in the camp of the Mazzinis of this world? The answer is 'no', as Mazzini's belief in fate ruling his life reinforces his feeble ability to control his situation ('Navigation,' says Shotover, 'Learn it and live; or leave it and be damned'[85]). Given Shaw's cynical view of society, he always tended to side with humanity over destiny and preferred a realistic approach to idealistic views. Similarly to Gorky, his message is projected very clearly in all his dramas, which he defined (referring to Ibsen and his followers – of whom he was one) as 'a forensic technique of recrimination, disillusion and penetration through ideals to the truth with a free use of all the rhetorical and lyrical arts of the orator, the preacher, the pleader and the rhapsodist.'[86] The preacher and the pleader were certainly two of the most favourite hypostases of the British playwright. Both Shaw and Gorky saw drama as didactic and the theatre as a forum for the heightened, almost spiritual awareness of its audience, and it was exactly these elements that they found particularly attractive in each other's works. The question as to whether this theatre of ideas was the most viable and progressive at the time is a slightly different matter, but it is worth bearing in mind that it is the ideas that 'have provided the most inflammatory of fuel for all the most inflammable mode of history. Violence has seldom been done on a large scale except on the score of ideas, and even today there is nothing that can so quickly upset a man's mental balance as a theory.'[87]

During the First World War Shaw became a contributor to the Social Democratic newspaper *New Life*, edited by Gorky, and the two writers maintained their friendship till the death of the Russian author in 1936. In 1921 Gorky decided to leave Russia, partly on account of his poor health

---

84   Shaw, Letter to Hugo Vallentin, 27 October 1917, in *Collected Letters*, vol. 3, 513.
85   Shaw, *Heartbreak House*, 177.
86   Quoted in J.L. Wisenthal, *Bernard Shaw's 'The Quintessence of Ibsenism' and Other Related Writings* (Toronto: University of Toronto Press, 1979), 220.
87   Eric Bentley, *The Life of Drama* (London: Methuen, 1965), 109.

(he had repeated attacks of tuberculosis) and partly because of his disagreement with Lenin: Gorky was known to be a committed supported of the Provisional Government and a strong opponent of the Red Terror. He then spent three years in Helsinki, Berlin, and Prague, before settling in Sorrento, where he maintained a vibrant lifestyle and was visited by an incessant flow of his Russian and foreign friends, including Chaliapin, Meyerhold, H.G. Wells and Shaw. In 1932 Gorky returned permanently to Russia, prompted by a personal invitation from Stalin to become the first Chairman of the Union of Soviet Writers. It was to Shaw's great regret that Gorky was unable to come to his seventy-fifth birthday gala celebration held in the House of Unions [Dom Soiuzov] during his trip to the Soviet Union in 1931 – the latter was staying in Russia at that time but was too ill to come to Moscow and sent a telegram that was publicly presented at the meeting:

> Dear Bernard Shaw! Illness – angina – prevents me from coming to Moscow to warmly grasp your hand – the hand of a brave fighter and gifted man. You have lived three fourths of a century, and with your sharp wit you have aimed countless, destructive blows at the conservatism and insipidness of men. I rejoice to know that your 75th birthday is celebrated in a country which values you so highly, among people who have begun the mighty struggle with the world you scorn, and are carrying that struggle to victory.[88]

There days later Shaw made a special trip to visit Gorky, who was recovering from his illness at his country cottage near Moscow, and when Shaw was informed of the death of the Russian author on 18 June 1936, his words were brief and sincere: 'I dare say it's time for all us nineteenth century writers to clear out. You'd better prepare my obituary. You never know.'[89]

---

88 'Shaw's Last Days in Moscow', *Moscow News* (3 August 1931).
89 'Tribute from London', *New York Times* (19 June 1936).

CHAPTER FOUR

'Mr Shaw Has Always Had a Weakness for Shrews': Shaw and *Annajanska, the Bolshevik Empress*

'Mr Shaw has always had a weakness for shrews' – wrote the correspondent of *The Times* on 22 January 1918.[1] His comment could hardly be regarded as flattering; in fact, it was not flattery at all, but somehow it managed to capture the key-note of the story of how Bernard Shaw came to write a one-act play about the Bolshevik Revolution just a matter of days after it happened in November (October, according to the Russian calendar of the time)[2] 1917. The play received its Lord Chamberlain's licence in December[3] and was presented to the public the following month under the gripping title of *Annajanska, the Wild Grand Duchess*. In 1919, however, it was changed to a more politicized version of *Annajanska, the Bolshevik Empress* when the text was published in Shaw's collection entitled *Heartbreak House, Great Catherine and the Playlets of the War* (Constable and Company, London).[4]

The play is set in the fictitious kingdom of Beotia, a thinly disguised version of Russia. A revolution has just occurred and General Strammfest at the front doesn't know which government he is supposed to take orders from.

1   'A Revolution Playlet', *The Times* (22 January 1918).
2   Imperial Russia operated on the 'old style' Julian calendar, which was 13 days behind the Gregorian calendar used in most Western European countries. The Gregorian calendar was adopted by the Bolshevik government in February 1918.
3   Lord Chamberlain's licence on the manuscript is dated December 1917; report and recommendation for licence by E.A. Bendall (British Library, manuscript Add 66183 G).
4   Bernard Shaw, 'Annajanska, the Bolshevik Empress', in *Heartbreak House, Great Catherine, and Playlets of the War* (London: Constable and Company, 1919), 251–66.

The action, such as it is, consists of a daughter of the deposed 'Panjandrum' – otherwise Tsar – bursting into his office, shaking off the soldiers who are supposed to be holding her, and, to the horror of the General (who is really an unreconstructed monarchist), declaring her allegiance to the Revolution. The play's central conceit involves the revelation that, contrary to the report, Annajanska did not elope with a revolutionary officer, but disguised herself in order to escape from the palace. In the climatic moment she reappears in a military uniform to prove that she herself was the officer.[5]

Why did Shaw produce this play, today so little known, at this juncture in the last year of the First World War? Apart from the obvious stimulus from current political affairs, the motivation was a matter of personal connections. Lillah McCarthy, who was one of the leading actresses of the day, and had indeed earlier starred in Shaw's *Man and Superman* as Ann Whitefield, had also appeared in several other of Shaw's plays, as she was married to one of Shaw's close collaborators, the playwright and director Harley Granville Barker. At the beginning of the First World War they had been on tour in the USA. During this tour Granville Barker abandoned McCarthy for the American heiress Helen Huntington, and they were divorced by 1917. McCarthy found herself back in England and needing to earn a living. Fortunately, as she recalls in her memoirs, she was able to call upon the services of the greatest playwrights of the day, who each wrote one-act plays for her. J.M. Barrie produced *Half an Hour*; John Galsworthy produced *The Little Man* and Shaw *Annajanska*. The play was first put on in January 1918 as part of variety bill at the Coliseum Theatre in St Martin's Lane, which at that date was still a music-hall; it was the ninth of twelve items in a programme which included the Herculean Gymnasts, Dainty Doris (a Comedienne), Neil Kenyon (Studies in Scottish Humour), Elastic Eccentric Dances, performing dogs and horses, and Vesta Tilley.[5]

Apart from Lillah McCarthy, the other members of the cast in 1918 were Randle Ayrton as General Strammfest, Henry Miller as his aide-de-camp Schneidekind, and a First Soldier played by an actor with an

---

5   Steve Nicholson, *British Theatre and the Red Peril: the Portrayal of Communism 1917–1945* (Exeter: University of Exeter Press, 1999), 173.

intriguing name Drelincourt Odum, which, curiously enough, seemed to anticipate one of *Saint Joan*'s (1923) characters – Robert de Baudricourt, known for having been the first stepping stone in the career of Joan of Arc. The connection might appear rather tenuous in its significance, but Shaw's *Annajanska* does actually anticipate *Saint Joan* in other more important ways – firstly as it shows Shaw sketching the idea of a young woman who is going to don military uniform and be prepared to lead her nation against the enemy. Secondly, because it uses as it were 'real-life' or historical subject-matter, rather than characters of the playwright's own invention. In this respect it follows the earlier 'historical' play *Caesar and Cleopatra* (1898) and, perhaps more pertinently, the one-act play produced just before the First World War, *Great Catherine* (1913), about Catherine the Great and Prince Potemkin (there is a key incident in *Annajanska* where the heroine bites the hand of one of the guards – this takes up a similar episode in *Great Catherine* where the character Claire bites a Russian soldier's hand). In a way, *Annajanska* is a history play with a difference in that it is about history in the making, written at the time when the Bolshevik campaign was still being waged and attracting close attention from all western observers.[6]

At the date of performance the play was still entitled *Annajanska, The Wild Grand Duchess* – with no explicit reference to Bolshevism in the title. Shaw also hid behind a pseudonym – Gregory Biessipoff[7] – which of course fooled no-one. As *The Times* put it, the play is 'dealing as it does with a certain development of the Russian Revolution. It is described as "from the Russian of Gregory Biessipoff", and possibly Mr Bernard Shaw may know who the author really is.'[8] In fact it was not the first time that

6   In her book *The Politics and Plays of Bernard Shaw* (Jefferson, NC: McFarland & Co Inc, 2003, 113) Judith Evans relates the playlet to the events of the February (March) Revolution of 1917, which is unlikely because the sketch was written in December 1917 after the Bolshevik Revolution had taken place in October (November) 1917; this reference is also supported by the change in the title *Annajanska, the Bolshevik Empress*.

7   Gregory Bi-es-si-p-off (BSCP-off) was a conspicuous pun on Shaw's initials – GBS, supplemented (one can only guess) by the initials of his wife, Charlotte Payne – Townshend.

8   'The Theatres', *The Times* (21 January 1918).

Shaw attempted to create a Slavic veneer through an explicitly stylized name. In a self-drafted interview on his earlier play *Arms and the Man* (1894), which was supposed to be an attack on Russian and Bulgarian militarism, he described the process of characterization he adopted as follows:

> I wanted a war as the background. Now I am absolutely ignorant of history and geography; so I went about among my friends and asked if they knew of any wars [...] At last Sidney Webb told me of the Servo-Bulgarian war, which was the very thing [...] So I looked up Bulgaria and Servia in an atlas, made all the names of the characters end in 'off', and the play was complete.[9]

Apart from a seemingly Russian author, no '-off' characters were employed in *Annajanska*; the atmosphere, nevertheless, was evoked through an unmistakable allusion to the famous Russian Empress Catherine the Great, who like the Wild Duchess was famed for appearing wearing male military uniform. And here the dramatist's claim regarding his apparent 'ignorance in history' should be taken as nothing but another of his elaborate literary ruses, for the text of the play contains a precise reference to the Preobrazhenskii regiment, which had a very special connection with the Russian Empress. The Preobrazhenskii regiment was one of the oldest and elite regiments of the Russian Army,[10] whose uniform the Empress used to wear, showing her allegiance to the squadron that played a crucial role in her accession to the Russian throne. Catherine the Great, in fact, held the military rank of Colonel of the Preobrazhenskii Hussars, and Shaw's carefully constructed pun on the name of the regiment – 'Panderobajensky' – leaves no doubt in the allusion: 'You must have seen him: the fellow is in the full dress court uniform of the Panderobajensky Hussars.'[11]

9   The interview was published in the *Pall Mall Budget* to advertise the forthcoming production of the play at Florence Farr's Avenue Theatre (quoted in Stoyan Tchaprazov, 'The Bulgarians of Bernard Shaw's *Arms and the Man*', SHAW *The Annual of Bernard Shaw Studies*, 31 [2011], 71).

10 The regiment was formed in the late seventeenth century by Tsar Peter the Great during his teens in the course of his military games near the village Preobrazhenskoe (which in Russian means 'named after Transfiguration').

11 Bernard Shaw, *Annajanska, the Bolshevik Empress*, in *Collected Plays*, vol. V, 237.

Speaking of the Russian dimension of the play, it is also worth pointing out that the character of the Wild Grand Duchess herself may well have been inspired by a young member of a rebellious (or indeed 'wild') Russian family. Aleksandra Kropotkina-Lebedeva (Kropotkin-Lebedeff), the only daughter of Prince Peter Kropotkin – one of the prominent leaders of the Russian Anarchist movement, was among the circle of Shaw's closest Russian acquaintances. Shaw knew her from childhood as Princess Sasha, and the male line of the family actually traced back to the legendary prince Rurik – the Royal dynasty which preceded the Romanovs.

Sasha was born and educated in England; she was named after Kropotkin's brother, Aleksandr – a revolutionary who committed suicide in Siberian exile a year before her birth. She was free-spirited and witty and very soon became the centre of her father's social gatherings. She was thought to have delicate manners and a distinctly aristocratic look so that the Russian symbolist poet Aleksandr Blok used to call her 'the ancient Riurikovna':[12]

Смех и брови, и голос светский	And laughter and eyebrows and the easy-
Этой древней Рюриковны	talk of this ancient Riurikovna

Shaw had always thought highly of the Kropotkin family, seeing in them the best embodiment of the Russian spirit. 'And here I must save my face with my personal friends who are either Russians or discoverers of the soul of the Russian people,' he wrote in *Common Sense about the War*,

> I hereby declare to Sasha Kropotkin and Cunninghame Graham that my heart is with their Russia, the Russia of Tolstoy and Turgenieff and Dostoeffskii, of Gorki and Tchekoff, of the Moscow Art Theatre and the Drury Lane Ballet, of Peter Kropotkin and all the great humanitarians, great artists, and charming people whom their very North German Tsars exile and imprison and flog and generally do what in them lies to suppress and abolish.[13]

---

12   Kornei Chukovskii, *Dnevnik 1901–1969* (Moscow: Olma-Press, 2003), vol. 2, 515.
13   Bernard Shaw, 'Common Sense about the War', in *Current History of the European War. What Men of Letters Say* (New York: The New York Times Company, 1914), vol. 1, 43.

Figure 3 Catherine the Great portrayed in the costume of the Preobrazhenskii Guard
by Vigilius Erichsen (c. 1762). The State Hermitage Museum, St Petersburg.

Long resident in London, Sasha made a striking impression on Somerset Maugham – the two even had a brief affair prior to Maugham's travelling to the Pacific, where he researched his novel *The Moon and Sixpence*
in 1916. Sir Gerald Kelly, a friend of the writer, painted Sasha's portrait,
and a series of Russian duchesses appeared in Maugham's writings of the
time: the Grand Duchess Anna Aleksandrovna in the unpublished play

The Road Uphill (1924); the Archduchess Anastasia in *Jack Straw* (1912) and another Archduchess Anastasia in *Penelope* (1912).

Sasha was a close friend of Shaw, and her husband Boris Lebedev (Lebedeff) became one of the first translators of Shaw's plays into Russian. In 1909 his version of *Caesar and Cleopatra* was staged in St Petersburg at the New Dramatic Theatre reopened under new management on Officers Street; in 1914 it was followed by an important production of *Pygmalion* at the Moscow Dramatic Theatre[14] – the production received the blessing of the author, who even recommended that they should reproduce the setting designed by Dennis Mackail for the London performance.[15] 'Бернардъ Шоу. That's your name in Russian,' wrote Sasha in one of her letters to Shaw, 'you ought to learn to sign it.'[16]

In May 1917, when the Bolshevik upheaval was already drawing inexorably closer, Sasha returned to Russia with her anarchist father upon the invitation of Aleksandr Kerenskii (the leader of the Russian Provisional Government), who was adamant to have Kropotkin as a member of the Cabinet. Through her father she became intimate with the most radical circles of Russian revolutionists, including Kerenskii and Boris Savinkov, the Russian revolutionary terrorist and the Deputy War Minister in the Provisional Government. Having volunteered to act as a translator, Sasha gladly introduced Maugham to the very heart of these circles during his espionage activities in Petrograd in the summer and autumn of 1917.[17] Never losing the chance to turn a real situation into a tale, Maugham made his

14   There had been a lot of controversy, regarding the translation used for this production of the play. In April 1914 Sasha wrote to Shaw that her husband's translation 'was sent to the Moscow Dramatic Theatre and was accepted', but then her brother-in-law informed them from Moscow 'that the same theatre has in hand two other translations of the play and up till now he has been unable to discover which translation has been accepted' (Sasha Kropotkin-Lebedeff, Letter to Bernard Shaw, 26 April 1914, LSE Archives, F. SHAW/15/3, list 13–14).

15   Senelick, '"More Looked at than Listened to": Shaw on the Prerevolutionary Russian Stage', 89, 93, 96.

16   Sasha Kropotkin-Lebedeff, Letter to Bernard Shaw, 27 February 1913, LSE Archive, F. SHAW/15/3, list 10–11.

17   Robert Lorin Calder, *W. Somerset Maugham and the Quest for Freedom* (London: Heinemann, 1972); Samuel J. Rogal, *A William Somerset Maugham Encyclopaedia* (London: Greenwood, 1997), 120.

spying experiences into a collection of *Ashenden Stories* (*Mr Harrington's Washing* in particular), where Sasha was depicted as mysterious Anastasia Leonidov:

> Anastasia Aleksandrovna Leonidov was the daughter of the revolutionary who had escaped from Siberia after being sentenced to penal servitude for life and had settled in England [...] Anastasia Aleksandrovna had fine eyes and a good, though for these days too voluptuous figure, high cheek bones and a snub nose [...] She dressed somewhat flamboyantly. In her dark melancholy eyes Ashenden saw the boundless steppes of Russia and the Kremlin with its pealing bells.[18]

After her departure from London, Sasha remained one of Shaw's closest friends and regular correspondents. Shaw kept sending her his plays, by mail and through friends, despite knowing that those that were posted had very little chance of reaching the addressee at the time: 'It seems that [George] Lansbury sent you a copy of Heartbreak House. I believe I sent you one myself; but I could only send it through the post in the ordinary way; and no doubt it got communized on the journey.'[19] On 20 June 1920, Sasha wrote back to Shaw, indicating that she had read both *Heartbreak House* and the *Bolshevik Empress*. Given that the play was only published in 1919, one can assume that she must have read it in the manuscript sent for her review (or indeed as a memento of their friendship) by the author.[20] In Shaw's view Sasha was a perfect example of an active revolutionist – decisive in her actions and persuasive in her views (all the qualities manifested in Annajanska), and in 1915 he wrote to Gorky: 'A little time ago a Russian lady [Sasha Kropotkin] brought up as an extreme revolutionist said to me with wild enthusiasm that the Russians would give the world back its lost soul. I quite understand that; it is not at all ridiculous to me.'[21]

---

18   Somerset Maugham, 'Love and Russian Literature', in *Ashenden or the British Agent* (Leipzig: Bernard Tauchnitz, 1928), 253.

19   Shaw, Letter to Sasha Kropotkin Lebedeff, 22 November 1920, in *Collected Letters*, vol. 3, 701.

20   The play was translated into Russian by Boris Lebedev as *Krasnaia Imperatritsa* (*The Red Empress*) and appeared in press in 1922 (Bernard Shou, *Krasnaia Imperatritsa* [Moscow: Bereg, 1922]).

21   Shaw, Letter to Maxim Gorky, 28 December 1915, in *Collected Letters*, vol. 3, 343.

Figure 4 Prince Peter Kropotkin, prominent émigré Russian anarchist and a friend
of Shaw for over thirty years, with his daughter Sasha.

110   CHAPTER FOUR

The Times critic – probably A.B. Walkley – was not persuaded that the *Bolshevik Empress* was one of Shaw's best efforts, claiming that the author had failed in ingenuity and exhibited a lack of nerve. 'Intellectual,' maintained the article,

> is somewhat too liberal an epithet for the new Molly[22] – or rather Anna-Janska at the Coliseum. For one reason, there is hardly room and verge enough for intellect within the limits of a music-hall 'sketch', and, for another, this is a shrew of the Russian Revolution, wherein intellect would find itself lamentably dépaysé. Perhaps that is why Mr. Shaw, too, has kept his own severely in check, venturing in that line upon nothing more dangerous than commonplaces about the revolutionary inconsistencies and incongruities. At any rate, there is nothing to our sense, peculiarly Shavian in the pious opinion which he expresses that what the Revolution needs is a common effort against a common danger, though one is quite content to see so handsome a champion as Miss Lillah McCarthy starting out to head the common effort in a wonderful white uniform designed by Mr. Charles Ricketts. But she should really be allowed to do her moujik-biting on the stage instead of off it; her revolver-shooting by no means consoles us for the loss of that.[23]

Shaw himself did not place much emphasis on the significance of the playlet, which in the preface he described as 'a frankly bravura piece'. '*Annajanska* has no literary importance,' he wrote to one of his publishers in 1920, 'and need not be published at all unless you have a few spare sheets to pad out a volume with.'[24] An author's views are never easy to contest, but the sketch, nonetheless, deserves a closer reading, especially when set in the context of Shaw's earlier and later career; and in this respect two points are particularly worthwhile. The first thing to notice is that *Annajanska, the Wild Grand Duchess* represents Shaw's first and almost spontaneous reaction to the Bolshevik experiment, which in a few years' time would turn into a life-long passion. Secondly, the Russian dimension of the play

22 The reference is to Molly Seagrim – an unfeminine and emancipated heroine in *The History of Tom Jones, a Foundling* by Henry Fielding.
23 'A Revolution Playlet', *The Times* (22 January 1918).
24 Shaw, Letter to Curt Otto, 20 March 1920, in Michel W. Pharand, *Bernard Shaw and His Publishers (Selected Correspondence of Bernard Shaw)* (Toronto: University of Toronto Press, 2009), 129–30.

sheds an interesting light on both Shaw's political position within the spectrum of the left, and the notion of his supposedly uncomplicated and unwavering pacifism.

The publication of Shaw's Anti-War pamphlet *Common Sense about the War* in 1914 led to him being widely vilified as unpatriotic. The newspapers advised their readers to boycott his plays; the booksellers withdrew his books from circulation. He was cold-shouldered even by the members of the Dramatists' Club; and after the meeting on 27 October 1915, the Secretary was instructed to write to him to the effect that 'he should absent himself for the present.'[25] With young men at this date queuing up across the country to enlist for service on the Western Front it is perhaps not surprising that this should have been the general reaction. But in fact Shaw had never been an uncomplicated and consistent pacifist. Back in February 1905, at a public meeting in London of the Society of Friends of Russian Freedom and the Social Democratic Federation, organized in response to the Bloody Sunday massacre by Tsarist troops of unarmed workers protesting outside the Winter Palace in St Petersburg, a resolution had been passed condemning this outrage. Shaw, by contrast, was reported by *The Times* as denouncing the peaceful nature of the protest as one of its strategic failures and the reason for the disaster:

> Mr Bernard Shaw said the strikers made a very great mistake in going unarmed to oppose the State. If they opposed the State the State would shoot them, and until all the working-class populations of the world understood thoroughly that when they stirred out of their ordinary round to oppose the State they must do it with arms in their hands it would be understood that none of them really meant business. He was not there to make a protest against the butchery and to sympathize with the victims. He was there to sympathize with the revolution.[26]

These are by no means the words of an unequivocal pacifist. Rather Shaw seems to be arguing that protest should have been backed up with arms.

Shaw had always been decidedly in favour of the use of force, provided that it was used for a good purpose. 'I like courage,' he claimed, 'and

25   Laurence, Editorial comments to *Bernard Shaw Collected Letters*, vol. 3, 315–16.
26   'The Crisis in Russia', *The Times* (2 February 1905).

the active use of strength for the salvation of the world, I think it is good to have a giant's strength, and not at all tyrannous to use it like a giant. What on earth is strength for, but to be used?'[27] Since the Boer War he had advocated conscription in peace time, as well as in war,[28] and when the Bolsheviks emerged he had never condemned them for using violence for their cause. Moreover, in his article 'The Dictatorship of the Proletariat', published in 1921, he excuses their slaughter of the counter-revolutionaries as justified by the extreme circumstances: 'A slight weakness regarding them may return the country to the tsarist regime when the workers lived in dungeons and earned pennies, when women were kept in prisons only because they taught their children how to read.'[29] Curiously enough, the wording in this quotation corresponds almost word for word with one of Annajanska's speeches, which shows a remarkable consistency in the dramatist's views: 'You flogged women for teaching children to read.'[30] The Soviet Ambassador in Britain, Ivan Maiskii, once challenged Shaw on this issue by saying: 'Bolsheviks, however, were far from treating the tsar and Russian bourgeoisie in a "fabianish" way.' To which Shaw replied, rather abruptly, as if it concerned some inconsequential annoying details: 'In tsarist Russia this was unavoidable, but this is all past, it is not worth coming back to this.'[31]

27   Bernard Shaw, 'The Peace in Europe and How to Attain It', quoted in Gordon N. Bergquist, *The Pen and the Sword: War and Peace in the Prose and Plays of Bernard Shaw* (Salzburg: University of Salzburg, 1977), vol. 28, 85.

28   Bernard Shaw, 'Is Conscription Necessary or Advisable?', *New Age*, 18/26 (1916), 464–6; quoted in Bergquist, *The Pen and the Sword: War and Peace in the Prose and Plays of Bernard Shaw*, 133.

29   Bernard Shaw 'The Dictatorship of the Proletariat', in R. Palme Dutt, *George Bernard Shaw: a memoir* (London: Labour Monthly, 1951), 17.

30   Shaw, *Annajanska, the Bolshevik Empress*, 248.

31   Ivan Maiskii, 'Bernard Shou', *Novyi mir*, 1 (1961), 220. In Shaw's views, expressed in a letter to Boris Lebedev, Lenin's government could not have done 'otherwise than it has done. To abandon so desperate a situation to the ballot box world have been to court the fate of Kerensky' (Shaw, Letter to Boris Lebedev, 22 November 1920, in *Collected Letters*, vol. 3, 702).

During World War I, Shaw's position was also far from that of an uncompromised and straightforward pacifist. For Shaw, the war represented not only the bankruptcy of the capitalist system, a tragic waste of young lives, all under the guise of patriotism, but the last desperate gasps of the nineteenth-century empires governed by tyrannical autocratic rulers who threatened the progress of European democracy. In *Common Sense about the War* he associated these imperial strongholds of despotism and 'junkerism'[32] with Germany and Russia and saw nothing wrong in using armed force against the latter. He therefore supported the British-French alliance in so far as it opposed the reactionary regimes; and when Woodrow Wilson brought the United States into the war on the side of the Anglo-French alliance, he thoroughly approved it as strengthening the coalition against Junkers: 'I esteem the entry of the United States into this war,' he wrote, 'as a first class moral asset to the common cause against junkerism.'[33] Joining the Triple Entente Agreement alongside Tsarist Russia was a completely different matter, for it meant allying with a state that in *Common Sense about the War* he singled out as 'the open enemy of every liberty we boast of.'[34] As he wrote to Gorky:

> The cause of France, the cause of Italy, and the cause of England may plausibly be represented as the cause of liberty and democracy, but how can the cause of Russia, with its autocracy, its bureaucracy, its maintenance of a form of personal despotism which England got rid of by a revolution in the seventeenth century, France in the eighteenth, and Italy in the nineteenth, be so represented? [...] At the moment when we point out that our institutions are so free that England is a paradise to the Jew, especially the German Jew, and that France is as hospitable to him as America, whilst Germany is notorious for its Judenhetze, the Russian Government engages in an unexampled persecution of Jews, enabling eminent Jewish authors and orators to rouse the Western audience to intense indignation by a recital of its horrors [...] And when it is apparent that the Central Empires could put the Western Powers in a very embarrassing position by making Poland an independent kingdom, and our

32   A Junker can be defined as a member of the Prussian landed aristocracy, a class associated with political reaction and militarism.
33   Bernard Shaw et al, 'Britain Indorses Wilson's Address', *The New York Times* (4 April 1917).
34   Shaw, 'Common Sense about the War', 43.

only chance of retaining Western sympathy on the Polish question is to persuade the west that Poland has more to hope from Russia than from Germany, the Russian generals show their contempt for Western democracy, or their ignorance of it, by Russianizing every part of Austrian or German Poland they invade, with ruthless disregard for Polish national sentiment.[35]

In his unpublished essay of 1915 *More Common Sense about the War*, Shaw refused Russia the right to enter the world-wide supranational organization, claiming that the moral standards in the country were below any acceptable level; moreover, it could hardly be regarded as a reliable international partner due to its antediluvian political structure, as he put it in the pamphlet, 'a set of international common agreements would not be made and broken at the whim of its aristocratic ruler.'[36] It was Russian autocracy, not German militarism, which he identified as the real enemy of these years and therefore considered a victory unattainable without Russian assistance as 'a defeat for Western European liberalism.'[37]

The situation, however, changed radically in March (February) 1917: the successful anti-tsarist revolution resulted in the abdication of Nicholas II and the formation of the Provisional Government, led initially by Prince Lvov, the representative of the Constitutional Democratic Party, who was then replaced by a more liberal Socialist-Revolutionary Aleksandr Kerenskii. When the news of the February Revolution reached Shaw he, like many of his fellow Fabians, became very enthusiastic because their associate was now a progressive force, as he remarked to Frank Harris: 'Good news from Russia, eh? Not quite what any of the belligerents intended, any more than Bismarck intended to make France a republic in 1870; but the Lord fulfils himself in many ways. It is probably not the last surprise he has up his sleeve for us.'[38] He also joined a group of the British liberals who sent an open message to democratic Russia to assure the Provisional Government of their sympathies for the new regime; the other contributors

35   Shaw, Letter to Maxim Gorky, 28 December 1915, in *Collected Letters*, vol. 3, 342–3.
36   Bernard Shaw, *More Common Sense about the War*, British Library, manuscript Add 63179–80, 140–6.
37   Shaw, 'Common Sense about the War', 57.
38   Shaw, Letter to Frank Harris, 30 March 1917, in *Collected Letters*, vol. 3, 463.

included H.G. Wells, Viscount Bryce, the Marquess of Crewe, a former
acting Secretary of State, and John Hodge, Minister for Labour. *The New
York Times* reported on Shaw's contribution as follows:

> Now that the Russian revolution is an accomplished fact, it is at last possible for us
> in the west to be entirely frank with our Russian friends. The truth, then, is that,
> although we could not afford to dispense with the military assistance of the Czar,
> our alliance with him was felt to be a disgrace in liberal circles, while even our reac-
> tionaries found it extremely embarrassing. We all knew that the Government of the
> Czar was ten times worse than the Government of the Kaiser, and when the Germans
> reproached us and held us up to contempt in America for combining with the most
> barbarous and bigoted autocracy in Europe to crush the most civilized power in the
> world, we had no reply to make except that the Russian Army was useful as a steam
> roller [...] Mr Shaw concludes with an appeal to the Russians for unity, so that 'the
> revolution shall not fall at home or in the field.'[39]

Given the changes, Shaw thought that the *Triple Entente* would now
make much more sense in the war effort, but his alleged pacifism was once
again complicated by the Russian case. Although broadly democratic,
the Provisional Government of Lvov, and later on Kerenskii, sought to
maintain the Tsarist obligation to the allies by continuing the country's
involvement in the War against Austria-Hungary and Germany, fearing
that the economy, already under huge stress from warfare, might become
increasingly unstable if vital supplies from France and the United Kingdom were to be cut off. Not only did Shaw support the decision, but in
his letter to Gorky (May 1917) he pointed out that the war, in fact, might
be quite handy for the newly established government, and referred to the
example of Catherine the Great who often used foreign threats as a successful means of keeping her 'unruly constituents in hand':

> How to prevent them [people] from changing the government every fortnight,
> since every act of government, every tax, every regulation that compels them to
> study their neighbours' interests as well as their own, every call on them for public
> service or self-sacrifice of any sort, seems to them a tyrannical inquiry? As far as I

---

39   Bernard Shaw et al, 'Assure New Russia of British Regard', *The New York Times* (1
     April 1917).

know, there is only one expedient that will effect this; and this is to confront them with a danger of such appalling magnitude that they will be terrified into recognizing that only a strong government can protect them from it. Now the only evil of this magnitude that a government can manufacture is a war. For this I can claim the authority of that very shrewd German ruler of Russia, Catherine II. But if Catherine, an anointed Tsarina, needed a war occasionally to keep her throne stable, how much more is a war necessary to your revolutionary government to keep its unruly constituents in hand?[40]

This point was made even more explicit in Shaw's article 'Russia's Interest in the War' published in *The Manchester Guardian* in July 1917. When soldiers and industrial workers in Petrograd rioted against the Government, whose indecisive policies as well as the lack of enforcement ability made it highly unpopular among Russia's war-weary people, Shaw's response to the events was in no way unequivocal: to avoid an outbreak of a civil war, the country had to concentrate on the foreign enemy. 'If the Russian Revolution is to be saved from reaction,' he maintained, 'and the Russian Republic from disruption by the discontent of the working class and the diversity of the ideals of its reformers, the revolutionary Government must fortify itself by a war, precisely as the French revolutionary Government had to. If there were no war, it would have to make one.'[41]

Several months later the same ideas were reiterated in *Annajanska*, which on the whole constitutes a fair reflection of Shaw's outlook on the events. It asserts the value of war from the point of view of cynical expediency and condones the use of violence for the right cause – the ordinary man must be bullied into submitting to positive government by somebody, as the Grand Duchess was to elaborate: 'I say that if the people cannot govern themselves, they must be governed by somebody. If they will not do their duty without being half forced and half humbugged, somebody must force them and humbug them.'[42] Moreover, as far as the war is concerned, it is regarded as a valuable political asset of the revolution – as a

---

40   Shaw, Letter to Maxim Gorky, 24 May 1917, in *Collected Letters*, vol. 3, 475.
41   Bernard Shaw, 'Russia's Interest in the War', *The Manchester Guardian* (7 July 1917).
42   Shaw, *Annajanska, the Bolshevik Empress*, 249.

means to secure national unity. 'What can save a mob in which every man is rushing in a different direction?', asks Strammfest, an old soldier who is used to obeying orders. The answer from the Duchess is that the war can: 'Yes, the war. Only a great common danger and a great common duty can unite us and weld these wrangling factions into a solid commonwealth;'[43] or

THE GRAND DUCHESS   [whip in hand] You flogged women for teaching children to read.
STRAMMFEST   To read sedition. To read Karl Marx.
THE GRAND DUCHESS   Pshaw! How could they learn to read the Bible without learning to read Karl Marx? Why do you not stand to your guns and justify what you did, instead of making silly excuses?[44]

We said earlier that *Annajanska* was a history play with a difference in that it was about history in the making – a comment on the current events, uninformed by any superior knowledge of their consequences. In this respect, it seems remarkably ironic that Shaw's argument about the Revolution and the right to read, using Karl Marx as an 'ABC-book', had a prophetic quality for Soviet Russia, where in the first years of the Bolshevik Revolution all religious books were withdrawn from circulation and replaced by the works of the ideologists of Marxism-Leninism. It is equally ironic that within the framework of such an ideological policy the USSR would indeed achieve high levels of adult literacy, later on praised by Shaw as a major achievement of the socialist experiment.[45] Perhaps too it is a play which took on a further poignancy of which Shaw could not have been aware when he was drafting it. In July 1918 all the Russian Royal family was murdered in Ekaterinburg, under the orders of Lenin and Sverdlov. No Romanov princess ever enjoyed the freedom of choice

---

43   Shaw, *Annajanska, the Bolshevik Empress*, 249.
44   Shaw, *Annajanska, the Bolshevik Empress*, 248.
45   In 1926, the literacy rate was 56.6 per cent of the population. By 1937, according to census data, the literacy rate was 86 per cent for men and 65 per cent for women, making a total literacy rate of 75 per cent (S. Fitzpatrick, *Stalin's peasants: resistance and survival in the Russian village after collectivization* [Oxford: Oxford University Press, 1994], 225–6, 363 footnote 78).

which Shaw offers his heroine; and in this context, a series of imposters, who emerged in the early twenties claiming to have survived the murder and presenting themselves as the Grand Duchesses of Russia 'in disguise',[46] make one think of the playlet as a harrowing example of inadvertent black humour. Furthermore, by the time Shaw published the playlet in 1919 the title had been made more explicitly political: *Annajanska, The Bolshevik Empress*; and it seems a sign of Shaw's growing commitment to Bolshevism that he should make this change given the circumstances of the Romanov murder. His early response in correspondence to the Bolshevik upheaval had in fact been distinctly tentative and by no means certain.

Initially the Bolshevik uprising took Shaw by surprise; for the first time he seemed to have difficulties in keeping up with the pace of political change. If the February Revolution instigated his spontaneous response in a series of press articles and public lectures, after his open message to the Provisional Government ('Assure New Russia of British Regard'), his views were widely sought after in Russia as well as in the West. The October events appear to have knocked him into silence. The fact that a group of ultra-left political adventurers could turn a vast country into a model socialist state made no sense to a reformist Fabian of the old school. The first public pronouncements of his support for the Bolsheviks did not appear until April 1919, when, in an article in *The Labour Leader* (24 April) which asked 'Are we Bolshevists?' Shaw definitively answered in the affirmative. The same kind of cautious silence can be traced in his private correspondence of the time, which contains no mention of Russian events. The first time Shaw claimed his allegiance to the Bolsheviks was once again two years later, when in his letter to Lena Shadwell (dated 31 October 1919) he conspicuously stated 'You are not a Bolshevik: I am.'[47]

---

46   The most famous survival story was that of Anastasia, the youngest daughter of the Romanovs; see, for instance, Robert K. Massie, *The Romanovs: the Final Chapter* (New York: Ballantine Books, 1996), 144–61.

47   Shaw, Letter to Lena Ashwell, 31 October 1919, in *Collected Letters*, vol. 3, 644. For Shaw's views on the Russian Revolution see also David Dunn, *Shaw's Russia: a Study of the Attitudes, Ideas and Beliefs of Bernard Shaw as They Affected and Were Modified by the Development of Soviet Russia* (PhD, 1984).

The constitutional principles of the Bolsheviks were not evident to Shaw; if they had been he would perhaps have joined in the public discussion. Only once, at a meeting of the Fabian Society in 1917, where the Bolsheviks were *anathematized and vilified* (while the Civil War was being waged), did Shaw raise his voice, saying 'We are socialists. The Russian side is our side' – his words were greeted with silence.[48] Curiously enough the same comment is made in *Annajanska*, which from this point of view turns out to be much more than 'a frankly bravura piece', for it presents a rare manifestation of Shaw's vision of the events:

THE GRAND DUCHESS Some energetic and capable minority must always be in power. Well, I am on the side of the energetic minority whose principles I agree with. The Revolution is as cruel as we were; but its aims are my aims. Therefore I stand for the Revolution.[49]

However the fact that he chose a young female member of the deposed royal family as a mouthpiece to comment on the advent of the first socialist revolution perhaps suggests an equivocal attitude to the proceedings (in this respect one also thinks of Shaw's earlier caricatural sketch *The Man of Destiny*, 1895, in which a 'respectable' general – Napoleon – is outmanoeuvred and outwitted by a woman). The setting of the playlet also contributes to the point: Shaw places the action in a fictitious country of Beotia, which, in fact, is not an invented country, but a region of ancient Greece, north of the eastern part of the Gulf of Corinth that came to be proverbial for the stupidity of its inhabitants.[50]

When considering Shaw's thoughts behind the play, two aspects must be taken into consideration: the seriousness of the content (Shaw's views on the Bolshevik Revolution) as opposed to the general spirit of farce and

---

48   Quoted in Allan Chappelow, *Shaw – 'The Chucker-out'* (London: George Allen and Unwin Ltd, 1969), 231.

49   Shaw, *Annajanska, the Bolshevik Empress*, 249.

50   'Boeotia', *Oxford English Dictionary*, <http://www.oed.com/view/Entry/20945?re directedFrom=Boeotia#eid>. The connotation of the name can be probably attributed to Athens's proud assertion of its cultural superiority compared to its rural neighbours; cf. the figure of the gullible Beotian deceived by the hero Dicaeopolis in Aristophanes *The Acharnians*.

theatricality that permeates the action. The device was not new. In his earlier works, the playwright had already employed this scheme in order to expose the falseness of the cause that motivates the characters. *Arms and the Man* (1894) is arguably the best example of this technique.

The title of that play is Dryden's paraphrase of Virgil's *Aeneid*: 'Of arms and the man I sing' ('Arma virumque cano'), which is used ironically in the context of Shaw's work. Rather than praising 'arms' and the men who use them, Shaw is dissecting the reality of war, showing the futile nature of taking up arms, as well as men in the service of the latter. The plot, therefore, is turned into a cliché-type heroic tale where a soldier, Sergius Saranoff, single-handedly forces the enemy into flight and his audacious deed becomes crucial for the outcome of the battle. In real life such a neglect of all elementary rules of warfare would lead to nothing but a disciplinary action, yet in the grotesque world of a burlesque Sergius ends up garnering military fame and success. In this respect *Arms and the Man* is a gem of characterization, for all characters in the play serve to underscore the traditional 'romanticism' of a war epic.

Sergius is rendered as a toy-soldier, whose marionette-like behaviour is outlined in every remark related to the character: 'Sergius immediately, like a repeating clock of which the spring has been touched, begins to fold his arms.'[51] The play opens when Raina is informed of the heroic exploits of her fiancé – this news seems to trigger her own internal mechanism; and she too assumes the demeanour of a fervent romantic icon: 'Raina, left alone, goes to the chest of drawers, and adores the portrait there with feelings that are beyond all expression. She does not kiss it or press it to her breast, or shew it any mark of bodily affection; but she takes it in her hands and elevates it like a priestess.'[52] When Sergius finally arrives they both stop talking in a normal human way, but begin to indulge themselves in some pompous theatrical rhetoric:

SERGIUS   Dearest, all my deeds have been yours. You inspired me. I have gone through
          the war like a knight in a tournament with his lady looking on at him!

51   Bernard Shaw, *Arms and the Man*, in *Collected Plays*, vol. I, 466.
52   Shaw, *Arms and the Man*, 394.

RAINA   And you have never been absent from my thoughts for a moment. (Very sol-
             emnly.) Sergius: I think we two have found the higher love. When I think of
             you, I feel that I could never do a base deed, or think an ignoble thought.[53]

Sergius is dismissed as an oversimplified romantic hero of a popular myth; his inner world is shallow and empty, that is why he becomes such a convenient 'vessel' for all possible truisms and clichés expected from a patriotic model. As far as reality is concerned, he is shown to be as incapable of real patriotism as of real love. He clearly is more attracted to the joyful Louka than the solemn and righteous Raina, but being totally controlled by his put-on role, he has to stick to the one that apparently suits better the criteria of 'the beloved of a hero'. Sergius is portrayed as a caricature, desperately clinging to his romanticized ideal; but even his bravery is quickly turned into a spoof when one realizes that the enemy troops that he defeated, were, in fact, supplied with faulty ammunition.

In the same vein, the revolutionary zeal in *Annajanska* is framed within the comedic setting of a farce, and the idea of theatricality manifests itself throughout the action. General Strammfest finds himself completely lost in the turmoil of the so-called 'political circus', not knowing even to whom to send his daily telegrams: to the provisional government or to some incomprehensible and equally unpronounceable revolutionary factions such as 'Maximilianists' or 'Oppidoshavians'[54] – a poorly disguised self-reference to the author. Shaw widely exploits verbal puns, and the ambiguity of tropes and saturates the text with figurative language to emphasize the notion of the topsy-turvy stage world. For instance, due to General Strammfest's excessive eloquence, Schneidekind imagines the worst about the fate of the monarch (dutifully affirmed by the General):

STRAMMFEST   A dagger has been struck through his heart
SCHNEIDEKIND   Good God!
STRAMMFEST   and through mine, through mine.
SCHNEIDEKIND   [relieved]. Oh, a metaphorical dagger! I thought you meant a real
                one. What has happened?[55]

53   Shaw, *Arms and the Man*, 424–5.
54   Shaw, *Annajanska, the Bolshevik Empress*, 234.
55   Shaw, *Annajanska, the Bolshevik Empress*, 236.

In a bravura setting, the dagger, of course, is supposed to be a trope – like the blank cartridges with which, according to Strammfest, the prime minister shot himself earlier in the day. On the one hand, these butaforic weapons remind us of the deceptive quality of the *buffonade*; on the other – such an emphatic misuse of language, especially when related to state affairs, invites a parallel with the misuse of power, which may well constitute a message implied by the author of this apparently not-so-trivial sketch.

The parallel between the Bolsheviks and a buffonade is conspicuously pronounced throughout the action, and Annajanska herself makes no distinction between being a revolutionary leader and a circus star: 'I am anything that will make the world less like a prison and more like a circus.'[56] It seems that for the author both the revolutionary zeal and the circus setting acquire the same dimension of an outrageous performance: Bolshevik eccentricities are foolish, their attitude is unprofessional, they are carried away by the excitement of the moment, and the whole thing is unreal.

Shaw always expressed his profound disapproval of an unprofessional approach to politics and state affairs, and his *Arms and the Man* has become a vivid manifestation of these views. Although the play does not fail to expose the realities of war – violence, confusion, hunger and fear – it has many obvious references other than the latter; one of these is the opposition of the professional (Captain Bluntschli) and the amateur (Major Sergius Saranoff), which in Shaw's view was not simply a matter of expertise, but a fundamental question of life principles. According to Shaw, it was this opposition, which he observed in two of his closest fellow Fabians, and not the increasingly militaristic climate of the time (the arms race with Germany was on its way), that gave him the idea of contrasting characters in the play. Cunninghame Graham became a prototype for the debonair and romantic Sergius, while the methodical and super-efficient Sidney Webb provided the model for Bluntschli. Shaw's private secretary remarked in her notes that 'Shaw once described Cunninghame Graham as "a story writer of genius: he figures in my play *Arms and the Man* with Webb in

---

56   Shaw, *Annajanska, the Bolshevik Empress*, 249.

strong contrast."[57] Shaw had always admired Cunninghame Graham's idealistic integrity, honour and fidelity to truth, but found his aspirations (especially when expected of others) dangerously unwarrantable, and the attitude attacked through Sergius is mainly that of amateurish enthusiasm, which for Shaw was tantamount to sheer incompetence.

In *Annajanska*, General Strammfest seems to be a mouthpiece for the same kind of theatrical quixoticism. In this context, it is sufficient to recollect his romantic readiness to salvage the world and even the revolution if there was nothing better to save at the time ('Stupid as I am, I have come to think that I had better save that [the Revolution] than save nothing.'[58]), his insistence on imperial etiquette, or his aristocratic scorn for modern fashionable abstractions like 'democracy' and 'liberty': 'You are young, young and heartless. You are excited by the revolution: you are attached to abstract things like liberty.'[59] In his extravagant rhetoric, however, he fails to grasp that the alternative which he reveres – the concreteness of an imperial sovereign – is equally devoid of any substance. He goes on lamenting the deportation of his monarch: 'O, my master, my master, my Panjandrum! [he is convulsed with sobs]'[60] – and his moaning, perhaps would be quite stirring, if the title of the ruler were any other than Panjandrum – the absurdity of the word (invented for a nonsense verse by Samuel Foote)[61]

---

57   Blanche Patch, *Thirty Years with G.B.S.*, Gollancz, London, 1951, p. 69. In the Notes to *Captain Brassbound's Conversion*, Shaw stated merely that he had taken one of Cunninghame Graham's parliamentary exclamations and given it to Sergius Saranoff: 'The House, strong in stupidity, did not understand him [Graham] until in an inspired moment he voiced a universal impulse by bluntly damming its hypocrisy. Of all the eloquence of that silly parliament, there remains only one single damn [...] The shocked House demanded that he should withdraw his cruel word. "I never withdraw", said he; and I promptly stole the potent phrase for the sake of its perfect style, and used it as a cockade for the Bulgarian hero of Arms and the Man. The theft prospered; and I naturally take the first opportunity of repeating it.' (Bernard Shaw, Notes to *Captain Brassbound's Conversion*, in *Collected Plays*, vol. III, 419).

58   Shaw, *Annajanska, the Bolshevik Empress*, 248.

59   Shaw, *Annajanska, the Bolshevik Empress*, 234.

60   Shaw, *Annajanska, the Bolshevik Empress*, 235.

61   'Panjandrum', in *Oxford English Dictionary*, <http://www.oed.com/view/Entry/136 877?redirectedFrom=panjandrum#eid>. The poem was composed by Foote in 1755

accentuates the absurdity of the antiquated rulers who make no real presence in the world that has already moved on. As observed by Annajanska: 'We are so decayed, so out of date, so feeble, so wicked in our own despite, that we have come at last to will our own destruction.'[62]

How serious was Shaw in this epitaph for the ruling classes? Was he hoping to change attitudes or simply amuse by outrageous foolery? Does the whole play draw attention to the madness of the revolutionary 'circus' or, in fact, is it subtly bent on justifying the Bolshevik cause? When approaching these questions, we should remind ourselves that *Annajanska* contains strong references to *Great Catherine*, Shaw's previous work on the Russian theme: in both plays the characters even address Her Royal Highness in the same affectionate way: 'little mother'.[63] Both plays are framed in a grotesque

---

to test the memory of the actor Charles Macklin, who had claimed he could read any paragraph once through and then recite it verbatim. It is not recorded whether or not Macklin was, in fact, able to memorize the passage at first reading, but he apparently took great pleasure in reciting both the anecdote and the passage in later life:

So she went into the garden to cut a cabbage-leaf to make an apple-pie; and at the same time a great she-bear, coming down the street, pops its head into the shop. What! no soap? So he died,	and she very imprudently married the Barber: and there were present the Picninnies, and the Joblillies, and the Garyulies, and the great Panjandrum himself, with the little round button at top; and they all fell to playing the game of catch-as-catch-can, till the gunpowder ran out at the heels of their boots

62   Shaw, *Annajanska, the Bolshevik Empress*, 245.
63   Apparently, Shaw's brave attempt to use a Russian idiom in this affectionate form of addressing was perceived as a *faux pas*. A correspondent of the Russian newspaper *Vechernee vremia* (*The Evening Time*), who attended the premier of *Great Catherine* in London, published a scathing critique of the play, calling it 'a vulgar farce worthy of a booth at a fair rather than a West-end theatre'; the critic specifically commented

comedic setting, but in *Great Catherine*, laughter also constitutes a major structural element of the plot. Edstaston, the English officer, who is as stiff in his convictions as his name in terms of its phonetic qualities, refuses to accept the views of Voltaire promoted by Catherine the Great, who was known to be in a friendly correspondence with the French author:

CATHERINE   [calmly] Do I understand you to say that Monsieur Voltaire is a great philan-
             thropist and a great philosopher as well as the wittiest man in Europe?
EDSTASTON   Certainly not. I say that his books ought to be burnt by the common
             hangman [her toe touches his ribs]. Yagh! Oh don't. I shall faint. I can't
             bear it.[64]

Being unaccustomed to any kind of objection, Catherine decides to convince the 'infidel' through a very special torture, which would consist of tickling him into laughter. This does the trick: not only does Edstaston agree to all the Tsarina's statements on Voltaire, he is converted to such an extent that he loses all his stiffness and starts calling her 'our darling little mother' – the affectionate name that Shaw initially reserved only for the Russian characters to mark out 'their manners from the less human formality of the English.'[65]

Catherine's ingenuity makes a strong impression on the court men, subtly alluding to the same kind of effect that the dramatist's mastery of conviction produces on his public. Taking the latter as a point of reference, let us consider what message the author was aspiring to put forward through the jarring buffoonery of *Annajanska*. What was the cause on behalf of which Shaw was trying to convince the audience (or, perhaps, himself) through laughter?

---

on the incorrectness of the idiom, saying that Catherine was called 'our little Russian mother' instead of a proper expression – 'our Russian little-mother' ('A Russian Criticism of Mr. Bernard Shaw', *The Times* [29 November 1913]). Having taken the point, perhaps, in *Annajanska*, Shaw simply reduced the phrase to 'little mother'.

64   Bernard Shaw, *Great Catherine*, in *Collected Plays*, vol. IV, 939.
65   John A. Bertolini, *The Playwriting Self of Bernard Shaw* (Carbondale, IL: Southern Illinois University, 1991), 154.

Shaw was not a revolutionary Marxist; as a member of the Fabian Society he attended a reading circle where a Russian woman would read *Das Kapital* to them in French.[66] He never met Lenin while the latter was living in London under the pseudonym Jacob Richter, nor had he ever encountered Karl Marx. Several times he found himself at the same meetings with Engels – in Hyde Park on successive May Days in the early 1890s – after which Engels reported to Karl Kautsky saying that he actually heard 'the paradoxical Shaw [...] a most talented and witty writer [...] speak on Bebel.' He also gave the opinion that as an economist and political scientist Shaw was 'absolutely useless.'[67] As far as Shaw's political views are concerned, Engels's remark was deeply ironic. Shaw's intellectual dexterity, his open-mindedness and ability to express sympathies with political positions differing from his own certainly contributed to his reputation for paradoxical duplicity. However, despite the seeming ambiguity or inconsistency of his statements, there were two things that he had always stood for – a political system based on the rule of law (democratic elections and universal suffrage) and a class of effective administrators capable of implementing a system of advanced planning.

During the February Revolution, Shaw supported the Provisional Government, which he saw as a democratic alternative to the barbaric anarchy of the tsarist regime in its final phase. If an identical revolution had happened in Germany at the time, it would have been welcomed equally by progressive forces as a move towards rooting out junkerism from totalitarian states. 'Germany, with her revolution still before her, and now made inevitable by the Russian example,' Shaw wrote in his open address to the Russian Government,

> still believes that she owes her military prestige to the Hohenzollerns: that the German armies have been victorious, and that, in spite of the devotion of the Russian people, the slaves of the Romanoffs cannot stand against them [...] Russia is on trial in this

66 Hesketh Pearson, *Bernard Shaw: His Life and Personality* (London: Collins, 1943), 79.
67 Friedrich Engels, *Friedrich Engels' Briefwechsel mit Karl Kautsky* (Wien: Danubia Verlag, 1955), 362.

matter, but nobody in the West doubts the result if Russia will hold together until the Hohenzollerns can no longer dream of conquering.[68]

Together with other liberal thinkers he placed high hopes on the Russian case, hoping that a constitutional form of government would evolve. The Bolshevik seizure of power effaced that perspective for the majority of its supporters. A minority left-wing clique, who professed to base their policies on the ideas of proletarian rule, did not seem to place much emphasis on the constitutional reforms (or as it is put in *Annajanska* – 'six different dictators, and not one gentleman among the lot of them'[69]). For Shaw it also had the air of an amateurish voluntaristic approach to state affairs, which was totally inconsistent with his views. Furthermore, Lenin's idea of turning the imperial war into a civil one on the general basis of class struggle threatened to spread the Bolshevik *coup d'état* to those countries which were not in fact controlled by corrupt autocracies. In this situation, revolution would no longer be a case of replacing political incompetence by the constitutional order, but the opposite; and Shaw's initial reaction to the Bolshevik venture was, therefore, not remotely assertive. In his article in *The Daily Chronicle* of January 1918 'The Falling Market in War Aims' (which was reprinted in the United States under a more explicit title 'Bernard Shaw Says Russia Not Only Country Ripe for Revolution'), he spoke about preventing the spread of revolution across Europe, speculating about the 'blaze of civil wars in England, France, and Italy' and the 'proletarians of all lands fighting to reproduce the Russian Revolution in their own country.'[70]

Moreover, when the whole structure of liberal democracy looked threatened, he appeared to alter his opinion on the distribution of forces in warfare and seemed to argue that regarding Russian affairs a separate peace with Germany would be more beneficial than a separate war ('not

68 Shaw et al, 'Assure New Russia of British Regard', *The New York Times* (1 April 1917).
69 Shaw, *Annajanska, the Bolshevik Empress*, 244.
70 Bernard Shaw, 'The Falling Market in War Aims', *The Daily Chronicle* (12 January 1918); reprinted as 'Bernard Shaw Says Russia Not Only Country Ripe for Revolution', *New York American* (24 February 1918).

only against Germany but all thrones'[71]). Taken at its face value, it was a shocking statement to make, for essentially it played along the Bolsheviks' lines and promoted Lenin's tactic of exiting the war as soon as possible (in the hope that the government could thus focus on the country's internal affairs). Most likely, however, this happened to be a sheer coincidence of interest, and Shaw's real concerns were, perhaps, of a completely different order. Far from asserting Russia's right to self-determination, he was simply trying to avoid an international class-based campaign against liberal western powers. On the other hand, it is important to bear in mind that in this context Shaw spoke not against Bolshevism as such, but against the disarray of a mindless revolution.

By 1921, however, the situation had changed – it was clear that Shaw's fear of the European-wide class-based battle had not been realized. On the contrary, the introduction of Lenin's New Economic Policy created an effective bridge-passage to Fabian reformist gradualism; and the first contacts with the leaders of the newly established state also prompted the Fabian idea of the intellectual administrative elite. As he summarized it later in 1945: 'None of us foresaw then that the revolution would be achieved in Russia (of all places!) by a minority of excessively sophisticated Marxists; and that they would make any possible catastrophic mistakes until they were driven by sheer force of facts to establish a Russo-Fabian state.'[72] British democratic socialists were soon pleased to realize that the frontrunners of the so-called proletarian revolution were, in fact, not proletarians at all, but rather a group of highly educated political activists. Georgii Chicherin, People's Commissar of Foreign Affairs, for instance, was an aristocrat by birth, a distant relative of Aleksandr Pushkin, and a nephew of Boris Chicherin – a well-known jurist and political philosopher, who worked out a Russia-based theory of liberal reforms (by the time of the Bolshevik uprising, he was probably the most reputable legal philosopher and historian in Russia). Chicherin had a degree in history and languages, and could have made a career as a trained competent musician; he spent

71   Shaw, 'The Falling Market in War Aims', *The Daily Chronicle* (12 January 1918).
72   Shaw, Letter to Harold Laski, 27 July 1945, in *Collected Letters*, vol. 4, 750.

thirteen years in Europe, being very active in émigré politics. Anatolii Lunacharskii, the People's Commissar of Enlightenment, was brought up in the family of a statesman. He received his education at the University of Zurich, where he entered the circles of the European Socialists (together with Rosa Luxemburg and Leo Jogiches). He was a playwright and an art critic, and produced a number of essays on the works of Western authors, including Marcel Proust and Shaw himself.[73] Lunacharskii spoke several foreign languages and was Shaw's official interpreter when the latter paid a visit to Russia in the early thirties. In one of her letters to H.G. Wells, Beatrice Webb remarked that Kamenev (Lenin's Deputy Chairman of the Council of People's Commissars) and Krassin (the People's Commissar of Foreign Trade), who arrived in London to conduct negotiations on the Anglo-Soviet trade and commercial agreement, pleasantly surprised her with their extensive knowledge of economic science, political professionalism and managerial skills:

> We had an hour's oration from each of them – one in French, the other in German – at a little private meeting of Fabians and Krassin struck me as a remarkable personality – quite the most remarkable Russian I have ever met. His account of Soviet industrial organisation as it was and as he wished it to be, is that of the most rigid form of state socialism, the dominant note being 'Working to a Plan', conceived by scientific men and applied without any regard to personal freedom or group autonomy.[74]

Given the circumstances, it became possible for Shaw to ponder seriously the emerging Bolshevik experiment. Able to sympathize with the communist cause, he became interested in the system for the simple reason that the Bolsheviks had been successful when he and his fellow socialists had not.

---

73   *Anatolii Lunacharskii, 'Bernard Shaw'*, in A.V. Lunacharskii, *Collected Works* (Moscow: Khudozhestvennaia literatura, 1965), vol. 6, 150–3 (*first published in Proletarskii avangard*, 8 [1931]).

74   Beatrice Webb, Letter to H.G. Wells, 8 September 1920, in *The Letters of Sidney and Beatrice Webb*, Norman Mackenzie, ed. (Cambridge: Cambridge University Press, 2008), vol. 3, 141. In his letter to Boris Lebedev (22 November 1920), Shaw also remarks that 'Krassin has made a very favourable impression here.' (*Collected Letters*, vol. 3, 702).

Since the time of the First World War the European Socialist movement had suffered from separatism and poor organization. In Shaw's *Annajanska*, this situation is reflected in the author's sarcastic remark on the non-event Peace Conference of 1917. Devastated with the chaotic frenzy, General Strammfest, who constantly receives conflicting telegrams and phone calls, points out that he is supposed to go to 'a damned Socialist Conference':

STRAMMFEST A third orders me to go to a damned Socialist Conference and explain that Beotia will allow no annexations and no indemnities, and merely wishes to establish the Kingdom of Heaven on Earth throughout the universe.[75]

The reference here is to the Stockholm Socialist Peace Conference, which was called for in Spring 1917 but never actually took place, due to indecisiveness and a conflict of interests among the parties involved. In the real life events, a telegram indeed exerted a crucial influence upon the standpoint of the British Socialists, deviously manipulated by Lloyd George, the Prime Minister, who personally was against Britain participating in the negotiations. When explaining his course of action regarding the Conference, he made reference to the Russian telegram which had repudiated the meeting as pointless. Aleksandr Kerenskii denied having made this communication, and the only justification that Lloyd George could produce at the time was another telegram attributed to the French Socialist leader Albert Thomas, which alluded to Kerenskii's reservations about the summit.[76]

The beginning of the 1920s bears witness to Shaw's approval of (if not admiration for) the effectiveness of the Bolshevik administration, especially compared with the affairs in his own country, characterized by the indolence of the Labour factions. In a lecture on 'Socialism and the Labour Party', on 29 January 1920, Shaw criticized the leaders of the British Labour Party for being 'immensely equipped for any kind of discussion, for the most violent electioneering, and for no action whatever'[77], and

---

75 Shaw, *Annajanska, the Bolshevik Empress*, 244–5.
76 Norman Mackenzie, Editorial comments to *The Letters of Sidney and Beatrice Webb*, vol. 3, 89–90.
77 Bernard Shaw, 'Socialism and the Labour Party' (National Guilds League lecture, 29 January 1920), in Bernard Shaw, *Practical Politics* (Lincoln and London: University

contrasted their approach with that of the Bolsheviks, who, he suggested, were perhaps less liberal but nevertheless showed more initiative:

> When Lenin saw a Constitutional Assembly muddling about doing nothing he did not wait but went ahead and like our governing classes there was no nonsense about democracy; he organised the thing in such a shape that it would work. He got his combination of Soviets, a certain method of indirect election which was not at all what we call a democratic method of election because it was vey indirect, it was doubly and triply indirect, but susceptible of being managed in such a way that Lenin got working with him the sorts of men he wanted to agree with him, which is precisely how our governing classes work elections in this country, and there was no nonsense about toleration at all.[78]

In this context, however, it is worth considering that the crucial point in Shaw's growing belief in the socialist experiment was not that he suddenly became a convinced Leninist; rather it is that he saw this regime producing people capable of effective administration – a group of activists who in no way could be associated with the mindless dilettantism which Shaw regarded as synonymous with weak management and incompetent government.[79] In his article 'The Dictatorship of the Proletariat' (1921) Shaw praised the achievements of the Soviets and claimed that the 'political machine of capitalism is incapable of producing socialism in the same way as a sewing machine is incapable of frying eggs.'[80] He characterized the new Russia as 'energetic, sober, and intellectual in the very modern sense of the word' and mentioned that it is becoming 'an independent, flourishing, and truly communist country.' As far as its leaders were concerned he later mentioned that 'if the future follows Lenin's predictions, one can smile and look at it without fear.'[81]

---

of Nebraska Press, 1976), 160; first published in the supplement to *The New Common Wealth* (6 February 1920).

78   Shaw, 'Socialism and the Labour Party', 158.
79   The fact that Shaw was interested in 'persons and not ideas' was also noted by Beatrice Webb back in 1913 (*The Letters of Sidney and Beatrice Webb*, vol. 3, 23).
80   Shaw 'The Dictatorship of the Proletariat', 17.
81   Quoted in E. H'yus, *Bernard Shou* (Moscow: Khudozhestvennaia literatura, 1968), 191.

In 1921 Shaw attempted to establish direct contact with Lenin by sending him an edition of his new play *Back to Methuselah* (1918–1920). Unfortunately the gesture, of a kind that Shaw had previously granted only to Lev Tolstoy, did not result in a letter to Shaw by way of reply. By the end of 1921 Lenin's health had deteriorated considerably, affected by enormous fatigue and a number of failed assassinations; he was forced to stay off work for some time. In 1922 he suffered a stroke from which he never fully recovered. It is recorded, nevertheless, that Lenin was a considerable enthusiast of Shaw's work. Arthur Ransome recalls that Lenin once heard somebody call Shaw a clown, 'Lenin abruptly turned around and remarked: "In a bourgeois state, he may well be a clown for the philistines, but he would certainly not be taken as such by the Revolution."'[82]

Shaw's *Back to Methuselah*, subtitled *A Metabiological Pentateuch*, consists of five major parts and revolves around the necessity of saving humanity from degradation, for which the Brothers Barnabas invented a new remedy with the properties of 'Methuselahic' longevity (*The Gospel of the Brothers Barnabas: Present Day*). This remedy has nothing to do with either medicine or pharmacology, but can be found in human beings themselves. Mankind must learn to live much longer through its utmost desire to live – the so-called 'life force', which is a means for mind and will, and for the human race, to achieve progress. Although one cannot seriously believe that *Back to Methuselah* is anything but a scientific utopia, it exemplifies the optimistic enthusiasm of the author – his faith in the triumph of the human spirit and its capacity to transform history – the evolutionary change occurs not because of natural selection, but because it is needed and wanted. It is not coincidental, therefore, that Shaw decided to send his monumental work to the Bolshevik leader. In paying respects to the achievements of the proletarian state, he was trying to initiate some kind of 'friendly polemics' on the future of humanity. While acknowledging the effectiveness of Lenin's ideas of revolutionary transformation, he suggested in this, his longest dramatic production, his own conception of evolutionary change controlled by intellect and scientific techniques. By

82   Arthur Ransome, 'Lenin and Shou', *Inostrannaia literatura*, 4 (1957), 24.

positing 'purpose and will' as the only hope for progress, he aspired to affirm that there were other methods of affecting history, but at the same time recognized Lenin as a kindred spirit, as a fellow collaborator in constant search of rational ways of transforming the world.

CHAPTER FIVE

'Russia Is All Right and We Are All Wrong': Shaw's Trip to the USSR

It took Shaw almost fourteen years to come to socialist Russia, which he had been supporting since its first appearance on the map in 1917. Compared with the reactions of his contemporaries, this was a relatively long period to wait. H.G. Wells, his erstwhile fellow Fabian, had visited Russia as early as 1918 (a trip commemorated in his book *Russia in the Shadows*), had a conversation with Lenin and was invited to come back in ten years to see the results of the socialist construction.[1] In his own words, Shaw wanted to avoid making a premature visit to a country suffering from the ravaging consequences of the Civil War; he was convinced that 'the Soviet system would not be seen at its best during the first flush of N.E.P. reactions to the excesses of war Communism.'[2] As usual, his reasoning was not easy to object to. Introduced in 1921 as a special measure to help the recovery of the war-devastated Russian economy, the New Economic Policy (NEP) hardly did justice to the socialist idea. It was essentially a mixed system, combining state-controlled large-scale industry with a limited proportion of private enterprise (mainly in agriculture and commerce). By the late twenties the situation had been radically transformed. In 1928 the NEP was abolished and replaced by the nationwide Five-Year Plan, which marked a distinct turn towards a centralized socialist economy. These developments, unique

---

1   H.G. Wells, *Russia in the Shadows* (New York: George H. Doran Co, 1921), 160. The very first account of the Soviet experiment – *Ten Days that Shook the World* (1919) – was written by the American journalist John Reed who was in Petrograd at the time and revealed his first-hand experience of the events.

2   Harry M. Geduld, 'Bernard Shaw in Russia', in Bernard Shaw, *The Rationalisation of Russia* (Bloomington: Indiana University Press, 1964), 12.

in their own right, attracted an influx of western observers interested in the economic aspects of the experiment or simply drawn by the basic impulse of natural curiosity.

Their visits, carefully filtered on the basis of the observers' *a priori* amiable attitude to the regime, were keenly supported at the highest level by the Soviet authorities, who were motivated to pursue better relations with the West in what was an exceedingly unfavourable (for Russia) political climate. In October 1926 Frank B. Kellogg, Secretary of State of the USA (which did not recognize the Soviet Union till 1933) rejected yet another offer of diplomatic negotiations, emphasizing that his country simply 'cannot recognize a régime whose very foundation principle is ultimately to bring about the overthrow of every foreign government by revolution.'[3] Anglo-Soviet relations also left much to be desired and were deteriorating rapidly towards the late twenties. After the Soviet government had provided substantial support for the General Strike of 1926 it was accused of interfering with the internal affairs of the United Kingdom. The situation was further exacerbated by the so-called Arcos affair (May 1927), when the employees of the All Russian Co-operative Society trade enterprise (Arcos) were charged with 'espionage and subversive activities throughout the British Empire.'[4] No evidence of subversion was found; however, and partly to cover the government's embarrassment over the incident, Britain still severed its diplomatic ties with the Soviet Union (to be restored only in October 1929, when a new minority Labour government returned to power). Relations with France looked no better; and although this time the Russian side was hardly to be blamed and the reason lay entirely in the red-baiting domestic policy of the French, it did not make things any

3   Kellogg to A.B. Houghton, US ambassador in London, no. 212, strictly personal and confidential for the ambassador, 4 November 1926, 861.01/1175, quoted in Michael Jabara Carley, 'Years of War in the East, 1939–45', *Europe-Asia Studies*, 58/2 (2007), 332–3.

4   Louis Fischer, *The Soviets in World Affairs* (Princeton, NJ: Princeton University Press, 1951), vol. 2, 688. On the account of the Arcos affair see also Christopher Andrew, *Defence of the Realm: The Authorized History of MI5* (London: Alen Lane, 2009), 152–5.

easier for the Soviets, who were trying to remain on acceptable terms with at least one of the great western powers. French national elections were to take place in spring 1928, and the conservative government of Raymond Poincaré decided to run an anti-communist campaign to diminish the electoral chances of the left.[5] With both Britain and France struck by insecurity about the perceived spread of communism, it was becoming increasingly difficult for Soviet diplomats to hold their position in the European political arena.

It was not surprising that in this context the recurrent visits of European public intellectuals became a desirable part of the Soviet political agenda. In 1918 the tradition was inaugurated by H.G. Wells, who then made a second appearance in 1934. The same journey was made by Romain Rolland (in 1935) – a Nobel Prize winner for literature, who became the conscience of the French nation, with his campaign against anti-Semitism in the wake of the Dreyfus affair – and by his compatriot, the communist writer Henri Barbusse, who was a frequent visitor to Moscow in the thirties and was indeed to die there in the summer of 1935. Among other such figures, Emil Ludwig, a world-renowned biographer, visited the USSR in 1931, followed the next year by the founders of the Fabian Society, Sidney and Beatrice Webb. The German-Jewish novelist, and founder of the newspaper *Der Spiegel*, Lion Feuchtwanger made the gesture in 1937, and there was also an unbroken succession of less eminent callers, hosted by the All-Union Society for Cultural Relations with Foreign Countries and the International Organization of Workers' Aid. The visitors were treated with a high degree of consequence, for in the fraught political climate of the age, their contribution to the positive image of the country was of vital importance. As *Izvestiia* (one of the central newspapers of the Soviet Union) presented the situation:

---

5   For more detailed information see for instance Michael Jabara Carley, 'Episodes from the Early Cold War: Franco-Soviet Relations, 1917–1927', *Europe-Asia Studies*, 52/7 (2000), 1275–1305; Michael Jabara Carley, *1939: The Alliance that Never Was and the Coming of World War II* (Chicago: Ivan R. Dee Publisher, 1999).

Some people are beginning to ponder over the 'experiment' being made in the USSR. Is it not amazing when such a thoroughly bourgeois, though liberal publication as the 'New Statesman and Nation' takes Churchill to task and tells him that instead of abusing and plotting against the USSR, it would be better to learn something from her? Or, is it not touching when Owen Young, author of the Young Plan, the snare in which Germany is tortured today, declares that he can criticize capitalism 'as well as any Bolshevik'? Or, when Professor Calvin Hoover declared Socialism, for good or evil, has ceased to be a theory and that it exists upon the face of the earth? Under such circumstances, the penetrating eye of the 'free man' will surely discern the real truth.[6]

Quite unexpectedly, an appeal for the 'real truth' came from a different side of the Russian political scales, which added a lot of controversy, not to say confusion, to the views of those concerned with the principles of socialist construction. In summer 1927, when Soviet relations with Britain and France were turning hastily from bad to worse, there appeared an anonymous letter addressed to the 'Writers of the World' which was sent to a number of French and Russian émigré newspapers:

> How to explain that you, whose gaze can pierce the depths of the human soul, the spirits of peoples and ages, pass us by and neglect us – Russians, condemned to gnaw at the shackles that bind us in this loathsome prison – the warden of the Free Word? You, who are raised on the creations of our masters of the word, why do you stand by and watch silently when, within this great country, great literature is choking to death? [...] Why did the writers, who had visited Russia – Mr Duhamel and Durten and others – not report anything about these matters upon their return? Were they not interested in the freedom of press in Russia? Or were they watching without seeing, and seeing without being able to understand? [...] We know that your sympathy, your moral condemnation of this most brutal tyranny, is all the aid you can offer us or our people. We ask for nothing more [...] But wherever you may be, and with all energy you may possess, do expose to the world the lies hidden behind the false and duplicitous mask covering the horrid face of communist rule in Russia. We ourselves are powerless to do so.[7]

6　A. Lunacharskii, 'Bernard Show, Our Guest', *Izvestiia* (21 July 1931), reprinted in English in *Moscow News* (23 July 1931).

7　Quoted in Nina Berberova, *Kursiv moi* (Moscow: Soglasie, 2001), 272, 274–5 ('Чем объяснить, что вы, прозорливцы, проникающие в глубины души человеческой, в душу эпох и народов, проходите мимо нас, русских, обреченных грызть цепи

Although *Pravda* declared the letter to be a fake, it triggered an emotional polemic by two Russian émigré writers, Konstantin Balmont and Ivan Bunin, a distinguished author who in 1933 became the first Russian winner of the Nobel Prize for Literature. In two open letters published in the Russian *Vozrozhdenie* (*Resurrection*) and the anti-communist daily *L'Avenir*, the exiled Russians accused western observers (and mainly Romain Rolland) of 'shaking hands with assassins.' According to Balmont, the Soviet regime was synonymous with large-scale destruction; the abuses included censoring all printed material, denying religious liberties, robbing the peasantry, putting millions out of work, and executing or destroying the sanity of leading Russian intellectuals.[8] Romain Rolland published his critical appreciation of the letters, but appealed to European intellectuals to be liberal-minded and objective in their judgement of the socialist future:

> You clear-sighted men, with your eyes washed of all illusions, it was not that ideal which has drawn allies to your side from Europe. Your allies are recruited from the worst reaction of the bourgeois 'moral order' and business imperialism [...] Are you unaware that between Russia and the rest of the world there is to-day a ceaseless flow of visitors and investigators? [...] Two – thirds of them have no tenderness for

---

страшной тюрьмы, воздвигнутой слову? Почему вы, воспитанные на творениях также и наших гениев слова, молчите, когда в великой стране идет удушение великой литературы в ее зрелых плодах и ее зародышах? [...] Но почему же писатели, посетившие Россию – господа Дюгамель, Дюртен и другие, – почему они, вернувшись домой, ничего не сообщили о ней? Или их не интересовало положение печати в России? Или они смотрели и не видели, видели и не поняли? [...] Мы знаем: кроме сочувствия, кроме моральной поддержки принципам и деятелям свободы, кроме морального осуждения жесточайшей из деспотий, вы ничем не можете помочь ни нам, ни нашему народу. Большего, однако, мы и не ждем [...] с энергией, всюду, всегда срывайте перед общественным сознанием мира искусную лицемерную маску с того страшного лика, который являет коммунистическая власть в России. Мы сами бессильны сделать это'). The letter was published in the Russian émigré newspapers in Paris (*Poslednie novosti* [10 July 1927]) and in Belgrade (*Novoe vremia* [10 July 1927]). For a more detailed account see René Gerra, 'Ostalis' neuslyshannymi', *Literaturnaia gazeta* (7 October 2009).

8   For a more detailed account see David James Fisher, *Romain Rolland and the Politics of Intellectual Engagement* (Berkeley: University of California Press, 1998), 211–12.

Communist ideas. They may be deceived by themselves, or by others, like all men. But they are sincere and without prejudice [...] you may learn – what we know already from our Russian friends – of the fine fever of work which burns in the students and in the professors down there, and the support given to their researches by the Soviet State [...] brilliant schools of young writers have sprung up – and ... they publish and they read down there a great deal more than ever before [...] *E pur si muove* ... And yet humanity marches forward. It is marching now. Over you. Over us.[9]

In practice, such well-informed and liberal objectivity did not come naturally even to those who were regarded as the most keen and lucid representatives of the western intellectual elite.

In a country which placed considerable restrictions on the movement of its own people, foreign visitors were offered a carefully packaged view of the estate (though sensibly designed to produce an impression of a fairly comprehensive outlook). The circuit comprised a visit to a factory or a collective farm; the guests were allowed to participate in public rallies and debates with a carefully selected group of Soviet intellectuals; free time in the evenings was filled with museums and theatre trips; the culmination of the stay often consisted of a private meeting with Josef Stalin, who in his mesmerizing pipe-smoking manner seemed to enthral even the most distrustful. What was expected of foreign pilgrims in return was good publicity in the eyes of the Western world, which usually took the form of a published testimony or a travelogue on their tour of the country. One has to admit that such a request was hardly unreasonable; Shaw himself came up with a similar idea back in 1922, when he wrote to Charles Sarolea:

> I hope you will be able to visit Russia [...] We want something from a capable observer and effective writer who is neither a fanatical Communist nor a scandalised bourgeois, and who has, moreover, a social and academic position, as well as a literary standing, which enables him to secure conspicuous publication in the Capitalist Press, without which no real publicity is possible in this country.[10]

---

9   Romain Rolland, 'Réponse à Constantin Balmont et à Ivan Bounine' (20 January
      1928), in Romain Rolland, *I Will Not Rest* (London: Selvin & Blount Ltd, 1933), 181,
      182, 183, 187 (first published in *L'Europe* [5 February 1928], 245–52).
10   Shaw, Letter to Charles Sarolea, 19 August 1922, in *Collected Letters*, vol. 3, 782.
      Dr Charles Sarolea, professor of French at the University of Edinburgh, published
      his *Impressions of Soviet Russia* in 1924.

This much awaited publicity appeared in a whole variety of forms, revealing, perhaps, the implicit proclivities of the authors. Barbusse produced a laudatory tract effectively entitled *Stalin: A New World Seen through One Man*, thus becoming the latter's first non-Russian biographer. Emil Ludwig issued no fewer than three versions of his eulogy to the Soviet leader – in 1933, 1940, and 1942; and the Webbs composed a mammoth treatise running to almost 1100 pages – *Soviet-Communism – a New Civilisation?* Sometimes, as in the case of Ludwig, the publication could be exploited further by the Soviet authorities – his interview with Stalin[11] would be incorporated into Stalin's seminal biography of Lenin. At other times, things did not work quite so neatly: for instance, Lion Feuchtwanger's book *Moscow 1937*, although published in the USSR with a huge print run of 200,000 copies, was subsequently censored and effaced from the pallet of the Soviet press.

All these testimonies were clearly aimed at presenting a positive image of the system, and the texts written by the foreign observers were thoroughly retouched and sieved by their Soviet hosts. There was a tacit agreement that the latter would have the right to proofread the work before its final publication, which commonly resulted in a glossy 'made-to-measure' account, well suited to the Soviet political aims. For example, the original script of the 1934 conversation between Stalin and H.G. Wells was cautiously adjusted from both sides. Stalin rectified a number of ambivalent comments and crossed out an entire passage that, in fact, was highly indicative of his manipulative techniques in conducting the meeting (he seemed to be well informed regarding the unspoken rivalry between Wells and Shaw):

STALIN   Not with the idea of flattering you, but absolutely honestly I have to tell you that my conversation with you gave me more pleasure than the one with Bernard Shaw.

WELLS   For sure, Lady Astor wouldn't allow anyone to say a word.

STALIN   Shaw demanded that she should be present.[12]

---

11   The full transcript of the interview was published in Russian and in English: Josef Stalin, *An Interview with the German Author Emil Ludwig* (Moscow: Co-operative Publishing Society of Foreign Workers in the USSR, 1932).

12   *Stalin-Wells talk: written transcript*, RGASPI (Russian State Archive of Social and Political History), F. 558, Op. 1, Ed. hr. 3151, List 23, quoted in Leonid Maksimenkov

Using the poetic licence extended by the Soviet leader, Wells decided to probe the idea of Russia joining the International PEN Club. As Galsworthy's death elevated him to the position of president, Wells wanted to discuss with the Soviet writers the possibility of their affiliating with the PEN. Being reluctant to put it across to Stalin in person, he now felt free to revise the text of the discussion, which later on he submitted by post. Such an oversensitive approach on behalf of the British author was highly ironic, for his actual conversation with Stalin contained (perhaps quite inadvertently) some far more risky statements regarding freedom of speech in the Soviet state: 'The organisation is still weak,' acknowledged Wells, 'but it has branches in many countries, and what is more important, the speeches of its members are widely reported in the press. It insists upon this free expression of opinion, even of opposition opinion. I hope to discuss this point with Gorky. I do not know if you are prepared yet for that much freedom here.'[13] According to the stenogram, Stalin preferred to leave the daring comment unanswered, but as the last word in any conversation was supposed to be his and his alone, he quickly scribbled a suitable conclusion, along the lines of 'We Bolsheviks call this "self-criticism" [*samokritika*]. It is widely applied in the USSR.'[14]

It can thus be seen that Shaw's trip to the USSR in 1931 was one of the links in this chain of foreign visitors to the Soviet country. However, it also differed in a number of key respects. Firstly, Shaw had the longest possible conversation with Stalin (comparable only with the similar exchange with H.G. Wells). Whereas other foreigners had been granted twenty minutes at most, he spent some two and a half hours with the Soviet leader. No records of their conversation survived and the contents of their talk are still

---

and Christopher Barnes, 'Boris Pasternak in August 1936 – An NKVD Memorandum', *Toronto Slavic Quarterly*, 6 (2003) <http://www.utoronto.ca/tsq/06/pasternak06. shtml>.

13   'Stalin-Wells Talk: The verbatim record', in *Stalin-Wells Talk* (London: New Statesman and Nation, 1934), 18.

14   *Stalin-Wells talk: Written transcript*, RGASPI, F. 558, Op. 1, Ed. hr. 3151, List 23, quoted in Leonid Maksimenkov and Christopher Barnes, 'Boris Pasternak in August 1936 – An NKVD Memorandum'.

unknown, but Shaw was profoundly moved by the discussion, reporting that when he met Stalin the very first thing he noticed about him was that he was a first-rate listener. 'I never met a man,' he claimed, 'who could talk so well and yet was in less of a hurry to talk than Stalin'.[15] Secondly, Shaw did not produce any formal account of his visit to Russia. In 1932, during his stay in South Africa, he started writing a book based on his journey, as a result of which a certain number of pages entitled *The Rationalisation of Russia* were sent to England to be typed by his secretary Blanche Patch.[16] The book remained unfinished, but the Soviet authorities seemed to be more than satisfied with a series of laudatory interviews that appeared in western newsprint shortly after Shaw's return to Great Britain. 'Russia is all right and we are all wrong,'[17] he claimed,

> Russia is what we call a great country, making a great experiment to which we our-selves have led up through many empirical but steadily converging paths. She is led by men of impressive ability and unprecedented freedom of thought, operating a system from which the disastrous frictions of our continual conflict of private interests, and the paralysing delays of our Parliamentary engines of opposition and obstruction, have been ruthlessly eliminated.[18]

Shaw's 1931 trip was not an official visit organized by the Fabians as a group. According to his description of the events, it had been devised and planned by Britain's first woman MP, Nancy Astor, a Conservative, and Lord Lothian (Philip Kerr), a Liberal and a former secretary to Lloyd

15   Bernard Shaw, 'Mr Bernard Shaw Comments', in *Stalin-Wells Talk*, 22. Some more detailed impressions are quoted in Pearson (*Bernard Shaw: His Life and Personality*, 364–5): 'Unlike the other dictators, Stalin has an irresistible sense of humour. He is not Russian: he is a handsome Georgian with the attractive dark eyes of his race. There is an odd mixture of the Pope and the field-marshal in him: you might guess him to be the illegitimate soldier-son of a cardinal. I should call his manners perfect, if only he had been able to conceal the fact that we amused him enormously.'

16   The text of Shaw's manuscript *The Rationalisation of Russia*, with the introduction and comments of Harry M. Geduld was published in 1964 (Bloomington: Indiana University Press).

17   '"We Are All Wrong", Says Bernard Shaw', *Moscow News* (8 August 1931).

18   Bernard Shaw, 'Mr Shaw on the Soviet', *The Times* (13 August 1931).

George. Shaw himself was persuaded to join the party only at a later stage, driven by the idea that in a few years' time he would be too frail to make the journey. 'My going is a bit of an accident,' he wrote,

> the Astors suddenly took it into their heads to see for themselves whether Russia is really the earthly paradise I had declared it to be; and they challenged me to go with them. I felt, at my age, that if I did not seize the opportunity, I should never see Russia at all; so I agreed. And now they have had to change their plans and nothing is left of the proposed party but myself, the Marquess Lothian (Phil Kerr) and Tennant, the head centre of Christian Science here.[19]

Lady Astor's biographers present a different version of the story, claiming that it was Shaw who received the invitation to visit the country, after his fame had grown very great in the USSR (related to the production of *The Apple Cart* in 1929).[20] What was odd about the entire venture was that this invitation was for midsummer when the heat in Moscow was intolerable, especially for Shaw's wife Charlotte, who had insufficient physical strength for such a journey at such a time. Shaw therefore wrote to the Embassy, saying that he would be happy to accept the invitation if he could be joined by some friends. The Ambassador looked favourably on the proposal, and the Astors immediately fell in with the plan.[21]

One would think that Nancy Astor was the very last person who should have been accompanying Shaw on his journey. Only the previous year Harold Laski, Professor at the London School of Economics, had denounced Nancy at a Fabian Committee meeting and then repeated the attack in *The Daily Herald*, calling her the 'Pollyanna of Politics'[22] – a type of ineffectual do-gooding political meddler. However, leaving aside her right wing stance, she fitted perfectly the mould of the Shavian New Woman, a manifestation in real life of those radical feminist figures in his dramas, such as Barbara in *Major Barbara*, Vivie, the Newnham-educated

---

19   Shaw, Letter to Horace Plunkett, 16 July 1931, in *Collected Letters*, vol. 4, 242.
20   Christopher Sykes, *Nancy: The Life of Lady Astor* (London: Collins, 1972), 325.
21   Anthony Masters, *Nancy Astor: A Biography* (New York: McGraw-Hill Book Company, 1981),. 167; Sykes, *Nancy: The Life of Lady Astor*, 325.
22   Quoted in J.W. Jones, 'A Mix of Members', *Parliamentary Affairs*, 33/1 (1979), 332.

career girl in *Mrs Warren's Profession*, or Candida in the eponymous play. Although she was indeed Britain's first woman to have taken her seat as an MP, Lady Astor was no progressive liberal; and, given Shaw's distinctly socialist orientation, nothing could seem more improbable than this oddly assorted pair. Shaw, nonetheless, admired Nancy as a 'conviction politician' and they remained very close from their first meeting in the twenties all the way through to the last years of Shaw's life.

Apart from the Astors and Lord Lothian, the group was to include J.W. Mallin, head of Toynbee Hall, the London social welfare centre, Sidney David Gamble, a sociologist from Cincinnati and Gertrude Ely of Philadelphia,[23] an American friend of Lady Astor, who finally did not make it to Moscow, having failed to obtain a valid visa for her passage through Poland. On 21 July 1931, after a two day train journey across Europe (via Berlin and Warsaw), the visitors arrived at the Belorusso-Baltic Station in Moscow. The station was amply decorated with red banners, bearing Shaw's portrait and his name; and when the distinguished visitor got off the train he was greeted by a brass band and a military guard of honour that escorted him through the enthusiastic crowd shouting 'Hail Shaw!' Waldorf Astor commented in his diary that 'the arrival at the station was unique;' and 'If one had told the late George Edwardes or the present Cochran to stage G.B.S.'s arrival in "Red" Moscow and his reception by the Proletariat they would have staged exactly what happened.'[24] The group of Soviet officials attending the meeting included Anatolii Lunacharskii, the former Minister of Enlightenment of the USSR,[25] Karl Radek, the leading journalist, and Maxim Litvinov, the Minister of Foreign Affairs, who, as it happened, had joined the travellers on the train as soon as they had crossed the Polish border.

And although all of this seemed to come as a complete 'surprise' for the British dramatist, who, apparently took pains to send a telegram to the

---

23   'Visitors to USSR', *Moscow News* (18 July 1931).
24   Quoted in Sykes, *Nancy: The Life of Lady Astor*, 329.
25   In 1929 Lunacharskii was dismissed from the position of Minister; at the time of Shaw's visit he was the director of the Institute of Literature and Arts and the Chairman of the Scholars Board of the Central Executive Committee of the USSR.

General Secretary of the International Union of Revolutionary Writers, Bélla Illés, emphasizing that 'under no circumstances should he be burdened with parades, receptions or banquets,'[26] the visit was widely celebrated by the Russian authorities and the Russian press.

Prior to Shaw's arrival in Moscow, Lunacharskii published a key-note article in *Izvestiia*, introducing the British author to the nation as 'the most brilliant European' who had made a major contribution to the 'great cause of liberty':

> Bernard Shaw's freedom has become a noted and a major factor of contemporary culture, because it is combined with a potential power of mind and sparkling sense of humour, which has been justly defined as the ability to discern the finest point of resemblance and the finest point of difference. Bernard Shaw carries his humour to the extent of paradoxes. His paradoxes compel thought, and the bright flashes of his illuminating humour quite frequently, quite unexpectedly, shed light on the thick twilight of the approaching night of capitalism.[27]

The article commented on the innate wit and natural sense of humour of the dramatist, but pointed out that it would be wrong to perceive him as a 'peculiar formalist in the realm of irony'. 'Bernard Shaw,' maintained Lunacharskii, 'is an enemy of capitalism, and frequently he applies a keen lancet to pierce bourgeois bubbles and to reveal that they are either empty or filled with malodorous gas.' In a rather diplomatic mode the former Minister touched upon Shaw's own wealth and standards of living. After all, the British dramatist was quite rich (and was to leave an estate valued at £367,000 after his death),[28] he lived like a middle-class 'bourgeois' and travelled in the company of reactionary aristocrats; according to the article, however:

> The power and brilliancy of his intellect has enabled him to disentangle himself from the cobwebs of bourgeois sophistry, bourgeois hypocrisy, and bourgeois prejudices [...] The bourgeoisie does not hate him. On the contrary, the English bourgeoisie forgets that Shaw is an Irishman and is inclined to take great pride in him. He has

26 A. Lunacharskii, 'Bernard Shaw, Our Guest', *Izvestiia* (21 July 1931).
27 Lunacharskii, 'Bernard Shaw, Our Guest', *Izvestiia* (21 July 1931).
28 'George Bernard Shaw', *Oxford Dictionary of National Biography*, <http://www.oxforddnb.com/view/article/36047?docPos=1>.

become a landmark of England, he is the great English word-magician, so to speak. 'Our Bernard Shaw,' one can hear from the lips of almost every Englishman. Of course, now and then, Bernard Shaw treats the fashionable bourgeoisie to such a slap in the face that it cannot help frowning, and even getting angry. Nevertheless, it soon becomes reassured: 'Oh, it is the witty Bernard Shaw, the unique old man. How can one be angry with him! He is so fond of paradoxes, and you can't expect him to spare the bourgeoisie or anyone else.'[29]

To emphasize Shaw's socialist orientation *Izvestiia* also presented a series of articles by Karl Radek, who in a virtual polemics with Shaw commented on the Fabian idea of reformist socialist transformation. Radek was a defiant extremist; and although at the beginning of the thirties he held the modest administrative position of Head of the International Information Office of the Central Committee, he had a turbulent experience of the revolutionary past. Not unlike Shaw, he was known for his non-conformist outlook and his fascination with strong leaders: in 1932 he produced a Russian translation of Hitler's *Mein Kampf* to be circulated within the narrow circles of the Soviet *nomenklatura*. In October 1923 Radek made an unsuccessful attempt to launch a second German revolution – Stalin did not approve the campaign, but it took place nevertheless, and the operation was called back only at the very last moment, due to the hostile political environment in the country. Radek was a great supporter of Trotskii's idea of the world-wide revolution – 'Communism will do away with frontiers.'[30] And although the concept and its author were already completely out of date by the late twenties,[31] it was exactly this very slogan that dazzled the travellers of Shaw's party as their train passed through the big iron arch at the Polish-Russian border, marking the entrance to what Shaw (if not the Astors) considered the promised land of the bright future.[32]

29   Lunacharskii, 'Bernard Shaw, Our Guest', *Izvestiia* (21 July 1931).
30   Karl Radek perished tragically in Stalin's purges of 1937; his show-trial was attended and approved of by Lion Feuchtwanger, who considered it a necessary step towards political democratization.
31   In 1928, due to his opposition to Stalin's idea of building communism in one country, Lev Trotskii was expelled from the Communist Party and exiled from the Soviet Union.
32   Shaw, Letter to Charlotte F. Shaw, 21 July 1931, in *Collected Letters*, vol. 4, 246.

Figure 5   Bernard Shaw given a highly orchestrated mass greeting
upon his arrival by train in Moscow, July 1931. LSE Archives.

As mentioned, Shaw did not produce any formal account of his visit
to Russia, but the trip was widely covered in the Soviet press, as well as
in several major western newspapers (*The Times*, *The Observer*, *The New
Leader* and *The New York Times*), which, together with the letters to his
wife Charlotte, present an extensive basis for the following reconstruction
of and reflection on his nine-day journey.

The travellers' agenda was heavily loaded with events that embraced a
broad spectrum of activities (though not very different from those offered
to other visitors). *Moscow News* (28 July 1931) reported that on the first
day in Moscow the party visited the Kremlin, the Park of Culture and the
Museum of the Revolution. In the evening they attended *The Beggar's
Opera* at the Chamber Theatre (Kamernyi Teatr), where an enthusiastic
demonstration took place upon Shaw's appearance in the auditorium. The
whole troupe came out on stage, over which had been hung a red banner
bearing (in English) the words: 'To brilliant master. Bernard Shaw – a

warm welcome to Soviet soil.' Aleksandr Tairov, director of the Chamber
Theatre, made a welcome speech and presented Shaw with a set of photographs of the theatre's production of his play *St Joan*. Tairov was in his
prime at the time, and his colourful spectacles had been highly acclaimed
in Moscow and abroad (in 1923 the theatre made a seven-month tour in
Germany and in France). In distinction to the Moscow Art Theatre, where
productions were led by the director's vision of the play, Tairov's company
was founded on a more 'democratic' principle akin to the 'collective' spirit
of the early twenties: his shows were conceived as an upshot of the joint
effort with an equal input from every actor, the designer and the producer
himself. Tairov was a master of so-called synthetic art, combining music,
pantomime and the performance. This resulted in a somewhat 'jazzy' spirit
in his productions. According to *The Times*:

> The critics of the Kamerny Theatre dislike the very modern and somewhat restless
> futurism of the scenery in many of the plays [...] but the real merit of the perform-
> ances as a whole, and the wonderful techniques of the actors, gradually won recogni-
> tion, and this year in Moscow the Kamerny Theatre was invited to give the annual
> performance in aid of the home for retired actors – an honour which falls to the
> most popular theatre.[33]

Shaw's *St Joan*, staged in October 1924, was also designed in the best avant-
garde tradition of the theatre, which certainly would not have been to the
taste of the British dramatist, who was sufficiently dismayed by the amazing
and, as he put it, 'at points disgusting perversion of the Beggar's Opera.'[34]
Tairov, on the other hand, was deeply inspired by Shaw's presence – a year
later he felt free to write to the British dramatist inquiring about certain
interpretations of his early play *Caesar and Cleopatra*,[35] which was subsequently staged at the Chamber Theatre in December 1934.

33   'Russian Players. The Moscow Kamerny Theatre', *The Times* (6 March 1923).
34   Shaw, Letter to Charlotte F. Shaw, 22 July 1931, in *Collected Letters*, vol. 4, 247. The
     production was based on Brecht's adaptation of the original *Die Dreigroschenoper*,
     Tairov received the text personally from the author during his visit to Germany in
     1929.
35   Aleksandr Tairov, Letter to Bernard Shaw, July 1932, RGALI, F.1923, Op. 2, Ed. hr.
     593.

Figure 6 Bernard Shaw with Lady Nancy Astor and Russian Communists,
Moscow 1931 (from left to right: Karl Radek, Anatolii Lunacharskii,
Lady Nancy Astor, Bernard Shaw, Artemii Khalatov). LSE Archives.

Figure 7 Bernard Shaw on his Moscow trip 1931, meeting Anatolii
Lunacharskii and Konstantin Stanislavskii. LSE Archives.

Figure 8   Sergei F. Sokolov and George Bernard Shaw visiting a Moscow factory
(1937, oil on canvas).

During his first three days in Moscow Shaw also met with a group of Soviet
writers in the office of Khalatov, the president of the State Publishing
House. The British dramatist jokingly proposed that literary subjects should
be excluded from conversation during the interview. All present agreed
willingly enough, but neither side kept to the agreement. The conversation was concluded by one of Shaw's usual prophetic statements, which in

its glamorous rhetoric could, perhaps, rival the best examples of the Party slogans (and, of course, was in no way derived from personal experience – after all, Tolstoy also preached poverty and lived well): 'We must get away from the mistaken idea that a writer is a superman,' he maintained. 'The writer should at the same time work in a factory at the bench, at actual productive labour. Absolutely nothing should be permitted to free him from this work.'[36]

Other people to whom Shaw paid a visit included Maxim Gorky, who was recovering from illness in his house in the suburbs near Moscow, and the legendary theatre director and head of the Moscow Art Theatre Konstantin Stanislavskii. At that time Stanislavskii was already very ill: in October 1928 he had suffered a heart attack at a gala performance of *The Three Sisters* and never returned to active stage work again. In terms of drama, however, the consequences of Shaw's visit which are of greater interest arguably concern the Russian writer Andrei Platonov. Platonov is most famous for his novels *Chevengur* and *The Foundation Pit*, which bitterly satirize the collectivization process, but in 1932 he also produced a play entitled *Fourteen Little Red Huts*. The play was not staged in Platonov's own lifetime; indeed it was not published until the eighties, long after the author's own death in 1951 (for years Platonov remained a banned writer and was severely persecuted by the regime). The play features a superannuated Edward-Johann-Louis-Bos – 'a world-renowned scholar, chairman of the League of Nations Commission for the Resolution of the Riddle of the World Economy and so Forth, 101 years old' – who is widely regarded as a thinly disguised parody of Shaw on his Russian trip the previous year.[37] A number of telling details contribute to this point. For instance, not unlike the omniscient Bos, Shaw was also happy to make the headline for almost any domain of politics and art. At the time of his visit, the British dramatist was already very old (by the standards of the 1930s) – hence the reference to his loss of critical perception. Platonov's Bos drinks milk at all times, reverting to the routine (and psychology) of a little child; the remark, of

36   'G.B.S. In Moscow and Leningrad', *Moscow News* (28 July 1931).
37   Robert Chandler, 'An Introductory note to Andrei Platonov's *Fourteen Little Red Huts*', in *The Portable Platonov* (Moscow: GLAS Publishers, 1999), 110.

course, has an indicative double meaning, for Shaw was known to be a strict teetotaller. As far as the opening scene of the drama is concerned – the arrival of Edward-Johann Bos in the country – the similarity with Shaw's pompous reception in Moscow cannot be missed:

STATION MASTER   [in his official voice] The Stolbtsy-Vladivostok express, 'The Mighty Bird', is now drawing up alongside platform one. Travelling in the first class coach is Mister Johann Louis Edward Bos, an honorary member of the Stockholm Academy, chairman of the League of Nations Commission for the Resolution of the Riddle of the World Economy and So Forth. (*Looks at his wrist-watch*). The delay: half a minute! The driver: comrade Vitalov!

The whistle of an engine, now inside the station. The sound of brakes. The train stops. Hubbub from the crowd. Greetings. A fanfare. The Station Master, drawing himself up to his full height, goes out onto the platform. The official greeter adopts an alert pose. With Interhom on his arm. Johann Bos comes out onto the station concourse. Interhom is carrying a small suitcase. They are followed by two writers Latrinov and Glutonov. Then the station master. The official greeter welcomes Bos. He introduces himself to him and his companion, and says a short sentence of welcome in French

BOS   [irritably] I know, I know ... I know Russian all right. What don't I know! There's more of the stuff than I can remember. Russian, Indian, Mexican, Jewish, astronomy, psychotechnics, hydraulics ... I'm a hundred and one years old, and you, a boy (*more and more irritably*) – a mere boy! – have the nerve to address me in French.

OFFICIAL GREETER   Greetings to you, Mister Johann Bos, great philosopher of declining capitalism, brilliant master of opportunistic ploys, and may I wish you –

INTERHOM   Become an infant, a preschool child, a young pioneer, a dear friend of the new world.

OFFICIAL GREETER   [to Interhom grimly] True, but only partly so. (*To Bos*) I welcome you – in the name of the working people who are building happiness and truth for both you and themselves – to this still unknown, gigantic country. We are happy to meet you in our common home!

BOS   I doubt if I will make you happy. [...] Where can I see Socialism? Show it to me at once. Capitalism irritates me.[38]

---

38   Andrei Platonov, *Fourteen Little Red Huts*, Robert Chandler, trans., in *The Portable Platonov*, 112–15.

The very last phrase is particularly striking in the way it echoes Shaw's own statement in his interview with *The New York Times*, in which when answering the question why he decided to go to Russia, he claimed that 'hitherto I have only been in capitalist countries, and surely' would be interested to go to the Communist one.[39]

The Communist country offered Shaw all the trappings of its warmest welcome. In Leningrad he was conducted through 'miles and miles of pictures at the Hermitage';[40] and made 50,000 feet of talking film on Lenin for *The Union of Cineastes* (*Soiuzkino*), convinced that his 'English will be lost on a Russian audience'.[41] He was entertained to a special performance at one of the cinemas, where the fragments of the best Soviet films were run off – *Battleship Potemkin, The Last Days of St Petersburg, Road to Life* and others; and the Association of Proletarian Writers gave a dinner in his honour at the Europa Hotel, with Anatolii Lunacharskii travelling specially from Moscow to preside at the feast.

On the following day the House of Unions hosted a gala concert on the occasion of Shaw's 75th birthday, where thousands gave him an ovation and the best artists of the stage took part in the spectacle. Shaw started his speech with the Russian word 'tovarishch' ('comrade'), pointing out that this was the only Russian word he knew so far, but which had acquired for him 'a particularly friendly sound.'[42] He said that during his conversations, many expressed their hope that upon his return to England he would tell the truth about Russia. Shaw perceived it as a sort of misunderstanding. 'Comrades,' he said,

> The idea of this whole journey to Soviet Russia is not to be able to tell the English something which I didn't know before; it is so that I can answer them on those occasions when they say to me: 'So, you consider Soviet Russia a remarkable country,

---

39   'Shaw Eager to Visit Non-Capitalist Land', *The New York Times* (1 July 1931).

40   Shaw, Letter to Charlotte F. Shaw, 24 July 1931, in *Collected Letters*, vol. 4, 251.

41   Shaw, Letter to Charlotte F. Shaw, 25 July 1931, in *Collected Letters*, vol. 4, 253.

42   It is highly ironic that back in the 1880s, Shaw disdained this very word with considerable aplomb (see Chapter One, footnote 16).

but you've not actually been there yourself, you haven't seen all its terrors'. Now upon my return I can say: Yes, I have seen all the 'terrors', and I was terribly pleased by them.[43]

Among the assortment of the venues that allowed the British dramatists to testify to the 'terrors' of the socialist experiment were Bolshevo – the labour commune for young criminals, where former juvenile offenders were educated and reformed – the Moscow Electric Factory, and the Lenin collective farm in Central Russia.[44] The necessity to found the labour commune as well as many other similar organizations in Russia had been caused by the rapid increase in juvenile delinquency after the end of the Civil War. Young criminals stole, robbed and presented a serious social danger. The Bolshevo labour commune (situated near Moscow) was founded in 1924. The basic principle behind it was self-management and self-sufficiency, and the task of the teachers was to train adolescents for a profession. For this

43   Bernard Shaw, speech at the Moscow House of Unions, 26 July, 1931. The text of the speech was published in *Pravda* (27 July 1931); the English translation appeared in *Moscow News* ('Bernard Shaw Speaks at Dom Soiuzov', *Moscow News* [28 July 1931]) and can be also found in *Collected Letters*, vol. 4, 256–8 [257]; here and hereafter we refer to the text in the *Collected Letters*. Dom Soiuzov (House of Unions) is a major congress building in Moscow; after the Revolution it was assigned to the Moscow council of Trade Unions, hence the name; the building hosted a number of major social and political events, such as state funerals (of Lenin and Stalin), and Communist Party conferences, as well as a series of Stalin's show trials.

44   The visit was, however, not without its funny moments. Mikhail Shatrov (born in Moscow, 3 April 1932), a well known Soviet dramatist and script-writer, claims that he owes his life and talent to the British dramatist. When his mother was expecting a child, his parents had a protracted argument and she decided to terminate the pregnancy. She was placed in the Grauerman Hospital – one of the central clinics on Arbat Street. This coincided precisely with the days of Shaw's Moscow visit, and the administration of the clinic was told to be ready to greet the distinguished foreign guests. Instantly it was decided that the very existence of an abortion clinic did not highlight the benefits of the socialist system, and all the women were sent home and advised to come back in a week. During this week, however, Shatrov's parents sorted out their affairs, and in a couple of months Mikhail successfully made his appearance in the world (Iurii Bezelianskii, 'The Revolution, Bernard Shaw and Mikhail Shatrov', *Alef*, 1002 [2010], <http://www.alefmagazine.com/pub2274.html>).

purpose, joiners' and shoemakers' workshops were set up, which later on expanded and mastered knitted goods, timber and metal-processing production. During the fifteen years of its existence, Bolshevo gained considerable pedagogical experience, which many Soviet and western specialists came to adopt. Overall, it was an exemplary community, which was widely discussed in the Soviet press of the time;[45] and the fact that it belonged to the OGPU jurisdiction (the State Political Directorate – secret police force) made it a very 'secure' place to show foreigners. 'We dined on cabbage soup (stchi) and black bread [...] which I find an ideal diet,' wrote Shaw, 'The first smile came on the faces of the criminals,' wrote Shaw, 'when I told them that I had begun by committing juvenile crimes for which I should have been sent to prison if the police had caught me.'[46] In the evening of the same day he watched the newly-created feature film, *Road to Life* (premiered 1 June 1931), which was largely based on the practice of the Bolshevo institution.[47]

Similarly, Shaw was profoundly impressed by his tour of the Elektrozavod (Electric Factory). The director, as Shaw put it, 'wore a beautiful silk skirt and a jacket of Conduit St-Savile Row cut, and had splendidly manicured hands,'[48] but told the visitors of the heroic struggle of the workers that had led to the completion of their Five-Year Plan in two and a half years. 'While I was in this factory,' Shaw recollected later,

> a young man, with an air of conscious virtue, was presented to me. He had an Order of some sort pinned to his coat, and he was the young man who had set the pace in that factory in the carrying out of the Five Year Plan. He had done more than any other, and I said to him, 'Young man, if you were in England, and you set up about double the pace of your fellow workers, you would not be a popular character, you would be called a 'slogger' – at least, that was the old fashioned word, I don't know what it

45   A. Avtonomov, 'Bolshevskaia commuana OGPU', *Nashi dostizheniia*, 7 (1930), 35.

46   Shaw, Letter to Charlotte F. Shaw, 23 July 1931, in *Collected Letters*, vol. 4, 249.

47   *Road to Life* was directed and written by Nikolai Ekk. The film won an award at the 1932 Venice International Film Festival, which went to Nikolai Ekk for Most Convincing Director.

48   Shaw, Letter to Charlotte F. Shaw, 23 July 1931, in *Collected Letters*, vol. 4, 249.

may be now – and you would run the risk of a brick being dropped on your head in a dark lane. If you are going on in this way, my friend, you stay in Russia.' Certainly there the young man was popular. He led for efficiency.[49]

As the party was leaving, Lady Astor became involved in a compelling debate with the workers who gathered in the courtyard of the factory. The latter were not shy of opposing the British Conservative on political issues 'to the diabolical amusement of Lunacharskii,' most evidently shared by the British dramatist.[50] *Moscow News* gave the following report on the incident, published under the eye-catching title 'Workers Respond to Lady Astor':

> A meeting was organized and a truck standing in the courtyard became the tribunal, from which workers greeted Shaw and the visitors. Lady Astor energetically requested that she be permitted to speak on how well the people live in England. From the crowd came a worker's voice: 'Who lives well? The workers or capitalists?' However the workers helped Lady Astor to climb up on the truck, and Shaw also mounted. Lady Astor said that although she was a member of the Conservative party, with all her heart she was sympathetic with the Soviet Union. 'You have done some good things,' she said 'for which I'm very glad, and I hope you will go from strength to strength. The Soviet Union must get in step with the whole world and then the world will march with you.' The heckling, which went on all through her talk, broke out afresh at this:
> – 'We'll march with the world proletariat, but not with the world bourgeoisie.'
> – 'While you have had great success,' continued Lady Astor, 'you are too conceited.'
> – 'We have a right to be conceited,' came voices from the crowd. 'We're building Socialism. We are proud because the Elektrozavod has finished its Five-Year Plan in two and a half years.'
> In leaving Shaw spoke the final word to the workers: 'Comrades, I am very glad to see such great enthusiasm here. When I return to England, I shall try to persuade the English workers to do the same as you have done.'[51]

49 Bernard Shaw, Lecture delivered at the Independent Labour Party National Summer School, Digswell Park, 5 August 1931, reprinted in *The New Leader* (7 August 1931).
50 Shaw, Letter to Charlotte F. Shaw, 23 July 1931, in *Collected Letters*, vol. 4, 249.
51 'G.B.S. In Moscow and Leningrad', *Moscow News* (28 July 1931).

Soviet farmers seemed to be no less persuasive than the socialist workers, when the party visited the Lenin Commune in the Kirsanovskii district (situated in the Tambov region, 480 km southeast from Moscow). The whole day was devoted to the study of the agricultural industry of the commune and special attention was given to its social facilities – day nurseries, children's quarters, laundries, kitchens and dining rooms. The head of the Lenin Commune, who had lived a long time in America, told the guests about the work organized nine years ago. The commune was established by a group of sixty-five American farmers, who came to Russia in 1922 and settled in the region in the small village of Ira.[52] Their commendable endeavour was approved personally by Lenin, and at the beginning of the thirties the collective farm became one of the most successful establishments shown to foreigners, partly because of its international dimension and connections with Lenin. Several American farmers talked about their life in the commune, and both Shaw and Lady Astor commented on its splendid organization.

It is at this point that Shaw's trip becomes highly controversial. The real objective of the journey – aside from the celebration of his seventy-fifth birthday that coincided with it – was to report on the success of the first Five Year Plan, one of the cornerstones of which, apart from the electrification of the USSR and the setting up of advanced industry, was the merging of the old-style smaller households into enormous, state-run, centrally-planned collective farms – the 'kolkhoz'. This was a massive undertaking, beginning in the late 1920s shortly after Stalin dismissed Trotskii and seized power. It was not just a rationalizing process but also an occasion to break the so-called 'kulaks', the wealthier, land-owning peasants – particularly widespread in the Ukraine – who as a sort of peasant bourgeoisie were perceived as putting up the most recalcitrant resistance to communism. A large element of Russia's population, as peasants, had been serfs on feudal estates until the emancipation of 1861. The kulaks were a minority stratum of wealthier, capitalist farmers who owned land and employed poorer peasants, and had been promoted in the latter years of tsarism. It has often been suggested that the Soviet authorities deliberately

52   'U eksponatov kolkhoznogo muzeia', *Leninets* (21 September 1977).

shielded Shaw and other western visitors from the worst aspects of the collectivization process. After all, this was a process which resulted in extermination, even by official Soviet figures, of some 700,000 people. The situation was aggravated by the famines of the early 1930s; and the so-called 'holodomor' in the Ukraine may have led to the death, whether through imprisonment, deportation or engineered starvation, of as many as 10 million peasants.

Sidney and Beatrice Webb, the most devoted Fabians and the founders of the Society, visited the Soviet Union in May–June 1932, travelling to the Ukraine for a more intensive study of collectivization (they were there for two months) than Shaw had been able to undertake on his mere nine day tour in 1931. It has to be said that Shaw arrived before the worst of the famine, but there were already undoubtedly mass deaths occurring during his visit to the country.[53] By the time the Webbs arrived the following year, things had got still worse, according to the testimony of such reporters as Gareth Jones, who visited the Soviet Union on three occasions (1930–1933) and wrote a series of articles for a number of newspapers on the conditions resulting from Stalin's Five-Year Plan.[54] Nevertheless, the importance of Shaw's visit in 1931 cannot be overestimated. In a speech after his return he completely countered the rumours of the famine mainly on the grounds of his visit to a 'show-off' collective farm, which, in fact, was run by Americans, and a series of splendid dinners that he was offered at the best hotels in Leningrad and Moscow. 'Food was good and there was plenty of it,' he stated.[55]

---

53   To add to the controversy of the situation in 1931 there appeared a book by Mrs Cecil Chesterton (G.K. Chesterton's sister-in-law), *My Russian Venture*. Mrs Chesterton travelled with a religious mission through Belorussia and Ukraine without any privileged treatment of the state visitors, but emerged from her ordeal, 'which had been as hard and bug-ridden as the other had been officially soften, with much the same starry-eyed belief in the ultimate beneficence of the Soviet system' (Sykes, *Nancy: The Life of Lady Astor*, 147).

54   Gareth Jones, 'The Two Russias', *The Times* (13–16 October 1930); 'The Real Russia', *The Times* (14–16 October 1931), 'Will There be Soup?', *The Western Mail, Cardiff* (15, 17 October 1932).

55   'They Say – Reality in Russia', *The New York Times* (2 August 1931).

Доклад Бернарда Шоу о СССР

Рис. Бор. Ефимов

Figure 9 'Bernard Shaw on the USSR: the English bourgeoisie
is extremely *shawcked*', *Moscow News*, 8 August 1931.

Was Shaw aware of the problem? The answer is undoubtedly 'yes', since the reports of the famine that reached the West independently[56] were known to the members of his close circle, and while describing his departure to Russia, he specifically pointed out their concerns about the food problem: 'Weeping relatives crowded around us when they learned that we were going to make this journey and warned us against it, saying that we would surely be killed. They gave us boxes of food, bedding, and even a tent so that we would have a roof over our heads. We have been dropping the food out of the windows of railway trains ever since.'[57]

In discussing the Moscow trip, Patrick Wright highlights Shaw's preposterous remarks connected with this episode.[58] Over the lunch at the Moscow Metropole Hotel, William Chamberlain, who at that time acted as a Moscow correspondent for the *Christian Science Monitor*, tried to convince Shaw that the people in his audience were indeed going hungry and must have been very shocked to hear that he disposed of his tins of food on the way. In response Shaw is said to have looked around the hotel restaurant and asked: 'Where do you see any food shortage?' And when Mr Chamberlain told him that children in Russia were going without milk he uttered something to the effect that Soviet mothers should, perhaps, follow the examples of the Eskimos who suckled their children until they were a good twenty years of age. Moreover, it is highly indicative in this context that Lord Lothian, Shaw's fellow traveller to Moscow, who was given exactly the same tour of the country, did not turn a blind eye to the crisis. 'The whole of Russia to-day was on war rations, as we were in 1917, and the staple diet of the towns was black bread and cabbage soup,' he admitted in his report to the Liberal Summer School in Cambridge.[59]

---

56   Apart from Gareth Jones, who was already writing his reports for the British press, there were, for instance, Donald Day's testimonies in *The Chicago Tribune* and an interview with a British consulting engineer Frank Easton Woodhead in *The Daily Telegraph* (28 November, 1930). For a more detailed account on the reports of the western correspondents see Patrick Wright, *Iron Curtain* (Oxford: Oxford University Press, 2007) 304–12.

57   Shaw, Speech at the Moscow House of Unions, in *Collected Letters*, vol. 4, 256; *Moscow News* (28 July 1931).

58   Patrick Wright, *Iron Curtain*, 297.

59   'A Liberal's Impression of Russia', *The Times* (6 August, 1931).

Shaw, on the other hand, was still sticking to his 'optimistic' views even two years later, when reports on the famine were extensively published in the British press (for instance by Gareth Jones and the young Malcolm Muggeridge).[60] 'Particularly offensive and ridiculous,' he wrote to the *Manchester Guardian*,

> is the revival of the old attempts to represent the condition of Russian workers as one of slavery and starvation, the Five-Year Plan as a failure, the new enterprises as bankrupt and the Communist regime as tottering to its fall. Although such inflammatory irresponsibility is easily laughed at, we must not forget that there are many people not sufficiently well informed politically to be proof against it, and that there are diehards among our diplomats who still dream of starting a counter-revolutionary war anywhere and anyhow, if only they can stampede public opinion into the necessary panic through the press.[61]

Ever since his return from the Russian trip, he had been filled with admiration for the factories he saw and the amazing progress they had made. He poured out his laudatory report on 'the only hope of the world' to the Fabian Society, as well as to the Independent Labour Party National Summer School, which later on was reprinted in major western newspapers,[62] maintaining that: 'here at last is a country which has established Socialism, made it the basis of its political system, definitely thrown over private property, and turned its back on Capitalism – a country which has succeeded in conducting industry successfully, and in achieving a political constitution.'[63]

---

60   Gareth Jones, 'Millions Starving in Russia', *The Daily Express* (30 March 1933); Gareth Jones, 'Famine Rules Russia', *The Evening Standard* (31 March 1933); Malcolm Muggeridge, three unsigned articles 'The Soviet and the Peasantry', *Manchester Guardian* (25, 27–28 March 1933).

61   Bernard Shaw, 'Social Conditions in Russia', *The Manchester Guardian* (2 March 1933).

62   Bernard Shaw, 'The Only Hope of the World' Lecture delivered at the Independent Labour Party National Summer School, Digswell Park, 5 August 1931; *Fabian News* 42/9 (September 1931); the excerpts reprinted in *The New Leader* (7 August 1931); *The New York Times* (6 August 1931); 'Mr Shaw's Comparison', *The Times* (6 August 1931).

63   Shaw, 'The Only Hope of the World', *The New Leader* (7 August 1931).

In many respects Shaw was an archetypal fellow traveller. According to David Caute, the characteristic features of this notion consisted of contempt for the Communist Party of one's own country, coupled with a revolutionary commitment (geographical, emotional and intellectual) to a distant cause.[64] Both components manifested vividly in Shaw's attitude to socialist Russia. Since 1917 he had been an ardent supporter of the Soviet experiment – as he put it in his Moscow speech: 'I believed you would win through, and I knew further that whether you were victorious or suffered defeat, it was my duty to back you to the limit.'[65] He also assured the audience that as an old socialist, he was deeply ashamed of England for being unable 'to lead the way, instead of Russia,'[66] and that it was almost a duty for everyone who had been 'preaching Socialism in the wilderness to go over and find out exactly how the things are being done.'[67]

Shaw's wholesale approval of the system was uncritical to the extent that it mystified even 'the converted'. Beatrice Webb, for instance, found it completely odd to discover from his statements that Soviet communism was merely Fabianism under a new name, that it was essentially a 'religious system all through' and that it was largely inspired by the modern political economy developed by Sidney Webb at the London School of Economics. The Webbs' name indeed had a solid reputation in Soviet Communist party circles: in 1898, the first volume of their major work, *The History of Trade Unionism* (1894), had been translated into Russian by Lenin,[68] but to consider Stalin's authoritarian policies as gradualism in the best Fabian tradition was a bit too much even for her sympathetic views. According to the note in Beatrice's diary:

---

64   D. Caute, *The Fellow Travellers* (London: Weidenfeld and Nicolson, 1973), 3.
65   Shaw, Speech at the Moscow House of Unions, in *Collected Letters*, vol. 4, 257; *Moscow News* (28 July 1931).
66   Shaw, Speech at the Moscow House of Unions, in *Collected Letters*, vol. 4, 258; *Moscow News* (28 July 1931).
67   Shaw, 'The Only Hope of the World', *The New Leader* (7 August 1931).
68   Lenin translated the first volume of the book during his exile in Siberia; later on, he also edited the second volume.

GBS spent two nights here and gave his pleasant chatty address on Russia to the
Fabian summer school. He was tired and excited by his visit to Russia; carried away
by the newness and the violence of the changes wrought. Here is tragedy – comedy
– melodrama, all magnificently staged on a huge scale. It must be right! The paradox of the speech: the Russian Revolution was pure Fabianism – Lenin and Stalin
had recognised the 'inevitability of gradualness'! Also they had given up 'workers'
control for the Webbs' conception of the threefold state – citizens, consumers and
producers' organisation [...] It is odd that it is this domination by a creed that seems
so attractive to GBS; he being that great destroyer of existing codes, creeds and conventions, seems in his old age to hanker for some credo to be enforced from birth
onwards on the whole population.[69]

Lord Lothian and Lady Astor were also intrigued by the fact that during
their stay in Moscow, Shaw remained so entirely 'deaf' to the oppression
of human rights they witnessed in the country. 'The Communist religion,
convinced that it could create a heaven for humanity in this world, had no
mercy for its opponents,' wrote Lord Lothian, 'The OGPU was an uncon-
trollable body, which had no Courts. People were tapped on the shoulder
and disappeared. They might come back, or they might not. There was no
such thing as freedom of the press in Russia, nor were there any of the things
which we call freedom at all.'[70] His perception was triggered by a revealing
incident that happened in Moscow when Shaw and Lady Astor received a
telegram from a Russian émigré Dmitrii Krynine, professor at Yale University, begging them, on behalf of himself and his son, to use their influence
on the Soviet authorities to help him reunite with his wife, who was refused
permission to leave the Soviet Union. Lady Astor tried forcefully to negotiate
the case with Litvinov, which led to nothing apart from the sudden disap-
pearance of Mrs Krynine when the journalists tried to interview her a few
days later. Shaw, on the other hand, showed little concern for the matter,
to the utmost dismay of the other members of the group.[71]

The question of why Shaw – one of the most cultured and intelligent
men of his time – was prepared to overlook so much and to accept so much
of the Soviet propaganda is not easy to answer. On the one hand, his letters

69   *The Diary of Beatrice Webb*, 8 August 1931, vol. 4, 249–50.
70   'A Liberal's Impression of Russia', *The Times* (6 August, 1931).
71   Sykes, *Nancy: The Life of Lady Astor*, 332.

to Charlotte are full of irony about the grand spectacle that had been laid on for his benefit: 'my arrival having been kept carefully secret there were only a few hundred people crowded round the carriage door to receive me with cheers and a salvo of fifty cameras'[72] or 'the audience had been instructed to receive me with tumultuous applause, which I acknowledged in Chaliapin's best manner';[73] and the fact that he was prepared to 'play along' shows that he was neither naïve nor blind: 'Nancy [...] finally let way to her loudly expressed disgust at my playing to the gallery. I smiled and waved and posed and posed – on the great gun (seated on three monster cannon balls), on the great bell, on every staircase and every doorway.'[74] Somehow his tone completely changed in the official reports on the trip that were presented to the public audience. With a great deal of sarcasm he vilified those who even dared to suggest that he was completely taken in by the very carefully packaged view of the system. 'Nobody seems, so far,' he wrote to *The New York Times*,

> to have taken in the full significance of Mr Westgarth's statement that when I visited Russia last year I saw not the real Russia, but an elaborate show staged for my special benefit, like the operatic Russia staged for Catharine II by Patiomkin when she took a holiday tour through her dominions. If Mr Westgarth is right, then all I can say is that the Soviet Government has achieved a feat of which no other Government in the world is capable. Just think of it! According to Mr Westgarth, the Russian Government, at a fortnight's notice (for my journey was unpremeditated), built two enormous cities, presumably of *papier maché* and painted canvas, each swarming with millions of inhabitants, all specially washed, dressed, and fed up for me; and passed off these two scenic impostures on me as Moscow and Petersburg ... When I say that I was completely taken in, it must be remembered that as a professional playwright of forty years' experience, I am an expert in theatrical illusion, and know all the tricks of the actor, scene-painter, property man, and producer inside and out. To have deceived me is a triumph of Soviet administration.[75]

72   Shaw, Letter to Charlotte F. Shaw, 21 July 1931, in *Collected Letters*, vol. 4, 246.
73   Shaw, Letter to Charlotte F. Shaw, 23 July 1931, in *Collected Letters*, vol. 4, 249.
74   Shaw, Letter to Charlotte F. Shaw, 21 July 1931, in *Collected Letters*, vol. 4, 246.
75   'My Reply [to J.R. Westgarth's "How Stalin Bluffed Shaw"]', *Daily Express* (13 June 1932).

This rift between the public and the private was not uncommon for Shaw's statements, becoming even more palpable when the dramatist started drifting into his later life. Thus, for instance, privately he admitted to Beatrice Webb that he found the whole business of the show trials 'very puzzling', saying that 'a conspiracy to kill him [Stalin] by level headed men like Sokolnikoff suggests the one real danger to Communism that its leaders have not minds of the necessary size to take it in and are relapsing into a pre-Marxian conception of politics.'[76] Publicly, however, he accepted the Stalinist account of the show trials as exposing a treasonous conspiracy on the part of old Bolsheviks, and the following passage was added to the first edition (1928) of *The Intelligent Woman's Guide to Socialism*, reprinted in 1937 under a slightly extended title: 'old Bolsheviks had to be executed,' he wrote, 'for revolutionary habits are hard to change; it still holds good that one of the first jobs of a successful revolution is to get rid of the revolutionists.'[77]

Does this all mean that Shaw was perfectly aware of the reality in Stalin's Russia, but, like, for instance, Romain Rolland, who placed a publishing embargo (until 1985) on his critical reflections on Russian affairs, he was adamant to suppress the truth in order to protect the socialist cause from its many foes? Or maybe, like Lion Feuchtwanger, he was defending the Soviet regime in preference to what he saw as the far worse menace of fascism in the late 1930s? Or perhaps, like the Webbs, he was simply waiting for Russia to prove its case? As Shaw put it in his testimony: 'The things I wanted to see were precisely the things I did see. I did not want to see

---

76 Shaw, Letter to Beatrice Webb, 4 September, 1936, in *Collected Letters*, vol. 4, 441.

77 Bernard Shaw, *The Intelligent Woman's Guide to Socialism, Capitalism, Sovietism and Fascism* (London: Penguin Books, 1937), 424. See also Will Bennett, 'How Shaw Defended Stalin's Mass Killing' (*The Daily Telegraph* [18 June 2003]) – The article refers to the questionnaire sent to Shaw by the journalist Dorothy Royal, where he justified Stalin's execution of many of those who had led the Bolshevik revolution in 1917. When asked whether he believed that the revolution had 'attracted degenerate types', Shaw replied: 'On the contrary it has attracted superior types all the world over to an extraordinary extent wherever it has been understood. But the top of the ladder is a very trying place for old revolutionists who have had no administrative experience, who have had no financial experience, who have been trained as penniless hunted fugitives with Karl Marx on the brain and not as statesmen. They often have to be pushed off the ladder with a rope around their necks.'

poverty and other remains of the capitalist system they have not been able to remove. I said I can see that within 20 minutes of my home in London.'[78] It is worth bearing in mind that Shaw and the Webbs were by no means revolutionary communists but reforming Fabians, who placed their faith in scientific administration and expanded education of the masses. They were therefore interested in the potential – not in the present, but in the best that could be done in the future. Moreover, when both Shaw and the Webbs visited Stalin's Russia, Britain, most of Europe and the USA were all in the depths of economic recession on a scale unknown in modern times. While the Depression was entering its worst phase, and the Labour government of Ramsay MacDonald was widely regarded as selling out its social-ist principles to the existing political establishment, Shaw, Wells, Keynes, and the Webbs seem to regard capitalism, at least in its existing form, as having failed, and looked to Russia as offering the way to be pursued. 'Communism,' maintained Keynes, 'is not a reaction against the failure of the nineteenth century to organise optimal economic output. It is a reac-tion against its comparative success. It is a protest against the emptiness of economic welfare, an appeal to the ascetic in us all to other values.'[79] In this respect, it is not surprising that the majority of western sympathizers saw exactly what they wanted to see. Shaw went to the Soviet Union wishing to be convinced of the conclusions he had already drawn – namely that this system was the only 'hope of the world.' And he was certainly not alone in such an intended approach, for the fact that the Webbs drafted their major treatise on Soviet Communism even before they ever visited the country speaks for itself.

The issue of Shaw's backing the Soviets as a potential ally against the rise of Fascism is a slightly different matter, for he was known to be sup-portive of both. At times his fascination with the most despotic leaders (Stalin as well as Hitler and Mussolini)[80] produced a shocking impression even on those who were among the closest in his circle of friends. Beatrice Webb, for instance, wrote in her diary:

78   Shaw, 'The Only Hope of the World', *The New Leader* (7 August 1931).
79   Maynard Keynes, 'Mr Keynes Replies to Mr Shaw', in *Stalin-Wells Talk*, 35–6.
80   See a revealing article by Stanley Weintraub, 'GBS and the Despots', *The Times Literary Supplement* (27 July 2011).

Shaw's apparent wholesale approval of Russian Communism is a little discounted
by his equally demonstrative admiration of Italian Fascism three years ago; their net
conclusion being that what he admires is neither of their several social ideals (seeing
that they are diametrically opposite, alike in economic principles and in metaphysical method), but their one common political constitution – the dictatorship of a
creed oligarchy, a way of government that not only disenfranchises but persecutes
those who object, in Russia to Communism, in Italy to capitalism. However, as I am
sympathetic to the social aim of Soviet Russia [...] – very different from my intense
irritation when listening to his [Shaw's] praise of Fascism![81]

It does seem that since the end of the First World War, Shaw had gone
from being a lone sane voice of pacifism at its outbreak in *Common Sense
About the War* (for which he was vilified as unpatriotic) to being disillusioned by the penal terms of the Versailles Treaty – an outspoken critic
of western governments and also of the very democratic process which he
seemed to have supported at the turn of the century. That led in turn to
a reverence for the figure of the strong individual, who had the power of
getting things done;[82] and in this respect, Shaw's veneration for Stalin was
only an extension of his earlier reverence for Mussolini, whom he had met
in the late twenties. Moreover, it has to be said that even after World War
II Shaw was remarkably forgiving of Hitler – perhaps to be expected of the
playwright, who was so influenced by Nietzsche's idea of the *Übermensch*
in *Also Sprach Zarathustra* when he wrote his own *Man and Superman*.

The audience with Stalin was the climax of Shaw's trip to Russia, and
he was very much looking forward to this meeting. As he claimed in his
speech in the House of Unions: 'Before I leave Moscow I intend, by hook
or by crook, that Stalin shall also become a living man to me and not merely
a name. Couldn't those of you who are personally acquainted with Stalin
ask him to help me out in this matter?'[83] At 8 p.m. on the evening of 29
July, he had his much coveted interview with the Soviet Leader, which

81   *The Diary of Beatrice Webb*, 28 July 1931, vol. 4, 248.
82   'Shaw Heaps Praise upon the Dictators; While Parliaments Get Nowhere, He Says,
     Hitler, Mussolini and Stalin Do Things', *The New York Times* (10 December 1933).
83   Shaw, Speech at the Moscow House of Unions, in *Collected Letters*, vol. 4, 257–8;
     Moscow News (28 July 1931).

lasted no less than two and a half hours. With him were Lord and Lady Astor, Lord Lothian and Maxim Litvinov. The honours of the occasion were won by Lady Astor, who, having no veneration for dictators or any awe of eminent persons, frightened the wits out of the interpreters during an interview with Stalin by asking the leader why he had slaughtered so many Russians. The interpreters were loth to translate this, nor did they do so until Stalin, observing their fearful embarrassment, demanded to be told what Lady Astor had asked. He took it very quietly, replying that some slaughter is inevitable when the constitution of a country is fundamentally disrupted. The violent death of a large number of people was necessary before the Communist state could be firmly established.[84] The entire content of Shaw's conversation with Stalin has never been revealed to the public. Foreign correspondents, impatiently waiting in the lobby of the Metropole Hotel for Shaw's return, were disappointed when the stately, white-bearded Irishman laughingly brushed them all aside and passed upstairs. 'He has a black moustache,' he called back mischievously, when half a dozen reporters eagerly plied him with questions about the evening. The varying accounts of the interview can be gleaned obliquely from the pamphlet *Stalin-Wells Talk*, a reprint of articles in the *New Statesman* by Shaw, Maynard Keynes, H.G. Wells and Ernst Toller, as well as from Shaw's other reports on the trip that appeared in the western press. His own verdict, however, was unequivocal: 'Stalin is one of the world's outstanding personalities. The Western World has nothing like him.'[85] Quizzical to the end, the British dramatist never changed this opinion throughout his life.

---

84   Sykes, *Nancy: The Life of Lady Astor*, 339. This version of the meeting was the one related by Shaw to his biographer, St John Ervine. Waldorf Astor conveyed it differently in his diary: 'Stalin evaded by quoting a case when some engineers had been convicted of intercourse with some foreign country with a view of sabotage, and assured her that he hoped the need for dealing with political prisoners drastically would soon cease' (quoted in Masters, *Nancy Astor, A Biography*, 173). The remainder of the interview involved a number of questions concerning Churchill and his adverse attitude to Russia.

85   'They Say – Reality in Russia', *The New York Times* (2 August 1931).

The sentiment was clearly reciprocated on the other side of the Iron Curtain, for none of his plays were ever included in the list of banned writings under the infamous decree 'On the Repertoire of Dramatic Theatres' (26 August 1946),[86] when the theatres were criticized for omitting ideological content, as well as for their predilection for a bourgeois foreign repertoire.[87] In 1946 Goslitizdat (The State Publishing House) reprinted a volume comprising Shaw's selected plays (with a significant print run of 50,000 copies), and the publication of his dramas continued even throughout the years of Stalin's ruthless anti-cosmopolitanist and anti-Westernist campaign (1948–1953).[88] During this time, Shaw's *Pygmalion* was staged at no fewer than eighty theatres all over the country, which was rivalled only by the communist best-sellers of Anatolii Safronov and Vadim Kozhevnikov, the literary editor of the *Pravda* newspaper.

Somehow Shaw learned about this and requested royalties – he was known to be very efficient and scrupulous in business; he never sold his rights to anyone and was much better informed in legal matters than the publishers whom he had to deal with. According to Hesketh Pearson, he was well aware that 'the money value of a work of art is what it will fetch

---

86   'O repertuare dramaticheskikh teatrov i merakh po ego uluchsheniiu', *Bolshevik*, 16 (1946); reprinted in A.N. Iakovlev, ed., *Vlast' i khudozhestvennaia intelligentsia. Dokumenty TsK RKP(b) – VKP(b), VChK – OGPU – NKVD o kul'turnoi politike. 1917–1953* (Moscow: Mezhdunarodnyi fond 'Demokratiia', 1999), 591–6.

87   In line with the new state cultural policy promoted by Zhdanov, the focus of attention was to be the Soviet man, depicted with all the virtues and heroism he had displayed during war-time.

88   The aggressive state-wide campaign was led by A.A. Zhdanov, the Secretary of the Central Committee of the Communist Party. In February 1948 he delivered a speech where he justified a radical turn from 'internationalism as a manifestation of certain socialist cosmopolitanism' to 'internationalism as an utmost expression of socialist patriotism' 'Internationalism originates from national, indigenous art' he claimed, 'to forget this is [...] to become a rootless cosmopolitan' (A.A. Zhdanov, *Vstupitel'naia reh' i vystuplenie na soveshchanii deiatelei sovetskoi muzyki v TsK BKP(b)* [Moscow: Gospolitizdat, 1952], 20) ('Интернационализм рождается там, где расцветает национальное искусство. Забыть эту истину – означает потерять руководящую линию, потерять свое лицо, стать безродным космополитом').

and has nothing to do with its merits as such. His *esprit de corps* was inflexible: to exact less than the market price of his work or to obtain a production by underselling his competitors was to him the crime of a blackleg [...] When his plays were demanded abroad, later on, he ascertained the highest fee paid to native authors and insisted on this for himself [...] This was the sort of trade-union triumph that he thoroughly enjoyed.'[89] But to ascertain the fees from Russia was a rather daring undertaking on his behalf. Neither tsarist Russia nor its Soviet successor joined the Berne copyright convention of 1886, and strictly speaking, the question of royalties was not on the agenda. Throughout the thirties, however, the Soviet authorities had their own mechanisms for remunerating their Western supporters, more precisely those in whom they were particularly interested. Thus, for instance, in July 1936, in preparation for his visit to the USSR, Lion Feuchtwanger was allocated 5,000 dollars for the screenplay of his trilogy *The Oppermanns*.[90] The screenplay was authorized by the writer but, in fact, produced by Serafima Roshal', a distant relative of Grigorii Roshal', the film director. Three years later, in July 1939, Feuchtwanger – a defiant adversary of the Hitler regime, now living in exile in France – was allocated another 35,000 francs for the screen adaptation of his anti-Nazi novel *Exile*, a most peculiar decision given the fact that the Molotov-Ribbentrop pact was signed just three weeks later.

Royalties, therefore, had never been paid directly, always remaining at the discretion of the system, but the British dramatist presented a rare exception to the rule. On 20 August 1949 the Foreign Policy Committee informed Stalin that the Art Committee of the Council of Ministers of the USSR (which was the line-manager of all theatres) expressed its consent to transfer 750,000 roubles to Mr Bernard Shaw as payment for the

89   Pearson, *Bernard Shaw: His Life and Personality*, 353.
90   The Politburo: memo regarding payment for the screenplay 'Semia Oppengeim', RGASPI, F. 17, Op. 163, Ed. hr. 1116, List 119–20; and Fond 17, Op. 163, Ed. hr. 1233, List 98; quoted in Leonid Maksimenkov, 'Ocherki nomenklaturnoi istorii sovetskoi literatury. Zapadnye piligrimy u stalinskogo prestola (Feuichtwanger i drugie)', part II, *Voprosy literatury*, 3 (2004), 332.

production of his plays by the Soviet theatres.[91] The decision was made at the request of the author (put forward during his conversation with the members of staff of the Soviet Embassy), as well as regarding his 'friendly attitude towards our country'. The payment was also supplemented by a relatively modest contribution of 90,000 roubles allocated from the budget of 'Khudozhestvennaia literatura' [Fiction] – one of the leading publishing houses of the state. This was an astronomical sum of money at the time, which immediately turned Shaw into one of the most highly paid Soviet dramatists. However, and not unreasonably, he was not interested in roubles, with which he had already had some trouble in the past when in 1922, due to strong inflation (the rouble was devalued 10,000 fold) all his savings were turned into nothing: 'I have a couple of million roubles in Moscow,' Shaw wrote to Frank Harris on this occasion, 'which cannot be sent to me because they are not sufficient to pay for a draft and a registered letter.'[92] Shaw therefore sent a letter to the Russian Embassy in London requesting conversion of his payment into pound sterling. The authorization was soon granted with a somewhat dubious exchange rate that resulted in £10,000 – still an enormous sum for these years – and the Soviet Ambassador Zarubin was instructed to arrange a meeting with Mr Shaw or 'in case there were no objections from the author, Mr Shaw was asked to provide details of the account to which the transfer could be made.'[93]

In this context, it is worth mentioning that this extraordinary incident coincided with the warm invitation to the First All-Union Congress for Peace Supporters in Moscow (25–27 August 1949) issued to Shaw (together with his Irish compatriot, the playwright *Sean O'Casey*) in exactly the same year. The 93-year-old Shaw declined the invitation; he was already too old to make the journey, but promised to send a welcoming address to

91   V.G. Grigor'ian, Note to Stalin, 20 August 1949, RGASPI, F. 17, Op. 163, Ed. hr. 1529, List 204; quoted in Maksimenkov, 'Ocherki nomenklaturnoi istorii sovetskoi literatury', *Voprosy literatury*, 3 (2004), 335–6.
92   Shaw, Letter to Frank Harris, 5 April 1923, in *Collected Letters*, vol. 3, 819.
93   Grigor'ian, Note to Stalin, RGASPI, F. 17, Op. 163, Ed. hr. 1529, List 204, quoted in Maksimenkov, 'Ocherki nomenklaturnoi istorii sovetskoi literatury', *Voprosy literatury*, 3 (2004), 335–6.

the Congress, thus once again affirming his long-lasting allegiance to the system. It has to be admitted that among the entire cohort of his fellow travellers to the Soviet Union, Shaw was, perhaps, the most loyal. Many of the others had already turned their back on Stalin's policies in the thirties, sliding peacefully into the domain of liberal politics like André Malraux and H.G. Wells, or causing conspicuous scandal in the process, like André Gide. Shaw, apparently, was unrepentant; up to the last days of his life he was convinced that Stalin was a man of very great ability – 'much more able than those who are running capitalism'[94] – and died with his portrait on the mantelpiece – a silent gesture of stoic loyalty that against all odds, or by some irony of fate did not remain downright unreciprocated. On 25 December 1952 Bernard Shaw's private photographer, John Graham, wrote to the Soviet Embassy in London, asking to pass a personal letter to Joseph Stalin. The letter also contained a photograph, made 13 August 1950 – the very last portrait of Bernard Shaw, taken when the playwright was already 94 years old. 'As a frequent guest at Shaw's house,' said the letter, 'I know how pleased he would have been if he had known that you have this photograph. Mr Shaw was a great admirer of your Highness.'[95]

94   '"We Are All Wrong", Says Bernard Shaw', *Moscow News* (8 August 1931).
95   John Graham, Letter to Stalin, 25 December 1952, RGASPI, F. 558, Op. 11, Ed. hr. 1703, List 1–2, quoted in Maksimenkov, 'Ocherki nomenklaturnoi istorii sovetskoi literatury, *Voprosy literatury*, 3 (2004), 336–7.

CHAPTER SIX

'Dear Liar': Shaw's Last Plays

> Rembrandt, Mozart and George Bernard Shaw are to appear on a series
> of stamps announced by the Russian Post Office to commemorate the
> thirty-ninth anniversary of the October revolution of 1917. Several pre-
> vious anniversaries of this event have resulted in issues of stamps, but
> hitherto the designs have been restricted to events and personalities of a
> domestic character or have emphasized the three-sided developments of
> Russia in a military, agricultural, and manufacturing sense. The depar-
> ture from custom for this oddly chosen thirty-ninth anniversary is the
> second occasion on which a British writer has been portrayed on a Rus-
> sian stamp.[1]

The Times correspondent may certainly be right in his ironic comment on
the 'oddly chosen' anniversary of the birth of the socialist country, but one
can hardly deny the worth of the gesture that marked a centenary of the
British dramatist and paid tribute to all his bona fide support for the Soviet
State. Shaw's 100-year jubilee was widely celebrated in international cultural
circles. London theatres renewed their productions of his major dramas;
on Broadway, one of the most well-known plays written by the dramatist
was turned into the musical best-seller of the century – *My Fair Lady*;
in Bulgaria, according to *The Times*, Shaw was included 'in a long series
of stamps honouring internationally famous figures in the arts,'[2] and The
Malvern Drama Festival held a Shaw centenary week. Established in 1929
at the initiative of Sir Barry Jackson, the Festival was dedicated specifically
to Shaw's creative output. Over the years a number of his plays had their
first performances at Malvern, including *In Good King Charles's Golden*

---

1   'G.B.S. To Appear on Russian Stamps', *The Times* (15 October 1956).
2   'G.B.S. To Appear on Russian Stamps', *The Times* (15 October 1956).

Days in 1939, *Geneva* in 1938 and the English premiere of *The Apple Cart*
(1929), which marked an important step in Shaw's rapport with Russia, for
in the words of Nancy Astor, it was this play that won him an invitation
for his legendary trip to the USSR.[3]

Outwardly the play presents a conflict between a squabbling cabinet
of Ministers, led by a hysterical Proteus, and the slippery King Magnus,
reluctant to be reduced to a mere constitutional dummy, with each side
trying to 'upset the apple cart' of their respective opponents. Framed in the
hermetic setting of a farce, the play offers a convenient platform for a discussion of the problems of power and in a capitalist economy; and although
it pits democracy against a presumed preference for monarchy, the essence
of the joke is that real power is positioned elsewhere. Britain precariously
survives as a clearing house for international capital, while politics emerges
as a thankless drudgery that attracts only ineffectual second-raters – these
are but a few ideas that reverberate through Shaw's witty piece of social
satire, which, given that it was set in the future, bears out that its author
was nothing if not ironically prophetic. The play's perspective is enthralling
and eerily timely, for what Shaw actually traced in *The Apple Cart* was a
world where giant corporations would become bigger than governments,
and American cultural colonialism would dominate the globe.

Almost six years separate *The Apple Cart* from his last historical drama,
St Joan (1923), and as Shaw put it in one of his letters 'it is as unlike St Joan
as it possibly can be.'[4] It is difficult to say why Shaw suddenly turned to the
genre of political extravaganza – a new milestone in his dramatic career;
but somehow he seemed to be very keen on the idea of forthright bravura.
The play was almost completed within eight weeks,[5] and on 2 February
1929 he wrote to Molly Tompkins:

3   Sykes, *Nancy: The Life of Lady Astor*, 325.
4   Shaw, Letter to Theresa Helburn, 8 February 1929, in *Collected Letters*, vol. 4, 129.
5   C.B. Purdom, *A Guide to the plays of Bernard Shaw* (London: Methuen & Co, 1963),
     285 and Laurence, Editorial comments to *Bernard Shaw Collected Letters*, vol. 4, 125.

When that endless book [*The Intelligent Woman's Guide*] was finished (the one you took as a personal insult), I thought I was finished, but when Barry Jackson announced a festival of my plays at Malvern in August next year, with nothing newer than Joan and Methuselah and Heartbreak House, I erupted like a volcano and simply hurled out a new play inspiringly entitled The Apple Cart.[6]

Figure 10   A Soviet postal stamp, issued for the centenary of Bernard Shaw (1956).

6   Peter Tompkins, ed., *To a Young Actress. The Letters of Bernard Shaw to Molly Tompkins* (New York: C.N. Potter, 1960), 131.

In March 1929 he was already reading extracts of the text to a small group of connoisseurs at Lady Astor's.[7]

The idea of the play was supplied to the author by Beatrice Webb (much earlier she had also provided an inspiration for *Mrs Warren's Profession*), who suggested that he should write a satirical piece on the shortcomings of British democracy and the inefficiency of its Labour Party in particular. 'What shall my next play be about?' wrote Shaw to Beatrice Webb. 'The Apple Cart, like Mrs. Warren, was written to your order.'[8] In the course of writing, however, the setting was extensively modified and expanded, and the only line that contained traces of the original thematic core, in the words of Shaw, was the opening dialogue between the royal secretaries, Pamphilius and Sempronius:

> Sempronius *père* was a false start. I began with a notion of two great parties: the Ritualists and the Quakers, with the King balancing them one against the other and finally defeating the combination of them. But I discarded this, as there wasn't room for it. However I thought the opening would make a very good Mozartian overture to get the audience settled down and in the right attentive mood before the real fun began: hence its retention. But the whole affair is a frightful bag of stage tricks, as old as Sophocles. I blushed when I saw it.[9]

Despite the author's coy rendition of the evening, the English premiere of the play was very well received, the leading parts being performed by Cedric Hardwicke (King Magnus) and Edith Evans (Orinthia). The

---

7   This follows from Shaw's correspondence with Mrs Patrick Campbell (Alan Dent, ed., *Bernard Shaw & Mrs. Patrick Campbell. Their Correspondence* [New York: Knopf, 1952], 283); also mentioned in Sykes, *Nancy: The Life of Lady Astor*, 108.

8   Shaw, Letter to Beatrice Webb, 5 September 1939, in Archibald Henderson, *George Bernard Shaw: Man of the Century* (New York: Appleton-Century-Crofts, 1956), 650. The play also suggests an effective parallel with the reign of George III – 'the patriotic king', known for his controversial opposition to the Ministers; a seminal monograph on this subject, authored by L.B. Namier (*The Structure of Politics at the Accession of George III* [London: Macmillan, 1929]) was released a couple of months before Shaw started working on *The Apple Cart* and was widely discussed in press.

9   Shaw, Letter to Sutro, October 1929, quoted in Pearson, *Bernard Shaw: His Life and Personality*, 390.

audience reacted well to Shaw's searching intelligence, liberating wit and his uncannily accurate vision of contemporary politicians, easily traceable in the motley array of his characters. Profoundly flustered Proteus clearly referred to Ramsay Macdonald; Lysistrata, Powermistress General, was seen as an amusing replica of Margaret Bondfield – the first woman Cabinet minister in the United Kingdom and one of the first three female Labour MPs; while Billy Boanerges, President of the Board of Trade, called to mind the eloquent speaker and socialist trade unionist John Elliot Burns.[10] According to *The Times*, the play was 'good entertainment';[11] and its success grew stronger by each consecutive performance: 'The Apple Cart went with a roar from end to end,'[12] wrote Shaw to Beatrice Webb straight after the first night at the Malvern Festival of 1939. His correspondent, however, was less assertive in her first impressions of the premiere. 'The evening before our Brighton visit,' she remarked in the diary,

> we saw The Apple Cart, that amusing and annoying satire on democracy. Magnus and his saying are d____d clever inventions of GBS's skittish political philosophy, or pretence of philosophy, for I don't believe that he seriously believes in the dictatorship as an alternative to the political democracy of Great Britain. What struck me as odd was a very minor note of sex, even in the interlude. Magnus's relation to Orinthia is that of a prudish philanderer, clearly incapable of sexual passion in the sense it is now exploited by the Aldous Huxley-D.H. Lawrence school of novelists. No wonder our brilliant nephew Malcolm dismisses GBS as 'early Victorian'.[13]

The critics also remained unconvinced by the virtues of the play's romantic digression, and the most nit-picking remarks fell on the scene showing the King cavorting with and being mocked by his mistress Orinthia. While commenting on the brilliant acting, and paying tribute to Shaw's gaiety and gusto, as well as his ability to write good parts for actors, they

---

10   St John Ervine, *Bernard Shaw: His Life, Work and Friends* (London: Constable, 1956), 517; Laurence, Editorial comments to *Bernard Shaw Collected* Letters, vol. 4, 45, 776.

11   'Mr Shaw's New Play', *The Times* (20 August 1929).

12   Henderson, *George Bernard Shaw: Man of the Century*, 650.

13   *The Diary of Beatrice Webb*, 2 October 1929, vol. 4, 195–6.

found Orinthia's attempt to turn their intellectual argument into sexual foreplay 'most tiresomely mannered'. *The Times* stressed that it was 'dull and pointless' to the extent that it was 'hard to imagine what persuaded Mr Shaw to write it' at all.[14] The deep irony, of course, lay in the fact that this very interlude, which apparently moved neither friends nor painstaking critics, was inspired by Shaw's own feelings for the actress Mrs Patrick Campbell,[15] and may well have accounted for the amusing exuberance and gusto that, according to the observers, was one of the most alluring features of this work. 'There may be no dramatic illusion,' claimed *The Times*,

> you may not care a snap of the fingers whether these people live or die; but their argument is so to speak 'good to read'. It is properly sharpened by satire. Backed by reason and, though damaged now and then by buffoonery, undistorted by prejudice, it is, moreover, extremely well delivered, and holds the stage as much by its easy and brilliant manner as by the solidity of the matter contained in it.[16]

After four productions at Malvern, the company moved to Birmingham, where all performances were sold out until the end of the season; and from 17 September *The Apple Cart* had a flourishing run at the Queen's Theatre throughout the year.

Over the next couple of years the play enjoyed considerable international acclaim. After its world premiere in June 1929 at the Polsky Theatre in Warsaw (*Wielki Kram*, in Polish),[17] which actually predated the Malvern production by two months, *The Apple Cart* was staged in many venues all over the world. Due to its peculiar political slant, it had a controver-

---

14   'Mr Shaw's New Play', *The Times* (20 August 1929).
15   Pearson, *Bernard Shaw: His Life and Personality*, 293; Shaw, Letters to Mrs Patrick Campbell, 6 April 1929 (*Collected Letters*, vol. 4, 132–3), 20 June 1929 (*Collected Letters*, vol. 4, 148–9), 11 July 1929 (*Collected Letters*, vol. 4, 151–2), 12 July 1929 (*Collected Letters*, vol. 4, 152–3).
16   'Mr Shaw's New Play', *The Times* (20 August 1929).
17   The premiere, in fact, did not go smoothly, according to Shaw's letter, 'the lady in Warsaw got stage fright and forgot her lines, making a mess of it, as far as I can ascertain, on the first night. It puzzled the audience considerably.' (Shaw, Letter to Mrs Patrick Campbell, 27 June 1929, in *Collected Letters*, vol. 4, 150).

sial reception in Germany, where the polemics between dictatorship and democracy acquired a particular urgency throughout the thirties. The play was premiered in Berlin on 19 October 1929, under the title of *Der Kaiser von Amerika* (*The Emperor of all America*), which apparently was the last directorial work of Max Reinhardt, a great admirer of Shaw's literary and dramatic talent, who after many years was saying farewell to the German Theatre. *The Times* reported that the play delighted the German audience, but 'confused the critics', who unanimously recorded the enthusiastic reception, and severally awarded the credit for it to the author, the actors, and the production of Herr Reinhardt. One distinguished critic says gloomily, 'Those who have walked with Shaw through half a century, must take leave of him here.'[18] Intrigued by the hostility of the reviews, Shaw made some inquiries about the staging only to realize that the text had, in fact, been severely modified by the director's hand, that several speeches had been inserted and that 'a lot of scandalous business' had been introduced. Infuriated by Max Reinhardt's liberties, he wrote a note to the press pointing out that 'R's Apple Cart is not my Apple Cart.'[19] Perhaps not surprisingly, the former Kaiser Wilhelm II (who at this time was living in the Netherlands in exile) was very enthusiastic about Shaw's new piece: 'it is a great play of the great satirist of our time,' he wrote, 'What a genius! What humour!'[20] At the same time, the Dresden municipal council was quick to ban the production at the local theatre on the grounds of its political controversy and an attempt to undermine 'republican ideals.'[21] The play also came under severe attack in the USA, where it was staged by Philip Muller at the Guild Theatre on 24 February 1930, with Tom Powers and Violet Campbell Cooper in the leading roles.

---

18 '"The Apple Cart" in Berlin', *The Times* (22 October 1929).
19 Laurence, Editorial comments to *Bernard Shaw Collected Letters*, vol. 4, 166.
20 Ervine, *Bernard Shaw: His Life, Work and Friends*, 110.
21 'The municipal fathers in Dresden decided that the play was subversive of republican ideals and that the production would be a real danger to young democracies. Shaw an unbridled Conservative!' ('The World of the Theatre', *Theatre Arts Monthly*, 14/3 [1930], 184).

In the Soviet Union, Shaw's reputation as a sage was, by contrast, greatly enhanced after the premiere of *The Apple Cart*. Although there was very little overt communism in this drama, it contained potent and destructive criticism of government by a parliamentary cabinet, and, consequently, of the liberal system. This made a positive impression on the Soviet authorities, and as Christopher Sykes puts it in his comments on the dramatist's visit to the USSR: 'Shaw was seen as a hero, for it was assumed that he must have shown considerable courage in producing and publishing such a play in a parliamentarily governed country, in defiance of the parliamentary police.'[22] The fact that its royalist aspect was completely, and perhaps suitably, condoned was, of course, not so surprising, for the ideological platform of *The Apple Cart* had little to do with the author's commendation of the indisputable assets of monarchy. The play bears witness to his impatience with democracy, as well as a growing belief in rule by 'a strong man', which the Soviet State was experiencing more and more overtly under the leadership of Josef Stalin.

What is therefore intriguing in the given circumstances was the practical inertia demonstrated by the Russian cultural authorities. With all their votes of confidence and acclaim, they were not quick to stage Shaw's new political satire at the major venues of the Soviet stage. Shaw's *Pygmalion* had been thriving at Soviet theatres since 1925, when it was first produced by the Leningrad Drama Theatre (a major production of this play was also mounted at the Moscow Maly Theatre in 1943). *Great Catherine* (under the title of *Reckless Catherine*), which ridiculed the now obsolete Imperial regime, was a popular choice straight after the Revolution. In 1920 a

22   Sykes, *Nancy. The Life of Lady Astor*, 325. Shaw, however, had always been respected by the Soviet *nomenklatura*. When in 1920 the English sculptress, Clare Sheridan had been commissioned to sculpt leading members of the fledgling Bolshevik cabinet, including both Lenin and Trotskii, she was struck by their high regard for Shaw, writing in the introduction to her memoir *Mayfair to Moscow*: 'I do not pretend to present a picture of Russia. I was only in Moscow where portrait work, not politics, was my concern. What I learnt about Bolshevism and the point of view of its leaders can come from illustrative remarks, often quite casually made, as for instance when I was solemnly asked one day what position Bernard Shaw would hold in the new Labor Cabinet, and they were surprised when I giggled' (Clare Sheridan, *Mayfair to Moscow – Clare Sheridan's Diary* [New York: Boni and Liveright, 1921], 11).

production of his *Man and Superman* was mounted briefly at the State Theatre of Comic Opera; and Meyerhold attempted *Heartbreak House* in 1921 (the setting was created by Sergei Eisenstein);[23] the plan, unfortunately, came to nothing, to the great regret of the director, who later on pointed out to his fellow colleagues: 'It is a shame that I did not stage Shaw's *Heartbreak House*.[24] I have been thinking of this wonderful play quite a lot; give me some decent actors, and I would stage it in three weeks right now and right away.'[25] There were some notable productions of *Caesar and Cleopatra*: in 1923 at The Leningrad Drama Theatre, and in 1934 as part of Aleksandr Tairov's topical montage that also included fragments of Pushkin's *Egyptian Nights* and Shakespeare's *Antony and Cleopatra*. In 1924 Tairov also created an avant-garde modernist version of *St Joan* at his Chamber Theatre, which was followed in 1933 by *The Devil's Disciple*, directed by Iurii Zavadskii in his Theatre-Studio. Zavadskii was a true admirer of Shaw's talent as a dramatist and commented on the unforgettable impression produced on him by his plays:

> I remember how fascinated and moved we were by the paradoxical nature and caustic sharpness of Shaw – the philosopher, and Shaw – the artist [...] In my opinion, he not only allows, but also appeals for a playful and daring directorial treatment of his works, an arrangement that would reveal all the defiant essence of his art. For the

23   S. Eisenstein, Setting and costume design for Shaw's *Heartbreak House*, with Meyerhold's comments on the characters, January-June 1922, RGALI, F. 963, Op. 1, Ed. hr. 870.

24   It is a great pity that in Russia there was no major production of *Heartbreak House* – the most 'Russian' of Shaw's plays; Estonia (Tallin) – 'boasts of the best production of this play' (Anna Obraztsova, 'Bernard Shaw and Russian Culture', in E.W. Connolly and Ellen M. Pearson, eds, *Bernard Shaw on Stage* [Guelph: University of Guelph, 1991], 55). Aleksandr Sokurov, a prominent Russian film director, responded to *Heartbreak House* in his incisive adaptation *Mournful Unconcern*. Banned in 1983 by the Soviet censors, it was released to the audience in 1987 (Birgit Beumers and Nancy Condee, eds, *The Cinema of Alexander Sokurov* [New York: Palgrave Macmillan, 2011], 242).

25   Aleksandr Gladkov, *Meyerhold* (Moscow: Soiuz teatral'nykh deiatelei, 1990), vol. 2, 145 ('Очень жалею, что не поставил "Дом, где разбиваются сердца" Шоу. Много думал об этой замечательной пьесе и с хорошими актерами мог бы сейчас поставить ее в три недели').

main feature of Shaw is his intolerance of philistinism, his fight with hypocrisy and lies with the flagellating weapon of irony.[26]

None of Shaw's major pieces, however, had been staged or revived specifically for his nine-day stay in the USSR in 1931. Moreover, the monograph on the life and work of the British dramatist (written by S.S. Dinamov), which was supposed to inaugurate his visit, but for some reason was delayed for about two months,[27] contained some severe criticism of Shaw's apparently 'opportunistic bourgeois position'. In his review of the book, published by *Izvestiia*, Lunacharskii maintained that:

> Shaw calls himself an old revolutionary, and refers to the fact that he read Marx from a young age. He refers to the 'biting' quality of almost each one of his plays. And indeed, the comediography of Bernard Shaw has always been sharp, caustic and anti-bourgeois. But the question is how one tends to bite. One can bite like a tiger and one can bite like a mosquito. Shaw's bites have always been very unpleasant; however, they are more the bites of a mosquito rather than those of a lion. Such a bite will never be a lethal one for the bourgeoisie. While understanding all the hypocrisy of the bourgeois, as well as the absurdity of the capitalist system, Shaw's major problem is his disbelief in the revolution: not only has he never promoted it, but he has disparaged and even mocked it. As a result, Shaw does not acknowledge this radical way of improving society. Using the power of his intellect and satire, he wanted to promote the idea of some intelligent associations, which may produce some powerful personalities, similar to King Magnus in his comedy 'The Apple Cart'.[28]

26   Iu. Zavadskii, 'O filosofskikh dramakh Shou i sovremennoi teatral'noi estetike', *Voprosy filosofii*, 11 (1966), 94 ('Помню, как восхитили и увлекли нас парадоксальность и едкая острота философа и художника [...] На мой взгляд, Шоу не только допускает, но и требует озорного, дерзкого режиссерского обращения с ним, такого, который выявлял бы воинствующую сущность его искусства. Ведь, главное в Шоу – его антимещанская непримиримость, борьба с лицемерием, ложью бичующим орудием иронии').

27   The typed manuscript of the article contained the following phrase, which was omitted in the published version: 'Originally, it was planned that the book would be launched at the time of Shaw's visit, but a bit of a delay would not do any harm.' (RGASPI, F. 142, Op. 1, Ed. hr. 209).

28   Anatolii Lunacharskii, 'The review of the book by S.S. Dinamov "Bernard Shaw"', *Izvestiia* (26 September 1931) ('Сам Б. Шоу называет себя старым революционером.

The authorities clearly had some reservations with regard to Shaw's flirting with communism and his advances towards the socialist system; as Lunacharskii pointed out in the article, so far the dramatist was only capable of giving some mild satisfaction to the people's frustration in order 'to preserve a faction of the oppositionists within the framework of the system. [...] Shaw's plays seem neither convincing nor appropriate for us, but his new outlook is already the first step along the staircase, leading up and to the left.'[29] Shaw was looked upon as a sympathetic fellow traveller, whose works were entertaining, ideologically probing, but not resounding enough to be recommended to the mass viewer; and it was not until the Brezhnev seventies – a time when unprecedented censorship had nearly killed the output of domestic authors,[30] that Shaw's *Apple Cart* finally found its way to the Soviet public.

Он ссылается на то, что смолоду изучал Маркса. Он указывает на кусательный характер почти всех своих пьес. Действительно, комедиография Б. Шоу была вся остра, едка и антибуржуазна. Но вопрос в том, как кусать. Можно кусать как тигр, и можно кусать как комар. Укусы Б. Шоу были очень неприятными укусами, однако более приближающимися к комариным, чем к львиным. От укусов Б. Шоу буржуазия никоим образом не могла умереть. Беда Б. Шоу в том и заключалась, что, прекрасно понимая лицемерие буржуазии, нелепость всего капиталистического строя, он вместе с тем отнюдь не верил в революцию, не звал к ней, даже осуждал ее, даже посмеивался над нею. Благодаря этому у Б. Шоу не осталось пути к коренному улучшению общества. Он хотел силой разума, силой насмешки убедить, что создадутся интеллигентные союзы, в которых, может быть, выделится какой-нибудь сильный человек, вроде Магнуса из знаменитой комедии "Тележка с яблоками"').

29   Lunacharskii, 'The review of the book by S.S. Dinamov "Bernard Shaw"', *Izvestiia* (26 September 1931) ('давать удовлетворение недовольству масс и тем самым удерживать их хотя бы в качестве оппозиционно настроенных в рамках целого [...] Пьесы Б. Шоу не являются для нас приемлемыми и убедительными, но с точки зрения его новой позиции это – уже первая ступень лестницы, ведущей вверх и налево').

30   When describing these years of unprecedented banning, Julian Graffy points out that films were 'found to contain too much drinking, too much bad language, or too many jokes. Andrei Smirnov's *Autumn* (*Osen'*, 1973) was found to contain too much

The play premiered on 28 March 1972 at the Leningrad Academic Theatre of Comedy, and was immediately commended as one of the best productions of the year.[31] The reviews praised Sergei Kokovkin in the role of Magnus, who displayed just the right mix of comic buoyancy and specific gravity, as well as Olga Volkova's Orinthia for her teasing loftiness and the refined tones with which she delivered Shaw's sparkling prose. Overall, the performance was distinguished by its 'joyful and daring theatricality', but the most flattering comments concerned the directorial work of Vadim Golikov, whose artistic dexterity and 'remarkable ingenuity'[32] won this show a very special place in the history of Shavian theatre.

As mentioned, in *The Apple Cart*'s satire on the British parliamentary system, the main character – King Magnus – conducts a risky game with his political adversaries, the ministers. In his usual paradoxical manner, Shaw, a left-wing socialist, makes the king the only sane character in the play. The essence of the paradox is that in the world of political corruption and headhunting for votes, the only person who is capable of free thinking is the one who in no way is dependent on financial capital – a monopoly corporation (the Pentland Firth Syndicate), the main sponsor of the country's politicians, and, in fact, the de facto ruler of the country itself. It was precisely this element of political play, conducted largely for the personal amusement of the participants rather than for the benefit of unsuspecting subjects, that Golikov intended to highlight in his outstandingly lucid production of *The Apple Cart*.

The action of the play was presented as a chess-match, which provided the perfect means to allegorize the power and ambition of the political game. A big chess-board was installed directly on stage, and throughout the action the royal secretaries were involved in a game, moving their chess pieces and at the same time exchanging comments on the 'strategic' moves performed by other characters in the play. Golikov recollected that at the

bad weather' (Julian Graffy, 'Cinema', in Catriona Kelly and David Shepherd, eds, *Russian Cultural Studies* [Oxford: Oxford University Press, 1998], 186–7).

31 V. Kalmanovskii, 'Zachem smeiat'sia?', *Smena* (8 June 1972); A. Romm, 'Telezhka s iablokami', *Vechernii Leningrad* (22 April 1972).

32 N. Pliatskovskaia, 'Telezhka s iablokami', *Teatr*, 1 (1973), 86.

beginning he thought of this device from a purely technical perspective – as a convenient trick to occupy these two, mostly static, figures in the play, who in comparison to other characters always seemed to be slightly out of action: 'I therefore outlined the task for these two, mostly passive, characters of the play who, apart from taking minutes at the meetings, did not have any other occupation in the course of the play. With the introduction of the chess-game, they could now take minutes in turns: while one was making notes, the other one was thinking out the next move.'[33] In the course of rehearsals, however, the metaphor was considerably elaborated and extended. The outline of a chess match accentuated the notion of opposing teams, which gave shape to the dramatic structure of the intrigue, and at the same time allowed the cast to find a symbol that incorporated all the complexity of its moral and political motifs. The King was seen as being metaphorically engaged in several simultaneous chess games with his ministers, but the latter were not free to devise their own moves: manipulated by the Pentland Firth Syndicate they were, in turn, identified with talking chess pieces – their armchairs were mounted on wheels, and they moved across the stage, being attached to their 'Ministerial seats'. The secretaries, on the other hand, were no longer regarded as a couple of helpless pawns. In the new context, they incarnated the idea of a 'political barometer', through which the strain and the pulse of the action were transmitted to the audience. This was a theatre within a theatre – a kind of internal mirror that reflected the true motifs of the characters and the emotional tension hidden behind the veneer of courtly etiquette. In the course of the play both games, the real one played by the secretaries and the symbolic one performed by the other characters, were foregrounded alternately and developed simultaneously, merging at times into an extraordinary multi-dimensional pattern.

33   'Interview with V. Golikov', *Teatral'nyi Leningrad*, 8 (1972), 9; also quoted in Vladimir Anzikeev, *Desiataia muza* (Moscow: Russkii shakhmatnyi dom, 2008), 21 ('Поначалу, – вспоминает Вадим Голиков, – я таким образом наметил сквозное действие лишь для этих самых пассивных персонажей, у которых по ходу пьесы не было никаких других занятий, кроме ведения протокола заседания. С появлением шахмат они уже протоколировали по очереди: пока один вел запись, другой обдумывал очередной ход').

The game played by the secretaries was, moreover, far from arbitrary. Everybody in the audience who possessed some basic knowledge of chess theory (and in Russia the proportion of this category had traditionally been quite high), was soon to realize that the opening of the match offered a classic Muzio gambit (a variation of a King's gambit), elaborated in the famous game between Chigorin and Davydov at the 1874 tournament in St Petersburg. This particular game was suggested to the director by the theatre chess-consultant Efim Stoliar, who, after careful consideration, decided to choose it as a perfect parallel to the dramatic twists and strategies employed in Shaw's play.

Golikov claimed that he would always keep the warmest memories of the company's tour in Riga, which by chance coincided with a chess tournament that took place in the city during this particular week. Having heard about a 'chess-comedy', the grandmasters decided to book the house for an evening outing; and, although many of them, according to Golikov, were not remotely interested in the virtues of the theatre, they were the most appreciative public the actors could dream of. All of them were scrupulously following all the nuances of the game, mapping it onto the actions of the characters and vividly reacting to their advances and 'faux pas'. Among the spectators was Mark Taimanov, the eminent International Grandmaster and World Championship quarter finalist. Upon arrival at the theatre, he was quick to grasp the chess diagram displayed in the playbill: 'I have not read the play,' he maintained, 'but judging from the opening, it should be a fascinating performance.'[34]

For all the efforts of the best grandmasters who had attempted to capitalize on this type of chess-debut, the Muzio Gambit usually leads to defeat (or a draw in the best possible scenario). From the first minutes, therefore, King Magnus (White) was shown to be pushed into a desperate game, with the Prime Minister Proteus (Black) in a very strong position, with a straightforward opportunity to blockade the King, to manoeuvre him into a stalemate and to force him to resign. In the hope of achieving a gainful exchange, neutralizing the major figures of the Black pieces and

34   Anzikeev, *Desiataia muza* (Moscow: Russkii shakhmatnyi dom, 2008), 22.

restraining their mobility, Magnus has to sacrifice a lot of material, but his chances of escaping a checkmate are considerably diminished. Not only does he receive little help from the figures of his colour, but at times he is clearly pushed into an epaulette checkmate created by his own lot.[35]

The action unfolds slowly, lingering on every move of the carefully executed middlegame, but suddenly a real hazard comes from an unexpected foe – in the last act, America decides to annexe Britain by announcing that it wishes to tear up the Declaration of Independence and become a colony again, with King Magnus as a puppet emperor. The country is already full of American ideas and American goods, so this union will, in fact, merely ratify what is already essentially a fait accompli. The King understands that the project is promoted by the clapped-out Cabinet of Ministers, which is almost totally in the pocket of big business; the people are too apathetic to vote, and the country will soon be reduced to a provincial outpost of the financial capital of the USA. This marks the turning point of the play: King Magnus finds an opportunity to escape 'to the queenside' (hence the interlude with his quick-minded mistress); he gets rid of 'the epaulettes' and then suddenly turns the match into an endgame – where, in classic tradition, he is no longer hiding on the back row, but is transformed into a strong piece ready to attack at the very centre.

The endgame theory is finite, and Magnus makes a number of well-calculated moves. Instead of accepting the ultimatum, he prefers to resign in favour of his son. This situation is totally acceptable for the Cabinet – the new King may be more agreeable than the old one; but, as a consequence of his resignation, the King intends to dissolve Parliament and call new elections. There is a whirlwind of panic among the ranks of the Ministers, for none of them are remotely capable of surviving the squabbles and bribes of another expensive campaign, without which their chances of being elected are practically nonexistent. And this is not the end of the

---

35   Epaulette mate is, in its broadest definition, a checkmate where two parallel retreat squares for a checked king are occupied by his own pieces, preventing his escape. The most common Epaulette mate involves the king on his back rank, trapped between two rooks. The perceived visual similarity between the rooks and epaulettes worn on military uniforms, gives the checkmate its name.

story – Magnus carries out his attack in the spirit of a standard endgame. He gives up all his titles and honours and acquires the status of an ordinary citizen – he becomes a pawn advancing rapidly to the eighth row in order to be promoted to power once again. He intends to present his candidature for the elections in the House of Commons, to form his own Party and to become a Prime Minister (or maybe even the President) of the united Anglo-American States. The Ministers are speechless, and after a long ponderous pause Proteus destroys the ultimatum in full silence, accepting his faction's defeat.

The final scene of the play, brilliantly performed by Sergei Kokovkin, who brought dash, style and a hint of melancholy to King Magnus in this epilogue, was also truly chess-like. It seemed that the King looked upon his success in terms of a Pyrrhic victory (in this respect, it is worth bearing in mind that the Muzio gambit, as mentioned, rarely results in anything better than a draw). The chess-board is nearly empty; and the King is too tired for another game, with very few figures on the board. And if the new game is lost, was there any sense in winning the old one? Finally, it is at this point that the Queen enters and casually invites her husband for a cup of tea:

THE QUEEN   Now Magnus: it's time to dress for dinner.
MAGNUS   [much disturbed] Oh, not now. I have something very big to think about. I don't want any dinner.
THE QUEEN   [peremptorily] No dinner! Did anyone ever hear of such a thing! You know you will not sleep if you think after seven o'clock.
MAGNUS   [worried] But really, Jemima –
THE QUEEN   [going to him and taking his arm] Now, now, now! don't be naughty. I mustn't be late for dinner. Come on, like a good little boy.[36]

According to the author's text, 'the King, with a grimace of hopeless tenderness, allows himself to be led away'. Shaw, apparently, was quite keen on his ending and made a lot of fuss when his instructions were violated in Max Reinhardt's production of the play:

---

36   Bernard Show, *The Apple Cart*, in *Collected Plays*, vol. VI, 374–5.

To miss this echo of the scene with Orinthia, the king going like a lamb with his unpretentious wife after fighting like a lion with the goddess – the most popular stroke in the whole play with the wives who drag their husbands to the theatre (the men always want to stay at home) was a miracle of maladress, of utter incapacity of handling serious work or even of understanding the public taste.[37]

This, nevertheless, was not how Golikov, or, perhaps, the censor, saw the ending – since clear vision into the future was always a major requirement of Soviet art. As if by accident, the Queen comes to the unattended chess-board. She takes a figure, and, after twisting it for a second, to the amazement of Magnus puts it back on the first vacant space, without the slightest idea that by doing so she has suggested a marvellously original start for a new opening, a new beginning and a new game.

Upon his return from the Soviet Union, Shaw seemed to be even more convinced of the advantages of the socialist experiment and continued to condemn the failures of western liberal democracy. His plays became overtly politically orientated, especially taking into account their extensive and ideologically charged prefaces. It seemed that in general he was moving in the direction outlined in Lunacharskii's ironically 'prophetic' article: 'Now, when the edifice of capitalism is disintegrating,' wrote *Izvestiia*,

and when on the edifice of socialism has been erected on the other side [...] an old and brilliant polemicist, the most talented comediograph of our time, the most famous of authors writing in the English language is trying to find his place on our side of the barricades [...] When we congratulated Shaw on his seventy fifth birthday, we gave a largely positive characteristic to his work. And we could do this with sincerity, as we have already seen him rising towards his new revolutionary outlook [...] It would be great if he himself would [...] point out the weaknesses and shortcomings in his former oppositional satirical activity, but if he does not rise to this venture, we ought to do it ourselves.[38]

37   Shaw, Letter to Siegfried Trebitsch, 31 January 1929, in *Collected Letters*, vol. 4, 167.

38   Lunacharskii, 'The review of the book by S.S. Dinamov "Bernard Shaw"', *Izvestiia* (26 September 1931) ('Теперь, когда здание капитализма начинает валиться и когда, с другой стороны, растет здание социализма [...] старый блестящий полемист, талантливейший комедиограф нашего времени и знаменитейший писатель,

And Shaw did diligently rise to this 'challenging task'. In the series of his plays of the thirties, one finds a parade of almost indistinguishable 'talking-heads' obsessed with politics and constitutional monarchy, and making bold flattering advances towards the beneficence of the Soviet regime. In the preface to *On the Rocks* (1933), for instance, he tries to justify Stalin's repression of the so-called 'enemies of the people'; and in *Geneva* (1938),[39] the western characters represent almost exclusively the forces of hypocrisy and indolence, while the Commissar is the proponent of happiness, arguing that 'Russia – Holy Russia – will save the soul of the world by teaching it to feed its people instead of robbing them.'[40]

The idea of democracy on the wane, disintegrating under inertia and the lack of practical thinking, runs through all Shaw's dramas of these years. In order to find an artistic form appropriate for his thoughts, he turns to the stylized grotesque of political-extravaganza, stripped of any elements of realistic portrayal. In these pieces the wildest fantasy is combined with bare journalistic precision, and the theatricality of the characters becomes conspicuously accentuated. The plays are saturated with touches of burlesque and slapstick comedy, characterized by freedom of style, and absurd situations, as well as vigorous and violent reactions.[41] For instance, in *Too*

пишущий на английском языке, отыскивает свое место с нашей стороны баррикады [...] Когда мы поздравляли Б. Шоу с его семидесятипятилетием, мы говорили, конечно, главным образом положительно о нем. Мы могли это делать тем более искренне, что видели его уже на высоте его нынешней революционной позиции [...] Было бы чрезвычайно хорошо, если бы он сам [...] указал на слабость и недостатки своей прошлой оппозиционно–сатирической деятельности, но если он этого не сделает, мы это сделать обязаны').

39   The play is set as an imaginary international show-trial of the almighty leaders, who bear the rather transparent names of Bombardone, Battler and Flanko.

40   Bernard Shaw, *Geneva*, in *Collected Plays*, vol. VII, 152.

41   In his insightful account of Shaw's productions in pre-revolutionary Russia, Laurence Senelick points out that Meyerhold had always 'viewed Shaw as an ironist, whose work would benefit from attention to its grotesque elements' ('"More Looked at than Listened to": Shaw on the Prerevolutionary Russian Stage', 94) and his productions of *You Never Can Tell* (1912) and *Pygmalion* (1915) were acclaimed for their theatricality, carnivalesque subversiveness, and 'occasional exploitation of commedia dell'arte style' (Obraztsova, 'Bernard Shaw and Russian Culture', 51).

True to Be Good (1931), the gentle heroine who is struck with illness, suddenly jumps out of bed and knocks out the burglar with a boxer-type punch in the chest; while Colonel Tallboys, annoyed by the excessive advances of the elderly lady, smacks her over the head with a readily found umbrella. All these abrupt gestures and farce-type techniques bring to mind the clowning anarchy of a Punch and Judy show, where the actions of the characters are in no way dictated by the demands of the plot. Similarly, in Shaw's pieces, various episodes are performed in the illogical spirit of outrageous bravura: bewilderment is piled on bewilderment, creating an effective parallel to the paradoxical lunacy of the world, with all its defiant madness and absurdity. Curiously enough, Shaw's devoted left wing friends were not in favour of his grotesque political sketches. During a weekend visit in 1931, Shaw once read the first act of *Too True to Be Good* to the Webbs. 'What an extraordinary "fantasy" of a play,' Sidney Webb wrote later to Beatrice, 'but the extreme cleverness seems to me wasted on what is practically no thesis.'[42] 'Leading nowhere,' she added, 'a characteristic in itself representative of the present lack of purpose and consequent restless disgust with human nature.'[43]

Too True to Be Good (1931) is commonly regarded as one of Shaw's most unpredictable comedies, with a talking microbe announcing sniffily before the interval that the action is 'virtually over', but the others will continue 'to discuss it at great length for two more acts.'[44] This virus is the healthiest and definitely the most sane creature among the characters, who are desperately trying to find their bearings in the mad-house of the topsy-turvy world. The play opens in a sick room, with a rich young woman, Miss Mopply, dying for the want of a purpose in life, an overbearing mother, and a peculiar nurse, who instantly lets in a burglar (her lover) aiming at Miss Mopply's jewellery. However, instead of calling the police, they all decide to escape the cosseting mother and to live off the proceeds of their own fortuitous burglary. Revelling in the idle opulence of fabulous luxury

---

42   Sidney Webb, Letter to Beatrice Webb, 17 June 1931, in *The Letters of Sidney and Beatrice Webb*, 351.

43   *The Diary of Beatrice Webb*, 18 June 1931, 245.

44   Bernard Shaw, *Too True to Be Good*, in *Collected Plays*, vol. VI, 455–6.

and total freedom, they soon realize that cocktails and cocaine offer no satisfaction. But the play offers much more than a virulent attack on the moral vacuity of wealth. Every aspect of the world portrayed is deeply corrupt and turned into its own parody: the diseases are engendered and spread by humans (the microbe whines that Miss Mopply has given him measles rather than vice versa); while the only healthy 'species' are in fact the viruses (and, perhaps, some patients in the hospitals, who are classified as sick). All characters seem to do exactly the opposite of their wills and wishes: there is a bible-reading soldier; a colonel, who is pushed into water-colour painting, for which he has neither ability nor liking; and a robber, who is actually an ordained preacher precisely because his father was an atheist. Life has become a hopeless clutter; and Shaw's point is not merely that money buys unhappiness, but that humankind has lost its compass, and the disillusioned post-War generation, with their disorientated souls and distorted values, spiral into a belief-free abyss:

AUBREY   Less than nothing, compared to the things I have done with your approval. I was hardly more than a boy when I first dropped a bomb on a sleeping vil-lage. I cried all night after doing that. Later on I swooped into a street and sent machine gun bullets into a crowd of civilians: women, children, and all. I was past crying by that time. And now you preach to me about stealing a pearl necklace! Doesn't that seem a little ridiculous?[45]

The only remedy against this failure Shaw sees in everyday labour, 'recommended' to all his characters by the author. The Prime Minister in *On the Rocks* (1933), for instance, is advised to charge his idle brain with some practical thinking, which, in Shaw's views, was missing as such in the daily routine of those belonging to the world of Western politics. As the dramatist put it in one of his public statements, published under the forbidding title *The Politics of Unpolitical Animals*:

We have discovered that parliament, the central parliament with the party system at work, is an unparalleled invention for preventing anything being done whatever. It has grown up historically as an instrument to prevent a country to be governed, and in that, of course, it's an entirely and thoroughly representative institution.

45   Bernard Shaw, *Too True to Be Good*, 504–5.

Not only have you got our parliament extinguishing every effort to get toward socialism, but out of that grew the Parliament of Man at Geneva, the League of Nations. That is supposed to be a democratic institution. When one nation sends its delegation to Geneva the next nation immediately sends another to checkmate that delegation and they are all there to prevent one another from doing anything, the typical being that of disarmament.[46]

The Millionairess, written in 1934 during the economic collapse of the Great Depression, is another example of Shaw's bizarrely hilarious analysis of out-of-control wealth and idleness, for which, he reckons, no cure can be found. Following the author's fantasy, his heroine finds a simple job in a hotel kitchen and in a little family-owned sweatshop, gets to the bottom of their business and turns everything into a big and profitable commercial enterprise. In this context, it is worth mentioning that the practical particularities of these episodes were partly derived from Beatrice Webb's early experience, when some fifty years ago she had worked briefly in a tailor's sweat-shop in the East End of London. Beatrice found Shaw's play neither amusing nor convincing, and in one of her letters put forward plainly to the author:

> Frankly, I do not like it. – perhaps I am too obsessed with our highly specialised work, or too lacking in sense of humour, or both. My complaint is, its intolerable ugliness. In the *Unexpected Island* and *Too True to Be Good* there is a strain of beauty, which compensates for, or balances, the burlesque situations and lampooned personalities. But in *The Millionairess*, every character is detestable, and every scene is an ugly farce – which seems to lead nowhere. Of course the dialogue is often witty and illuminating – but even there you are not at your best. I hope the distinguished actress will not accept the part and that you will not stage it. Anyway it is too short to be more than a curtain-raiser. Leave it to be discovered after your death, as a neglected spark from the genius Bernard Shaw![47]

---

46   'Shaw Heaps Praise upon the Dictators', *The New York Times* (10 December 1933) – excerpts from the stenographic report of Shaw's lecture before the Fabian Society in London *The Politics of Unpolitical Animals*.

47   Beatrice Webb, Letter to Shaw, 30 July 1935, *The Letters of Sidney and Beatrice Webb*, 407–8.

Curiously enough, Beatrice's negative comment about 'an ugly farce – which seems to lead nowhere' was very much to the point and managed to capture the key-note of the message that Shaw aspired to project through the dazzling bravura of his allegorical sketch.

The apocalyptic atmosphere saturating Shaw's dramas of these years seems to find its gloomiest manifestation in *The Simpleton of the Unexpected Isles* (1934). In the allegorical form of a play within the play, Shaw presents the idea of a demise of the mindless civilization that has already degenerated insofar as it can be no longer revitalized even through the power of eugenics (the experiments to create a viable breed of human beings result in some impaired offspring that personify the futile demagogical ideals of Love, Pride, Heroism and Empire). With the arrival of the ultimate Judgement Day, on which the criterion for survival is 'a useful life', it becomes clear that earthly inhabitants have nothing to declare. They have 'splendid words', the meaning of which they do not understand, a vast volume of 'beauty' and no 'intellect'. The essence of western civilization is represented by a little cowardly clergyman – a simpleton of the Unexpected Isles ('I am a futile creature,'[48] he divulges); and his name, Iddy (a diminutive for Idiot), does not require any further comment.

Shaw's plays of the thirties, nevertheless, contain a reference to the place unaffected by the perilous spirit of the capitalist society. *The Simpleton of the Unexpected Isles* finishes with the appeal that could stand as an epigraph to the entire series of his writings of the time:

PRA   All hail, then, the life to come!
PROLA   All Hail. Let it come.[49]

The new life and the new beginning are affiliated with the socialist experiment. The characters of the play *Too True to Be Good* dream of reaching the place called UFSS – The Union of Federated Sensible Societies – 'an

---

48 Bernard Shaw, *The Simpleton of the Unexpected Isles*, in *Collected Plays*, vol. VI, 810.
49 Shaw, *The Simpleton of the Unexpected Isles*, 840.

outlandish place in which even property is not respected,'[50] but their aspirations are in vain, for idle demagogues and bluffers are not welcome to the
efficient land of the UFSS people. The gap between these two societies is
unbridgeable, but the author has neither misgivings nor regrets about such
a pessimistic prospect. Liberal democracy, in his view, has already been
relegated to the past; the future belongs to another system; and the UFSS
destination in his drama is nothing but a thinly disguised reference to the
USSR. In this context, it is certainly worth drawing attention to a small
detail that suggests an indicative link between two seemingly unconnected
pieces, written by the dramatist more than a decade earlier. In *Too True
to Be Good*, the UFSS territory is closely associated with the country of
Beotia – a place where *Annajanska, the Bolshevik Empress*, was conducting
the revolution, back at the time of the 1917 upheaval.

TALLBOYS	What is the meaning of this? Whose passports are these? What are you doing with them? Where did you get them?
MEEK	Everybody within fifty miles is asking me to get a passport visa'd.
TALLBOYS	Visa'd! For what country?
MEEK	For Beotia, sir.
TALLBOYS	Beotia?
MEEK	Yessir. The Union of Federated Sensible Societies, sir. The U.F.S.S. Everybody wants to go there now, sir.
THE COUNTESS	Well I never!
THE ELDER	And what is to become of our unhappy country if all its inhabitants desert it for an outlandish place in which even property is not respected?
MEEK	No fear, sir: they wont have us. They wont admit any more English, sir: they say their lunatic asylums are too full already. I couldn't get a single visa, except [to the Colonel] for you, sir.[51]

Notwithstanding Beatrice Webb's stringent comment that Shaw's
Millionairess should never be put on, the entire series of his plays of the
thirties had a very successful run on the stage of the Malvern Festival and
abroad. The position with the Soviet cultural authorities was however rather

50   Shaw, *Too True to Be Good*, 523.
51   Shaw, *Too True to Be Good*, 523.

different. Although these plays were translated into Russian remarkably quickly, they were rarely (if at all) staged in Soviet times. For instance, *Too True to Be Good*, which in Britain only appeared in print in 1932, was translated into Russian the same year; the manuscript also contains a positive review of the play (dated January 1933[52]) provided by Glavlit and Glavrepertcom – the two major government bodies that controlled respectively all printed and staged output in the USSR. The same can be said about *The Simpleton of the Unexpected Isles*: the play was premiered in Britain in 1935, but its printed version was published only the following year. By December 1935, several months prior to its publication in the United Kingdom, the Russian translation of the play (made by Boris Lebedev, the husband of Sasha Kropotkin and a personal friend of Shaw) had already received its comments from the political editor of the governing bodies.[53] All these texts were subsequently released in the collected volumes of Shaw's writings; they were regarded as a 'good read' for those interested in drama, but too remote from the major concerns of the Soviet viewer. As luck would have it, however, and here yet again one cannot miss the irony of Beatrice Webb's remarks, the only exception to this rule was to be *The Millionairess*, which from the mid-sixties had a highly successful run at the major venues of the Soviet stage.

The choice, in fact, may not seem so surprising, for the play contains an alternative ending intended by Shaw specifically for the audience in 'countries with Communist sympathies.'[54] The comedy focuses on one of Shaw's favourite motifs: capitalism, represented by a strong woman – the wealthy heiress Epifania Ognisanti di Parerga, who embodies the unstoppable distaff drive that he used to associate with the Life Force. Dazzling Epifania is far too glamorous and far too restless for her husband, her lover,

---

52   B. Shaw, 'Plokho, no pravda' (*Too True to Be Good*); letters from Glavlit and Glavrepertcom, 2 October 1932–14 January 1933, RGALI, F. 656, Op. 1, Ed. hr. 3150.

53   B. Shaw, 'Prostak s ostrovov Neozhidannosti' (*The Simpleton of the Unexpected Isles*), translated by B. Lebedev; the letter from the Political Editor of Glavrepertcom, 13 November–17 December 1935, RGALI, F. 656, Op. 2, Ed. hr. 952.

54   Bernard Shaw, *The Millionairess*, in *Collected Plays*, vol. VI, 967.

and the suave gentleman she sets her sights on – an Egyptian doctor, with whom she has at least one thing in common: they are both determined to live up to their parents' deathbed wishes. Epifania promised her dying father she would only marry after her fiancé has turned 150 pounds into 50,000 in six months. For his part, the doctor promised his dying mother he would only marry a hard-working woman (his prospective bride had to earn her living 'alone and unaided for six months'[55]). Dedicated to caring for the poor and totally uninterested in money, the doctor is the other side of Epifania's money worshipping personality. He seems completely immune to her irresistible charms but not for long ('Of a surety,' he reckons, 'there is no wit and no wisdom like that of a woman ensnaring the mate chosen for her by Allah'[56]). In Shaw's talky romantic comedy everything concludes happily ever after, but, as the dramatist put it, only 'in capitalist countries' that never require an 'edifying moral. In Russia, however, and in countries with Communist sympathies, the people demand that the tale shall have an edifying moral. Accordingly, when the doctor, feeling Epifania's pulse, says that he loves it and cannot give it up, Blenderbland continues the conversation as follows.'[57] The author did not seem to have any difficulties in supplying the moral: in the idealistic fervour Epifania and the doctor speak of commencing a new life in Russia, while professing the advantages of socialist labour (so ardently promoted by the British author):

> I am a capitalist here; but in Russia I should be a worker. And what a worker! My brains are wasted here: the wealth they create is thrown away on idlers and their parasites, whilst poverty, dirt, disease, misery and slavery surround me like a black sea in which I may be engulfed at any moment by a turn of the money market. Russia needs managing women like me. In Moscow I shall not be a millionairess; but I shall be in the Sovnarkom within six months and in the Politbureau before the end of the year.[58]

Finally they give up the idea of travel and decide to stay where they are in the hope of converting the British Empire into a 'Soviet republic', which

55   Shaw, *The Millionairess*, 929.
56   Shaw, *The Millionairess*, 966.
57   Shaw, *The Millionairess*, 967.
58   Shaw, *The Millionairess*, 968.

would be far more beneficial for mankind, because the Russians effectively would not make any use of their efforts – 'they have stayed at home and saved their own souls. Ought not we to stay at home and save ours?'[59]

In Russia, *The Millionairess* was premiered on 5 September 1964 at the Vakhtangov Theatre in Moscow (directed by Aleksandra Remizova)[60] and at the Leningrad Komissarzhevskii Theatre, produced by Aleksandr Belinskii the same year. To some extent the production was inspired by the release of the eponymous film-comedy in 1960; directed by Anthony Asquith,[61] the film had a great success at the time, starring Sophia Loren and Peter Sellers in the leading parts. In the Moscow production, seductive, efficient and utterly insufferable Epifania was performed by Iulia Borisova. Played with a verve that was simultaneously appealing and daunting, her dazzling elegance and striking beauty brought to mind the graphic acting of Sophia Lauren. She was charming, demanding and so ruthlessly capable that she could take over everything from conversations to struggling businesses she did not even really want to own. 'Can one live with a tornado? with an earthquake? with an avalanche?'[62] called out in desperation Sagamore, Epifania's lawyer (Vladimir Osenev), for neither he, nor her earthbound husband (Anatolii Katsynskii), the champion boxer and a tennis player, had a minute of rest. All three men, including Adrian Blenderbland, Epifania's lover, deliberately played down their parts, so that this dynamic or, more precisely, 'dynamite-like' woman was constantly under the spot-light. Such a setting, apparently, struck more than a few resonant chords with the Soviet public, where the image of an emancipated woman managing a household of docile, not to say feeble, men has always been something of a cultural

59   Shaw, *The Millionairess*, 968.
60   In 1974 this stage production was turned into a very successful film, directed by Boris Nirenburg and Aleksandra Remizova.
61   In 1938 Anthony Asquith directed a highly successful screen adaptation of *Pygmalion*; Shaw, who has always been very sceptical about cinema, retained full control over screen play.
62   Shaw, *The Millionairess*, 962.

cliché.[63] For this reason, Vladimir Etush, who created a mildly eccentric portrait of Epifania's lover, even performed his role 'against type'. Contrary to the author's remarks on the character, which suggested 'an imposing man in the prime of life' with considerable aplomb,[64] Etush accentuated Adrian's fastidious resentfulness, coloured by the ironic premonition of trauma and the fatal deceit. His breakup with Epifania was hilariously swift; and when it did happen, then he turned his character into a rude annoying egoist – a real contrast to the benign character of the Egyptian doctor, performed by Iurii Iakovlev in elegantly soft, but strategically firm tones.

Needless to say, the production employed the alternative 'moral' ending, and an attempt was made to turn Shaw's dazzling farce into a social drama of a capable woman, deprived of personal happiness through her worship of money. However, it was, after all, the Khrushchev Thaw of the liberal sixties; and the compulsory veneer of ideological correctness could not eclipse the hilarious bravura of all kinds of mischief with the necessities and evils of moneymaking, skillfully cloaked in the prickly terms of the light romantic pursuit. (Even the comment 'Then you are either a fool or a Bolshevik'[65] was not cut out by the scrupulous hand of the Soviet censor.) It was a very successful production, full of magnetic energy and the carefully measured flickers of warmth, that remained in the Soviet theatres' repertoire for many years.

Unfortunately, Shaw never had a chance to see his play produced in the country that he supported so ardently, so persistently and despite the weight of public opinion. One can say that, in terms of his political allegiance, the question mark, which he placed in the title of the 1944 political tract *Everybody's Political What's What?* (the author's account of socialism and the way it changed throughout the years) was never applicable to his own position. In the twenties, he defended the socialist experiment against

---

63   In this respect one can name a number of popular films, released in the early sixties *The Striped Trip* (*Polosatyi reis*, 1961, directed by Vladimir Fetin), *A Hussar Ballade* (*Gussarskaia ballada*, 1962, directed by Eldar Riazanov) and *The Optimistic Tragedy* (*Optimisticheskaia tragediia*, 1963, directed by Samson Samsonov).

64   Shaw, *The Millionairess*, 900.

65   Shaw, *The Millionairess*, 923.

all its opponents and foes; and in the thirties supported every single step
of Stalin's policies, to the astonishment and horror of his closest friends.
In 1939, everyone else was appalled by the news about the Soviet-German
non-aggression treaty; and Beatrice Webb put a note in her diary describing it as an epitome of international immorality:

> Yesterday morning the front page in *The Times* and *Daily Herald* gave the sinister
> news that the anti-aggression pact between U.S.S.R. and Germany had been nego-
> tiated and that Ribbentrop is flying to Moscow to sign it. A horrible thought for
> the friends of the Soviet Union: it looks a complete reversal of the foreign policy of
> the U.S.S.R. – all the more discreditable because of its secrecy and obvious incon-
> sistency with the anti-aggressive protestations of the Soviet government at Geneva
> and elsewhere.[66]

Yet Shaw commended the reports in his note to *The Times*, 'The joyful news
came,' he pointed out, 'Herr Hitler is under the powerful thumb of Stalin,
whose interest in peace is overwhelming. And every one except myself is
frightened out of his or her wits!'[67] The day before, he had confirmed his
optimism in a letter to Nancy Astor, saying 'I wrote to The Times about
the absurd jitter when Stalin took Führer by the scruff of the neck [...] we
should celebrate the news with illuminations.'[68]

In the forties, however, with the end of the Molotov-Ribbentrop pact
and the Soviet Union's entry into the alliance against the Axis powers in
1941, his views suddenly became more politically correct. British public
opinion passed through a phase of total transformation. The brutality of
Stalin's regime and his seemingly treacherous alliance with Nazism were
forgotten, and the Soviet Union became almost an object of open adula-
tion. In cultural circles these changes became quite noticeable. The Left
Book Club was on the rise. It had been set up by Victor Gollancz, John
Strachey, Stafford Cripps and others to promote primarily non-fiction but
also some fiction, which took an explicitly left-wing line. In fact, its line

66   *The Diary of Beatrice Webb*, 23 August 1939, 438.
67   Bernard Shaw, 'Can Anyone Explain?', *The Times* (28 August 1939).
68   Shaw, Letter to Nancy Astor, 27 August 1939, quoted in Sykes, *Nancy: The Life of
      Lady Astor*, 412.

was effectively pro-Stalinist, and George Orwell, after having published *The Road to Wigan Pier* through the Club, but having had a preface added by Gollancz dissociating himself from Orwell's anti-Soviet views, found that the Club then refused his subsequent *Homage to Catalonia*, because of its attack on Stalinist elements in the Spanish Civil War. In an age when Beaverbrook could publish booklets of Pro-Soviet cartoons for the readers of the *Daily Mail*, it looked as if Shaw found himself in an unusual position as a spokesman in tune with public passion. But it was one of these rare (not to say unique) occasions when, driven by the pull of paradoxes, he actually did not try to turn the vector upside down. His response to the German invasion of Russia was highlighted by *The New York Times*: 'Only yesterday we and America were faced with the tremendous job of smashing Hitler – with Russia looking on smiling. Today, owing to the inconceivable folly of Hitler, we've nothing to do but sit and smile while Stalin smashes Hitler. Now we'll see what will happen. Germany hasn't a dog's chance.'[69]

These were very difficult years for the dramatist: his wife Charlotte passed away in September 1943, and four months earlier Beatrice Webb had died. Shaw nevertheless made a couple of appropriate gestures: he contributed to the press coverage of the war, having the Soviet war news delivered to him daily,[70] and sent a message to the Union of Soviet Writers commemorating the anniversary of Chekhov's death.[71] He also promoted the new edition of the Webbs' life-work, their treatise *Soviet Communism: A New Civilisation* – a reverential study of Britain's new-found ally, which appeared in October 1941; he wrote a commendatory article to accompany a photograph of the Webbs published in *Picture Post*. After the war, in 1946 he condemned Churchill's 'Iron Curtain' speech at Fulton, claiming that it was in fact 'nothing short of a declaration of war on Russia,'[72] and in response to the former Prime Minister's message in the same year

69 'Shaw Sees Hitler's Doom; "We've Nothing to Do but Sit and Smile," He Declares', *The New York Times* (23 June 1941).

70 Shaw, Letter to Ivo Geikie-Cobb, 21 January 1942, in *Collected Letters*, vol. 4, 626.

71 'George Bernard Shaw and J.B. Priestley send messages to Soviet Writers Union', *The New York Times* (16 July 1944).

72 'Europe's Capitals Stirred by Speech', *The New York Times* (7 March 1946).

congratulating him on the occasion of his ninetieth birthday, he did not
miss the opportunity to point out that: 'the rock foundation of all possible
systems is pure Communism, and the man who questions this knowingly
is no gentleman.'[73]

Shaw's ninetieth birthday was celebrated with unprecedented festivity.
In New York, a dinner, sponsored by *The Saturday Review of Literature*,
was held in honour of the dramatist and transmitted to the nation. Four
hundred people representing the literary world, the theatre, moving pictures
and radio came to the hotel room which 'was flanked by the American flag
and the British Union Jack and in the centere, with the flag of the Irish
Free State draped beneath, was Jacob Epstein's massive bust of Shaw.'[74] In
London there was a special jubilee performance of *Don Juan in Hell* at the
Arts Theatre. The BBC broadcast *The Man of Destiny* (with Eric Portman
and Jean de Casalis in the cast) and surprised the audience with an unexpected television appearance of the great playwright, who was lured into
filming at his house in Ayot St Lawrence by Denis Johnston. In its editorial
article, entitled simply 'G.B.S' – no further comments were required for
these celebrated initials – *The Times* highlighted that the dramatist

> 'stimulates the youth of to-day as vigorously as he stimulated the youth of half a cen-
> tury ago', and commented that the extravagant nonsense with which he trumpeted his
> ideas were not the tricks of a literary tradesman but were in truth the expedients of a
> preacher so much in earnest that he dared not be dull and decorous and unpopular.
> Implicit in all his antics was the unresting urge to preach an exhilarating faith in the
> living spirit of man.[75]

A Festschrift, *G.B.S. 90*, was issued by his publishers; and a large exhibition
on Shaw's life and work was organized by the National Book League. The
exhibition contained first editions of all Shaw's major works, many original
manuscripts (some of which were in shorthand); copies of the first-night
programmes of all his plays were borrowed from the Gabrielle Enthoven

---

73   Shaw, Letter to Winston S. Churchill, August 1946, in *Collected Letters*, 778.
74   'Untamed Shaw, 90, Snaps at All Who Stop by "to See the Animal"', *The New York
     Times* (26 July 1946).
75   'G.B.S.', *The Times* (26 July 1946).

collection and there were also photographs of many of the original productions. John Masefield, the Poet Laureate, who presided at the opening
event, ended it by reading the verses he himself contributed to *G.B.S. 90*:

> Honour him living, all earth's brightest brains.
> Order him statues; let us have more sense,
> And call the grand man great while he remains.[76]

while Dean Inge, an old friend of Shaw, drew attention to his social stance
in declaring that 'G.B.S. had tried, quite seriously, to show the English
what absurd people they were' and 'wondered if G.B.S. still had his friends
the Russians. If he did, he must have faith that could remove an iron
curtain.'[77]

The 'Russian friends' were also ready to rise to the occasion. In 1946
Gosizdat (The State Publishing House) reprinted a volume of Shaw's
selected plays, in response to which Shaw wrote a warm letter of gratitude, suggesting a possibility of literary exchange between the two countries.[78] Performances of his plays were staged throughout his birthday week
in virtually every major city of the USSR.[79] This was an unprecedented
celebration for a foreign author, considering above all the fact that the
Cold War was by now being waged. The Soviet response to the dramatist's
centenary, when it came a decade later, at least in terms of the number of
events mounted, was carried out on a somewhat lower scale,[80] especially as

76   'In Honour of G.B.S.', *The Times* (27 July 1946).
77   'In Honour of G.B.S.', *The Times* (27 July 1946).
78   G.B. Shaw, Letter on the publication of his works in the USSR and a possibility of
     cultural exchange, 11 May 1947, RGALI, F. 631, Op. 14, Ed. hr. 276; the reports on
     the jubilee edition were published in *The New York Times* (19 April 1947).
79   Laurence, Editorial comments to *Bernard Shaw Collected Letters*, vol. 4, 691–2.
80   Shaw did appear on a Soviet postal stamp, but otherwise the main emphasis was
     on Russian scholars' response to Shaw's work: Aleksandr Anikst published a major
     article 'How to Become Bernard Shaw. Instead of a Jubilee Article' (*Theatre*, 7 [1956],
     127–32); the All-Union State Library of Foreign Literature produced a bibliographical
     index on scholarly studies of Bernard Shaw (Obraztsova, 'Bernard Shaw and Russian
     Culture', 56), and there was a new edition of his selected plays (Moscow: Goslitizdat,
     1956).

compared, for instance, to the accolades given to the playwright in London and New York. Curiously enough, at the beginning of the nineteen sixties some distant notes of these American festivities acquired a very specific resonance in Russia, and were shaped into a show that was to become a major event in the history of the Soviet stage.

A year after Shaw's hundredth anniversary, Jerome Kilty, an American scriptwriter and actor, authored a dialogue-play, based on the correspondence of Bernard Shaw and the leading actress Mrs Patrick Campbell, who for almost thirty years remained Shaw's muse, inspiration and love.[81] The play was called *Dear Liar* – a teasing nickname, given to the British dramatist by the glorious actress. It had a reasonable success (52 performances) on Broadway in 1960, with Brian Aherne and Katharine Cornell forming its cast; and two years later at the Criterion Theatre in London. By this time, however, the play had already been seen in Germany (staged at the Renaissance Theater in Berlin in 1957) and in France, where under the title *Cher Menteur* it was adapted by Jean Cocteau for the Athénée Theatre in Paris. *Cher Menteur* was premiered on 3 October 1960; and a year later it won the Prix du Brigadier for Maria Casarès and Pierre Brasseur, who starred in the roles of Mrs Patrick Campbell and Bernard Shaw.[82] In 1961, *Dear Liar* premiered in the Soviet Union and immediately became a firm favourite. The country's most renowned performers competed to act in

81   As a playwright, Jerome Kilty was keen on epistolary drama, and his other notable
      writings in the genre included *Dear Love* (1969) – a story based on the poems and
      letters of Elizabeth and Robert Browning; and *The Ides of March* (1962) – an adap-
      tation of the novel by Thornton Wilder into both English and German (*Die Iden
      des Maerz*), which centred on fictitious correspondence, this time at the time of
      Julius Caesar. Although both plays were mounted in the USA and Europe (*The Ides
      of March* was staged at the Renaissance Theatre [Berlin] in 1962, at the Haymarket
      Theatre [London] in 1963 and then published by S. French [New York City] in 1970;
      Dear Love was first produced in Boston, MA, in 1969, then at the Alley Theatre,
      Houston, Texas in 1970, and later in London in 1973) none of them came remotely
      close to the international acclaim of *Dear Liar*.
82   In 1982 there also appeared a TV adaptation of *Cher Menteur* (directed by Alexandre
      Tarta), casting the French film-stars Jean Marais and Edwige Feuillère.

this play.[83] It was a sold-out production at the leading venues of Leningrad and Moscow, including the Moscow Art Theatre, where it remained in the repertoire for fourteen years.

The play came to Russia from Paris, where it drew the attention of Elsa Triolet, the Russian-born wife of the French Communist writer Louis Aragon. Elsa Triolet had considerable literary talent (she was the first woman to be awarded the Prix Goncourt in 1944) and extensive connections in the Russian cultural milieu: she enjoyed the friendship of Vladimir Maiakovski (who later had a long-term relationship with her elder sister Lilia Brik) and was in regular correspondence with Gorky. Having been moved by the bitter-sweet tragedy of *Dear Liar*, Triolet volunteered to translate the play for the Soviet super-star Liubov' Orlova, in case the latter would fancy taking the part. 'Dear Liuba,' she wrote to Orlova,

> I would like you to come to Paris to watch a play [...] I would be happy to translate it for you. It is a very special play. It is composed from the letters of Bernard Shaw and the actress Patrick Campbell, out of forty years of their correspondence. The dialogues are their own verbatim words, taken from the letters [...] The audience is captured by this curious feeling of truthfulness [...] they go through love, through life, through quarrels, through the war and death, youth and glory, aging and oblivion ... Cynical Shaw is in love and at her feet ... but he does not leave his wife. She too may well be in love, but could anyone be eternally in waiting? – she marries somebody else ... but the correspondence, the desire and their pseudo-friendship still goes on.[84]

83 The most recent revivals include those in The St Petersburg Theatre of Comedy (2000) and The National Theatre of Russian Drama in Kiev (2007). It was turned into two fascinating screen adaptations: in 1976, based on the Moscow Art Theatre production; and in 2001 starring Vasilii Lanovoi and Iulia Borisova – a dazzling and unforgettable 'millionairess' of the seventies.

84 G.V. Aleksandrov, *Kino i epokha* (Moscow: Izdatel'stvo politicheskoi literatury 1976), 258–9 ('Милая Люба [...] мне хочется, чтобы Вы приехали в Париж посмотреть одну пьесу [...] Я бы ее для Вас перевела. Пьеса особенная. Она смонтирована из писем Бернарда Шоу и актрисы Патрик Кемпбелл, из сорокалетней переписки между ними. Диалог – это их настоящие слова, взятые из писем [...] У зрителя странное ощущение правды [...] проходят любовь, жизнь, ссоры, война, смерть, молодость, слава, старость и забвение ... Влюбленный циник Шоу у ее ног ... Но жены не бросает! Она, может быть, и любит, но не ждать же всю

Mrs Patrick Campbell (Stella) first met Shaw in 1912, and at his request she (although by then forty-seven years old) originated the role of Eliza in *Pygmalion*. This encounter gave rise to a fervent, though platonic, love affair, and to a revitalizing inspirational relationship which ended only with her death in 1940, in France: 'Stella, Stella,' Shaw wrote in one of his letters to the actress,

> don't you KNOW that you are so exacting, so exciting, so absorbing, so incessant that only a wooden Highlander from a tobacconist's shop could bear the enormous strain of living with you? ... Of course you are a pair of mountebanks; but why, oh why do you get nothing out of me, though I get everything out of you? Mrs Hesione Hushabye in Heartbreak House, the Serpent in Methuselah, whom I always hear speaking in your voice, and Orinthia: all you, to say nothing of Eliza, who was only a joke. You are the Vamp and I the victim; and yet it is I who suck your blood and fatten on it whilst you lose everything![85]

From considerations of discretion, Shaw had always refused permission to publish their personal correspondence unless in a heavily edited form; and it was not until 1952 (a year after Shaw's death) that these letters were revealed to the public.[86] 'She was a great enchantress,' he recollected. 'how or why I do not know, but [...] she enchanted me among the rest.'[87]

Already in her late-fifties, and acutely aware of the twilight of her own (unparalleled to date) cinematic career, Orlova took the commotions of the ageing Stella Campbell close to her heart. She and her husband, the eminent film director Grigorii Aleksandrov, were a legendary couple. In

жизнь – она выходит замуж за другого ... а переписка, влечение, псевдодружба продолжаются').

85   Shaw, Letter to Mrs Patrick Campbell, 28 July 1929, in *Collected Letters*, vol. 4, 157.
86   Alan Dent, ed., *Bernard Shaw and Mrs. Patrick Campbell: Their Correspondence* (New York: Alfred A. Knopf, 1952); also published by Victor Gollancz (London 1952). The memoirs of Mrs Patrick Campbell, containing photographs and some edited letters, appeared in print earlier, in 1922 (Mrs Patrick Campbell, *My Life and Some Letters* (New York: Dodd, Mead and Company, 1922). On the relationship between Mrs Patrick Campbell and Bernard Shaw, see Margot Peters, *Mrs. Pat: The Life of Mrs. Patrick Campbell* (New York: Alfred A. Knopf, 1984), 369–78.
87   Shaw, Letter to Ada Tyrrell, 17 April 1940, in *Collected Letters*, vol. 4, 553.

the thirties, Liubov' Orlova starred in five musical comedies directed by Aleksandrov,[88] which instantly became Soviet classics; and in 1941 she was awarded the Stalin Prize for her major achievements in this field. Although Aleksandrov had never before ventured into the role of theatre director, he too became very keen on the production, which brought back some of the most cherished recollections of his distant youth. During his film-studies in Hollywood and Europe, he had met both Bernard Shaw and Mrs Campbell, and, was eager to recreate his first-hand impressions on stage. Back in 1929, he had paid a couple of visits to Shaw's country house at Ayot St Lawrence, and retained the warmest memories of the evening gatherings at Charlie Chaplin's, coloured by Stella Campbell's mesmerizing piano playing.[89] Both Orlova and Aleksandrov were very keen to start the rehearsals at the Mossovet Theatre (where Orlova was acting at the time), but the Soviet bureaucratic machine was not quick to commission a work from a foreign translator; and by the time that Elsa Triolet managed to complete her Russian adaptation, the play had already been premiered twice (though in a different translation by E. Golysheva and B. Isakov). In 1961 it was directed by Nikolai Akimov at the Leningrad Academic Theatre of Comedy, casting Elena Iunger and Lev Kolesov, and the following year – at the Moscow Art Theatre with two of the most illustrious Soviet actors, Angelina Stepanova and Anatolii Ktorov; *Izvestiia* claimed that 'Ktorov's performance is an artistic discovery without any exaggeration. He produced such an intelligent, kind and good-hearted, such an egoistic, ironic, and deeply sensitive Bernard Shaw, that it is now absolutely impossible to imagine him anything different from that.'[90]

88 *Jolly Fellows* (1934), *Circus* (1936), *Volga-Volga* (1938), *Bright Path* (1940); at the peak of Stalin's purges, the comedy genre was particularly favoured by the Soviet cultural authorities for what they considered its uplifting spirit and an optimistic outlook on the people's struggle towards socialist progress.

89 Aleksandrov, *Kino i epokha*, 259 ('Его исполнение – без преувеличения – художественное открытие. Он сыграл такого умного, доброго, сердечного, такого эгоистичного, ироничного, так глубоко чувствующего Бернарда Шоу, что никаким иным его теперь уже представить просто и невозможно').

90 Dmitrii Shcheglov, *Liubov' i maska* (Rusich: Olimp, 1997), 284.

Figure 11 A scene from Jerome Kilty's play *Dear Liar* (based on
Shaw's letters to Mrs Patrick Campbell), which has run on the Russian
stage for half a century (Mossovet Theatre production, 1963, Shaw
– Rostislav Pliatt, Mrs Patrick Campbell – Liubov' Orlova).

Aleksandrov recollects that the stakes became very high.[91] The administration of the Mossovet Theatre could hardly see any point in spending time on yet another version of the dialogue-drama that had already been presented to the public, and on top of everything stood for a new type of chamber theatre (completely unknown to the Soviet viewer) which left practically no room for manoeuvre in staging. Given the circumstances, the idea of creating an original adaptation seemed practically out of the question. As a professional film director, Aleksandrov had nevertheless always believed that action was more generally understood than words. Having been brought up in the tradition of the Hollywood 'silent movies', he split the entire text into a series of separate frames, giving minute instructions to the actors and specifying what exactly they should perform when uttering each and every phrase of their parts (the type-written text of his 'framing' turned out to be five times longer than the entire play):

> at the utterance 'Darling, do not be silly ...' Campbell puts downs the telephone receiver [...] at this very moment Campbell puts on her dressing gown in complete darkness, takes a little stool from under the sofa, lies down on the sofa, placing her feet on the stool [...] during this piece of information, Campbell puts on her earrings, necklace and spectacles, starts smoking a cigarette, using a lighter, and goes through her papers puffing the clouds of smoke.[92]

Such an emphasis turned out to be highly rewarding, for it created a rich layer of implicit subtext, so intimate to the Russian tradition of psychological significance in acting. While rehearsing the play, Aleksandrov briefly met Charlie Chaplin in Vevey (Switzerland),[93] coming back with a new array of

91   For a detailed account of this production see Aleksandrov, *Kino i epokha*, 257–66; Shcheglov, *Liubov' i maska*, 281–9; Aleksandr Khort, *Liubov' Orlova* (Moscow: Molodaia gvardiia, 2007), 300–14.

92   G.V. Aleksandrov, stage-script of 'Milyi Lzhets' (*Dear Liar*) by J. Kilty, RGALI,.F. 2921, Op. 3, Ed. hr. 259 ('На реплике "Дорогой мой, не валяйте дурака ..." Кэмпбелл кладет телефонную трубку [...] Кэмпбелл в это время в темноте надевает пеньюар, выдвигает скамеечку из-под дивана, ложится на диван, положив ноги на скамеечку [...] Кэмпбелл во время этого информационного текста надевает серьги, бусы и очки, закуривает папиросу, зажигая ее зажигалкой, и разбирает бумаги, пуская клубы дыма').

93   Charlie Chaplin also volunteered to compose music for the performance, but the project came to nothing; Igor Iakushenko created a soundtrack for the performance.

nuances which were immediately incorporated into the portrayal of Shaw: a waist-coat with seven buttons, and a habit of accentuating the pace of his speeches by tapping with the edge of his right hand on the palm of the left. Mikhail Romanov (Bernard Shaw), who belonged to Stanislavskii's school of emotional identification, masterfully employed his techniques when creating an image of the British dramatist, which was coloured with the humanistic pathos and the overtones of restrained romantic passion.[94] Aleksandrov recalled that there were two things that were absolutely banned from the performance – 'hysteria and explicit sentiments.'[95] The stage was almost empty, and there were no major props and imposing decorations, while the elaborate use of light and music called attention to the unspoken feelings and kaleidoscopic thoughts on aging, human creativity and the passage of time – so close to the heart of every man and every artist.

Dear Liar had a jubilant run on the stage of Russian theatres, surviving the severe censorship of the Brezhnev era, and the swingeing revisionism of post-Soviet times, and growing in reputation with each successive production down to the present day. Moving, sensitive, at times amusing and infinitely poignant, the play struck a chord with many generations of Russian viewers, affirming the triumph of love over time, wisdom over circumstances and illuminating humour over mortality. For more than half a century after his death and notwithstanding numerous changes of political regime, 'dear Liar' continued talking to 'his Russians', who accepted so unresentfully his unorthodox ideas cloaked in flippancy, his paradoxical plots and assertive women, his intellectual discussions and eclectic philosophy, as well as his life-long passion for the 'strange intensive culture of the Russian soul.'[96]

94   Regrettably, Romanov passed away in September 1963, a couple of months after the premiere of the play, and the role was taken over by Rostislav Pliatt. His Shaw was an absolute tour de force: eccentric, paradoxical and effervescently witty, he had marvellous skills of interacting with the audience, capitalising on its immediate reaction to his teasing jokes (Aleksandrov, *Kino i epokha*, 262).

95   Aleksandrov, *Kino i epokha*, 264.

96   Shaw, Letter to Maxim Gorky, 28 December 1915, in *Collected Letters*, vol. 3, 343.

Bibliography

Primary Sources

Gorky, Maxim, *Collected Works*, 25 vols, L.M. Leonov, ed. (Moscow: Nauka, 1968–1970)

—— *Collected Works (with portraits and facsimiles)*, 30 vols (Moscow: Khudozhest-vennaia literatura, 1949–1955)

——*Dans les bas-fonds*, E. Séménoff, trans. (Paris: Société du 'Mercure de France', 1903)

—— *Five plays: The Lower Depths, Summerfolk, Children of the Sun, Barbarians, Enemies*, Kitty Hunter-Blair and Jeremy Brooks, trans. (London: Methuen, 1988)

——*In the Depth*, W.H.H. Chambers trans., in Alfred Bates, ed., *The Drama: Its History, Literature and Influence on Civilisation* (London: The Athenian Society, 1903), vol.18, 279–352

—— *Nachtasyl, Szenen aus der Tiefe in vier Akten*, August Scholz, trans. (München: F. Marchlewski, 1903)

——*Pis'ma*, F.F. Kuznetsov, ed. (Moscow: Nauka, 1998)

——*Sommergäste*, August Scholz, trans. (Berlin: J. Ladyschnikow, 1906)

Shaw, Bernard, 'Annajanska, the Bolshevik Empress', in *Heartbreak House, Great Catherine, and Playlets of the War* (London: Constable and Company, 1919), 251–66

——*Annajanska, the Wild Duchess*, British Library, manuscript Add 66183 G

——et al., 'Assure New Russia of British Regard', *The New York Times* (1 April 1917)

——*Bernard Shaw Collected Letters*, Dan H. Laurence, ed. (London: Max Reinhardt, 1965–1988)

——'Bernard Shaw Says Russia Not Only Country Ripe for Revolution', *New York American* (24 February 1918)

——*Bernard Shaw: The Diaries, 1885–1897*, Stanley Weintraub, ed. (University Park, PA: Pennsylvania State University Press, 1986)

——et al., 'Britain Indorses Wilson's Address', *The New York Times* (4 April 1917)

——*Collected Plays with their Prefaces*, Dan H. Laurence, ed. (London: Max Reinhardt, 1971)

Annajanska, the Bolshevik Empress, vol. V, 229–50

The Apple Cart, vol. VI, 245–394

The Apple Cart, Preface, vol. VI, 249–79

Arms and the Man, vol. I, 387–472

Augustus Does His Bit, vol. V, 199–226

Back to Methuselah, vol. V, 251–713

Captain Brassbound's Conversion, Notes, vol. II, 418–30.

Geneva, vol. VII, 9–176

Great Catherine, vol. IV, 895–948

Heartbreak House, vol. V, 59–181

Man and Superman, vol. II, 489–803.

Man and Superman, Epistle Dedicatory, vol. II, 493–530.

Man and Superman, The Revolutionist's Handbook, vol. II, 735–80

Millionairess vol. VI, 847–969

Misalliance, Preface 'Parents and Children', vol. IV, 13–142.

Plays Pleasant, Preface, vol. I, 371–85

The Shewing-up of Blanco Posnet vol. III, 669–812

The Simpleton of the Unexpected Isles, vol. VI, 741–846

Three Plays for Puritans, Preface, vol. II, 11–48.

Too True to Be Good, vol. VI, 395–534

Widowers' Houses, Preface, vol. I, 35–132

—— 'Common Sense about the War', in *Current History of the European War. What Men of Letters Say* (New York: The New York Times Company, 1914) vol.1, 11–59

—— 'The Dictatorship of the Proletariat', in R. Palme Dutt, *George Bernard Shaw: A Memoir* (London: Labour Monthly, 1951), 15–30

—— 'Is Conscription Necessary or Advisable?', *New Age*, 18/26 (1916), 464–6

—— 'The Falling Market in War Aims', *The Daily Chronicle* (12 January 1918)

—— *The Intelligent Woman's Guide to Socialism, Capitalism, Sovietism and Fascism* (London: Penguin Books, 1937)

—— *Krasnaia Imperatritsa (The Red Empress)*, trans. Boris Lebedev (Moscow: Bereg, 1922)

—— Lecture delivered at the Independent Labour Party National Summer School, Digswell Park, 5 August 1931, *The New Leader* (7 August 1931)

—— Letters to Peter Kropotkin, 1 January 1902, 16 February 1905, 25 April 1905, GARF (State Archive of the Russian Federation), F. 1129, Op. 2, Ed. hr. 2816

—— Letter on the publication of his works in the USSR and a possibility of cultural exchange, 11 May 1947, RGALI (Russian State Archive of Literature and Art), F. 631, Op. 14, Ed. hr. 276

—— *More Common Sense about the War*, British Library, manuscript Add 63179–80

—— 'Mr. Bernard Shaw Comments', in *Stalin-Wells Talk* (London: *New Statesman and Nation*, 1934), 21–2

—— 'Mr. Shaw's Clash with Tolstoy', *Evening Standard* (6 February 1928)

—— 'Mr. Shaw on the Soviet', *The Times* 13 August 1931)

—— 'My Reply [to J.R. Westgarth's "How Stalin Bluffed Shaw"]', *Daily Express* (13 June 1932)

—— 'The Only Hope of the World'. Lecture delivered at the Independent Labour Party National Summer School, Digswell Park, 5 August 1931; *Fabian News* 42/9 (September 1931); *The New Leader* (7 August 1931)

—— 'Our Bookshelf: The Life of Tolstoy: Later Years', in *Bernard Shaw's Book Reviews*, Brian Tyson, ed. (University Park: Pennsylvania State University, 1996), vol.2, 254–8

—— 'Our Theatres in the Nineties: Duse and Bernhardt', in Diarmuid Russell, ed. *Selected Prose* (New York: Dodd, Mead & Company, 1952), 426–32

—— *The Perfect Wagnerite: A Commentary on the Ring of the Niblungs* (London: Grant Richards, 1898)

—— 'Plokho, no pravda' (*Too True to be Good*); letters from Glavlit and Glavrepertcom, 2 October 1932–14 January 1933, RGALI (Russian State Archive if Literature and Art), F. 656, Op. 1, Ed. hr. 3150

—— 'Prostak s ostrovov Neozhidannosti' (*The Simpleton of the Unexpected Isles*), translated by B. Lebedev; the letter from the Political Editor of Glavrepertcom, 13 November-17 December 1935, RGALI, F. 656, Op. 2, Ed. hr. 952

—— *Quintessence of Ibsenism* (New York: Bretano's, 1928)

—— *Razoblachenie Blanko Pozneta. Stsena v adu*, L.P.Nikiforov and V.M. Shuliatikov, trans. (Moscow: Izd. S. Dorovatovskogo i A. Charushnikova, 1911)

—— 'Russia's Interest in the War', *The Manchester Guardian* (7 July 1917)

—— 'Social Conditions in Russia', *The Manchester Guardian* (2 March 1933)

—— 'Socialism and the Labour Party' (National Guilds League lecture, 29 January 1920), in Bernard Shaw, *Practical Politics* (Lincoln and London: University of Nebraska Press, 1976), 160; *The New Common Wealth* (6 February 1920)

—— Speech at the Moscow House of Unions, 26 July, 1931, *Moscow News* (28 July 1931); *Collected Letters*, Vol.4, 256–8

—— 'That Realism is the Goal of Fiction', a lecture to the Blackheath Essay and Debating Society, 18 January 1888, *SHAW: The Annual of Bernard Shaw Studies*, 16 (1996), 111–18

—— 'Tolstoy: Tragedian or Comedian?', *The London Mercury*, 4 (1921), 31–4.

Tolstoy, Lev Nikolaevich, *Collected Works*, 90 vols, V.G. Chertkov, ed. (Moscow: Khudozhestvennaia literatura, 1928–1958)

—— Extracts from Unpublished Diaries, in *The Complete Works of Count Tolstoy 1904–1912*, Leo Wiener, trans. (Boston: Dana Esters & Company, 1905), vol. 23

—— *The Novels and Other Works of Lyof N. Tolstoï*, Aylmer and Louise Maude, trans. (New York: Charles Scribner's Sons, 1902)

    The Death of Ivan Ilyitch, vol. 14, 1–71

    Power of Darkness, vol.16, 234–337.

    What Is Art?, vol. 19, 339–543.

    What Is to Be Done?, vol. 18, 1–283

—— *O literature. Stat'i. Pis'ma. Dnevniki* (Moscow: Khudozhestvennaia literatura, 1955)

—— *Tolstoy on Shakespeare*, Vladimir Tchertkoff, trans. (New York-London: Funk & Wagnalls Company, 1906), 3–126

Webb, Beatrice, *The Diary of Beatrice Webb*, Norman and Jeanne MacKenzie, eds (London: Virago Press Limited, 1985)

—— and Sidney, *The Letters of Sidney and Beatrice Webb*, Norman Mackenzie, ed. (Cambridge: Cambridge University Press, 2008)

Secondary Sources

Aleksandrov, G.V., *Kino i epokha* (Moscow: Izdatel'stvo politicheskoi literatury 1976)

Alston, Charlotte, 'Tolstoy's Guiding Light', *History Today*, 60/10 (2010), 32–8

Andrew, Christopher, *Defence of the Realm: The Authorized History of MI5* (London: Alen Lane, 2009)

Anikst, Aleksandr, 'How to Become Bernard Shaw. Instead of a Jubilee Article', *Theatre*, 7 (1956), 127–32

Antonova, Irina, and Merkert, Jörn, *Berlin – Moskau. 1900–1950* (Moscow-Berlin-Munich: Prestel, 1995)

Anzikeev, Vladimir, *Desiataia muza* (Moscow: Russkii shakhmatnyi dom, 2008)

'"The Apple Cart" in Berlin', *The Times* (22 October 1929).

Arnold, Matthew, 'Count Leo Tolstoi', *Fortnightly Review*, 42/252 (1887), 783–99

Avtonomov, A., 'Bolshevskaia commune OGPU', *Nashi dostizheniia*, 7 (1930), 35

Batyushkov, F., 'Teatral'nye zametki. "Dachniki" – stseny M. Gorkogo v dramaticheskom teatre im. Komissarzhevskoi', *Mir bozhii*, 12/2 (1904), 14–23

Bennett, Will, 'How Shaw Defended Stalin's Mass Killing', *The Daily Telegraph* (18 June 2003)

Bentley, Eric, *The Life of Drama* (London: Methuen, 1965)

'Beotia', *Oxford English Dictionary*, <http://www.oed.com/view/Entry/20945?redi rectedFrom=Boeotia#eid>

Berberova, Nina, Kursiv *moi* (Moscow: Soglasie, 2001)

Bergquist, Gordon N., *The Pen and the Sword: War and Peace in the Prose and Plays of Bernard Shaw* (Salzburg: University of Salzburg, 1977), vol. 28

Bertolini, John A., *The Playwriting Self of Bernard Shaw* (Carbondale, IL: Southern Illinois University Press, 1991)

Berzak, I., 'Pervye piesy Gorkogo na zapadnoi stsene', *Teatr*, 3 (1937), 65

Besant, Walter, and James, Henry, 'The Art of Fiction', *Longman's Magazine*, 4/23 (1884), 502–21

Beumers, Birgit, and Condee, Nancy, eds *The Cinema of Alexander Sokurov* (New York: Palgrave Macmillan, 2011)

Bezelianskii, Iurii, 'The Revolution, Bernard Shaw and Mikhail Shatrov', *Alef*, 1002 (2010), <http://www.alefmagazine.com/pub2274.html>

Bian, R. Nisbet, 'Maxim Gorky, *Monthly Review*, 5 (1901), 172

Borras, F.M., 'Maxim Gorky the Writer', in Colin Chambers, ed., *Continuum Companion to Twentieth Century Theatre*, 325

Botsyanovskii, V., 'Kriticheskie nabroski', *Rus'* (5 February 1905)

Breitburg, S., 'B. Shou v spore s Tolstym o Shekspire' in *Literaturnoe nasledstvo* (Moscow: Akademiia Nauk SSSR, 1939), 617–32

Burns, James, 'Maxim Gorky: A Voice from the Depth', *Westminster Review*, 160/August (1903), 148–56

Calder, Robert Lorin, *W. Somerset Maugham and the Quest for Freedom* (London: Heinemann, 1972)

Calvin, Judith S., 'The GBSsence', *Shaw Review*, 5/1 (1962), 21–35

Carley, Michael Jabara, *1939: The Alliance that Never Was and the Coming of World War II* (Chicago: Ivan R. Dee Publisher, 1999)

——'Episodes from the Early Cold War: Franco-Soviet Relations, 1917–1927', *Europe-Asia Studies*, 52/7 (2000), 1275–305

——'Years of War in the East, 1939–45', *Europe-Asia Studies*, 58/2 (2007), 331–52

Carlyle, Thomas, *Chartism* (London: James Fraser, 1840)

Caute, D., *The Fellow Travellers* (London: Weidenfeld and Nicolson, 1973)

The Chambers Dictionary (Edinburgh: Chambers, 1998)

Chandler, Robert, 'An Introductory note to Andrei Platonov's *Fourteen Little Red Huts*', in *The Portable Platonov* (Moscow, GLAS Publishers, 1999), 110

Chappelow, Allan, *Shaw –'The Chucker-out'* (London: George Allen and Unwin Ltd, 1969)

Chesterton, G.K., *George Bernard Shaw* (New York: John Lane Company, 1909).

Chukovskii, Kornei, *Dnevnik 1901–1969* (Moscow: Olma-Press, 2003)

'Contemporary Life and Thought in Russia', *The Contemporary Review*, 47 (1885), 727–36

'Count Tolstoi's Life and Works', *Westminster Review*, 130 (1888), 278–93

'The Crisis in Russia', *The Times* (2 February 1905)

Dent, Alan, ed., *Bernard Shaw & Mrs. Patrick Campbell. Their Correspondence* (New York: Knopf, 1952)

Dillon, E.J., *Maxim Gorky, his Life and Writings* (London: Isbister and Company, 1902)

Dinamov, S.S., 'M. Gorky i Zapad', *Krasnaia Nov'*, 10–11 (1931), 225

Dole, Nathan Haskell, Preface to Ernst Dupuy's *Great Masters of Russian Literature* (London: J & R Maxwell, 1888)

Dunn, David, *Shaw's Russia: A Study of the Attitudes, Ideas and Beliefs of Bernard Shaw as They Affected and Were Modified by the Development of Soviet Russia* (PhD, 1984)

Dupuy, Ernst, *Great Masters of Russian Literature*, Nathan Haskell Dole, trans. (London: J&R Maxwell, 1888)

Edmonds, Rosemary, Translator's Introduction, in Leo Tolstoy, *Resurrection* (London: Penguin, 1966)

Eisenstein, S., Setting and Costume Design for Shaw's *Heartbreak House*, with Meyerhold's comments on the characters, January-June 1922, RGALI (Russian State Archive of Literature and Art), F. 963, Op. 1, Ed. hr. 870

Eksteins, Modris, *Rites of Spring: The Great War and the Birth of the Modern Age* (New York: Mariner Books, 1989)

Engels, Friedrich, *Friedrich Engels' Briefwechsel mit Karl Kautsky* (Wien: Danubia-Verlag, 1955)

——'Real Imperial Russian Privy Dynamiters', *Der Sozialdemokrat* (29 January 1885)

Ervine, St John, *Bernard Shaw: His Life, Work and Friends* (London: Constable, 1956)

'Europe's Capitals Stirred by Speech', *The New York Times* (7 March 1946).

Evans, Judith, *The Politics and Plays of Bernard Shaw* (Jefferson, NC: McFarland & Co Inc., 2003)

Filosofov, D., 'Zavtrashnee meshchanstvo', *Novyi put'*, 11 (1904), 328–32

Fischer, Louis, *The Soviets in World Affairs* (Princeton, NJ: Princeton University Press, 1951)

Fisher, David James, *Romain Rolland and the Politics of Intellectual Engagement* (Berkley: University of California Press, 1998)

Fitzpatrick, S., *Stalin's Peasants: Resistance and Survival in the Russian Village after Collectivization* (Oxford: Oxford University Press, 1994)

Fitz-Simon, Christopher, 'Shaw, George Bernard', in Chambers, Colin, ed., *Continuum Companion to Twentieth Century Theatre* (New York: Continuum Press, 2002), 685–6

Frank, S.L., *Russkoe mirovozzrenie* (St. Petersburg,: Nauka, 1996)

Garnett, Edward, *The Golden Echo* (London: Chatto & Windus, 1953)

——'Maxim Gorky', *The Academy*, 60 (1901), 497

'G.B.S.', *The Times* (26 July 1946)

'G.B.S. To Appear on Russian Stamps', *The Times* (15 October 1956)

'G.B.S. In Moscow and Leningrad', *Moscow News* (28 July 1931)

Geduld, Harry M., 'Bernard Shaw in Russia', in Bernard Shaw, *The Rationalisation of Russia* (Bloomington: Indiana University Press, 1964), 7–32

'George Bernard Shaw', *Oxford Dictionary of National Biography*, <http://www.oxforddnb.com/view/article/36047?docPos=1>

'George Bernard Shaw and J.B. Priestley Send Messages to Soviet Writers Union', *The New York Times* (16 July 1944)

Gerra, René, 'Ostalis' neuslyshannymi', *Literaturnaia gazeta* (7 October 2009)

Gibbs, A.M., *A Bernard Shaw Chronology* (New York: Palgrave, 2001)

Gladkov, Aleksandr, *Meyerhold (Moscow: Soiuz teatral'nykh deiatelei, 1990)*

Graffy, Julian, 'Cinema', in Catriona Kelly and David Shepherd, eds, *Russian Cultural Studies* (Oxford: Oxford University Press, 1998)

Graham, John, Letter to Stalin, 25 December 1952, RGASPI (Russian State Archive of Social and Political History), F. 558, Op. 11, Ed. hr. 1703, List 1–2

Griffith, Gareth, *Socialism and Superior Brains* (London: Routledge, 1993)

Grigor'ian, V.G., Note to Stalin, 20 August 1949, RGASPI (Russian State Archive of Social and Political History), F. 17, Op. 163, Ed. hr. 1529, List 204

Gromov, M.P., and Dolotova, A.M., *Perepiska A.P. Chekhova* (Moscow: Khudozhestvennaia literatura, 1984)

Gruzinskii, A.E., ed., *Pis'ma gr. Tolstogo k zhene (1862–1910)* (Moscow: A.A. Evenson, 1915)

Gusev, N.N., *Lev Nikolaevich Tolstoy. Materialy k biografii, 1855–1869* (Moscow: Akademiia Nauk SSSR, 1957)

Hardy, Florence Emily, *The Later Years of Thomas Hardy, 1892–1928* (London: Macmillan, 1930)

Henderson, Archibald, *Bernard Shaw: Playboy and Prophet* (London: D. Appleton and Co., 1932)

——*George Bernard Shaw: His Life and Work* (London: Stewart and Kidd Co., 1911)

—— *George Bernard Shaw: Man of the Century* (New York: Appleton-Century-Crofts, 1956)

Henley, W.E., 'Count Tolstoi's Novels', *Saturday Review* (1 January 1887)

——'New Novels', *The Academy*, 329 (1878), 186–7

Holroyd, Michael, Bernard Shaw, 5 vols (London: Chatto & Windus, 1988–92)

H'yus, E., *Bernard Shou* (Moscow: Khudozhestvennaia literatura, 1968)

'In Honour of G.B.S.', *The Times* (27 July 1946)

'Interview with V. Golikov', *Teatral'nyi Leningrad*, 8 (1972), 9

James, Henry, 'Ivan Turgénieff', *Atlantic Monthly*, 53 (1884), 42–55

—— 'The New Novel', in *Notes on Novelists and Some Other Notes* (New York: Charles Scribner's Sons, 1914), 328–9

Jones, Gareth, 'Famine Rules Russia', *The Evening Standard* (31 March 1933)

—— 'Millions Starving in Russia', *The Daily Express* (30 March 1933)

—— 'The Real Russia', *The Times* (14–16 October 1931)

—— 'The Two Russias', *The Times* (13–16 October 1930)

—— 'Will There be Soup?', *The Western Mail, Cardiff* (15, 17 October 1932)

Jones, J.W., 'A Mix of Members', *Parliamentary Affairs*, 33/1 (1979), 332–6

Kalmanovskii, V., 'Zachem smeiat'sia?', *Smena* (8 June 1972)

Karlinsky, Simon, ed., *Anton Chekhov's Life and Thought: Selected Letters and Commentary* (Evanston, IL: Northwestern University Press, 1997)

Keynes, John Maynard, 'Mr Keynes Replies to Mr Shaw', in *Stalin-Wells Talk* (London: New Statesman and Nation, 1934), 30–6

Khort, Aleksandr, *Liubov' Orlova* (Moscow: Molodaia gvardiia, 2007)

Komarova, V.D., and Modzalevskii, V.L., eds, *Lev Tolstoy i V.V. Stasov. Perepiska, 1878–1906* (Leningrad: Priboi, 1929)

Kropotkin, Peter, 'Anarchism', in *Encyclopedia Britannica* (Cambridge: Cambridge University Press, 1910), 918.

Kropotkin-Lebedeff (Lebedev), Sasha, Letter to Bernard Shaw, 27 February 1913, LSE Archives, F. SHAW/15/3, list 10–11

—— Letter to Bernard Shaw, 26 April 1914, LSE Archives, F. SHAW/15/3, list 13–14

Kugel, A., 'Dachniki', *Teatr i iskusstvo*, 46 (1904), 814

Laurence, Dan H., 'Approaching the Challenge', *SHAW: The Annual of Bernard Shaw Studies*, 16 (1996), 17–34

—— *A Bibliography* (Oxford: Clarendon Press, 1983)

—— Editorial Comments to *Bernard Shaw Collected Letters* (London: Max Reinhardt, 1965–88)

Lebedev (Lebedeff), Boris, Letter to Bernard Shaw, 14/27 October 1915, LSE Archives, F. SHAW/15/3, list 21–2.

'A Liberal's Impression of Russia', *The Times* (6 August, 1931)

Limedorfer, Eugene, 'The First Translation of Gorky's Work', *The New York Times* (27 July 1901)

Lunacharskii, Anatolii, 'Bernard Shaw', in Lunacharskii, A.V., *Collected Works* (Moscow: Khudozhestvennaia literatura, 1965)

—— 'Bernard Shaw, Our Guest', *Izvestiia* (21 July, 1931)

——'Review of the book by S.S. Dinamov "Bernard Shaw"', *Izvestiia* (26 September 1931

——'Review of the book by S.S. Dinamov "Bernard Shaw"', manuscript, RGASPI (Russian State Archive of Social and Political History), F. 142, Op. 1, Ed. hr. 209

Mackenzie, Norman, Editorial comments to *The Letters of Sidney and Beatrice Webb* (Cambridge, Cambridge University Press, 2008)

Maiskii, Ivan, 'Bernard Shou', *Novyi mir*, 1 (1961), 208–25

Maksimenkov, Leonid, and Barnes, Christopher, 'Boris Pasternak in August 1936 – An NKVD Memorandum', *Toronto Slavic Quarterly*, 6 (2003) <http://www.utoronto.ca/tsq/06/pasternak06.shtml>

——'Ocherki nomenklaturnoi istorii sovetskoi literatury. Zapadnye piligrimy u stalinskogo prestola (Feuichtwanger i drugie)', part II, *Voprosy literatury*, 3 (2004), 274–342

Marsh, Cynthia, *The File on Gorky* (London: Methuen Drama, 1993)

——*Maxim Gorky Russian Dramatist* (Bern: Peter Lang, 2006)

Marx, Karl, and Engels, Frederick, *Collected Works*, K.M. Cook, trans. (New York: International Publishers, 1990)

Massie, Robert K., *The Romanovs: The Final Chapter* (New York: Ballantine Books, 1996)

Masters, Antony, *Nancy Astor: A Biography* (New York: McGraw-Hill Book Company, 1981)

Matual, David, 'Shaw's The Shewing-up of Blanco Posnet and Tolstoy's The Power of Darkness', in Charles A. Berst, ed., *Shaw and Religion* (University Park: Pennsylvania State University Press, 1981), 129–40

Maude, Aylmer, *The Life of Tolstoy. Later Years* (New York: Dodd, Mead and Company, 1911)

——*Tolstoy on Art* (Oxford: Humphrey Milford Oxford University Press, 1924)

——*Tolstoy on Art and Its Critics* (Oxford: Humphrey Milford Oxford University Press, 1925)

Maugham, Somerset, *Ashenden or the British Agent* (Leipzig: Bernard Tauchnitz, 1928)

Mein [Tsvetaeva], Anastasiia, 'Iz knigi o Gorkom', in Anastasiia Tsvetaeva, *Collected Works* (Moscow: Izograf, 1996), vol. 1, 63–209

Merezhkovskii, D.S., 'Gorky i Chekhov' (1906), in *Maksim Gorky: Pro et contra: Lichnost' i tvorchestvo Maksima Gorkogo v otsenke russkikh myslitelei i issledovatelei. 1890–1910-e gody* (St Petersburg: Izdatel'stvo Russkogo Khristianskogo gumanitarnogo institute, 1997), 643–86

Morfill, William Richard, 'Literature', *The Academy*, 866 (1888), 364

'Mr. Shaw's New Play', *The Times* (20 August 1929)

Muggeridge, Malcolm, 'The Soviet and the Peasantry', *Manchester Guardian* (25, 27–28 March 1933)

'"Na dne" M. Gorkogo na stsene berlinskogo Malogo teatra', *Vestnik inostrannoi literatury*, 3 (1903), 282

'"Na dne" M. Gorkogo v berlinskom teatre', *Mir Bozhii*, 3/2 (1903), 81

Namier, L.B., *The Structure of Politics at the Accession of George III* (London: Macmillan, 1929)

Nazar'ev, V., 'Zhizn' i liudi bylogo vremeni', *Istoricheskii vestnik*, 11 (1890), 442–4

Nemirovich-Danchenko, Vladimir, *Izbrannye pis'ma* (Moscow: Iskusstvo, 1954)

Nicholson, Steve, *British Theatre and the Red Peril: The Portrayal of Communism 1917–1945* (Exeter: University of Exeter Press, 1999)

'O repertuare dramaticheskikh teatrov i merakh po ego uluchsheniiu', in A.N. Iakovlev, ed., *Vlast' i khudozhestvennaia intelligentsia. Dokumenty TsK RKP(b) – VKP(b), VChK – OGPU – NKVD o kul'turnoi politike. 1917–1953* (Moscow: Mezhdunarodnyi fond 'Demokratiia', 1999), 591–6

Obraztsova, Anna, 'Bernard Shaw and Russian Culture', in E.W. Connolly and Ellen M. Pearson, eds, *Bernard Shaw on Stage* (Guelph: University of Guelph, 1991), 43–59

——Obraztsova, A.G., *Bernard Shou i russkaia khudozhestvennaia kultura na rubezhe IX–XX vekov* (Moscow: Nauka, 1992)

Oleinikov, Dmitrii, 'Kumiry chitaiushchei publiki nachala stoletiia', *Rodina*, 3 (1998), 72

Ostwald, Hans, *Maxim Gorki* (London: William Heinemann, 1905)

'Panjandrum', in *Oxford English Dictionary*, <http://oxforddictionaries.com/definition/panjandrum>

'Peace or War', *Izvestiia* (9 October 1939)

Pearson, Hesketh, *Bernard Shaw: His Life and Personality* (London: Collins, 1943)

Peters, Margot, *Mrs. Pat: The Life of Mrs. Patrick Campbell* (New York: Alfred A. Knopf, 1984)

Pitcher, Harvey J., *The Smiths of Moscow* (Cramer: The Swallow House Books, 1984)

Platonov, Andrei, *Fourteen Little Red Huts*, Robert Chandler, trans., in *The Portable Platonov* (Moscow, GLAS Publishers, 1999), 112–78

Pliatskovskaia, N., 'Telezhka s iablokami', *Teatr*, 1 (1973), 86

The Politburo: memo regarding payment for the screenplay 'Semia Oppengeim', RGASPI (Russian State Archive of Social and Political History), F. 17, Op. 163, Ed. hr. 1116, List 119–20; Fond 17, Op. 163, Ed. hr. 1233, List 98

Purdom, C.B., *A Guide to the Plays of Bernard Shaw* (London: Methuen & Co, 1963)

Ralston, W.R.S., 'Novels of Count Leo Tolstoy', *Nineteenth Century*, 5 (1879), 650–69

Ransome, Arthur, 'Lenin and Shou', *Inostrannaia literatura*, 4 (1957), 24–6

Revoliutsionnyi put' Gorkogo (Moscow-Leningrad: Khudozhestvennaia literatura, 1933)

'A Revolution Playlet', *The Times* (22 January 1918)

Rogal, Samuel J., *A William Somerset Maugham Encyclopaedia* (London: Greenwood, 1997)

Rolland, Romain, 'Réponse à Constantin Balmont et à Ivan Bounine' (20 January 1928), in Romain Rolland, *I Will Not Rest* (London: Selvin & Blount Ltd, 1933), 180–7

Romm, A., 'Telezhka s iablokami', *Vechernii Leningrad* (22 April 1972)

'A Russian Criticism of Mr. Bernard Shaw', *The Times* (29 November 1913)

'Russian Players. The Moscow Kamerny Theatre', *The Times* (6 March 1923)

Senelick, Laurence, '"More Looked at then Listened to": Shaw on the Prerevolutionary Russian Stage', *SHAW The Annual of Bernard Shaw Studies* 27 (2007), 87–104

Senese, Donald, *Stepniak-Kravchinskii* (Newtonville, MA: Oriental Research Partners, 1987)

'Sergey Kravchinsky', *Oxford Dictionary of National Biography*, <http://www.oxforddnb.com/view/article/62226>

Sharp, W., 'New Novels', *The Academy*, 871 (1889), 22

'Shaw Eager to Visit Non-Capitalist Land', *The New York Times* (1 July 1931)

'Shaw Heaps Praise upon the Dictators; While Parliaments Get Nowhere, He Says, Hitler, Mussolini and Stalin Do Things', *The New York Times* (10 December 1933)

'Shaw's Last Days in Moscow', *Moscow News* (3 August 1931)

'Shaw Sees Hitler's Doom; "We've Nothing to Do but Sit and Smile," He Declares', *The New York Times* (23 June 1941)

Shcheglov, Dmtrii, *Liubov' i maska* (Rusich: Olimp, 1997)

Sheridan, Clare, *Mayfair to Moscow – Clare Sheridan's Diary* (New York: Boni and Liveright, 1921)

Slatter, John, *Russian Political Emigrants in Britain, 1880–1917* (London: Frank Cass, 1984)

'Soviet Editorial on Hitler Peace', *The New York Times* (10 October 1939)

Stalin, Josef, *An Interview with the German Author Emil Ludwig* (Moscow: Co-operative Publishing Society of Foreign Workers in the USSR, 1932)

'Stalin-Wells Talk: The Verbatim record', in *Stalin-Wells Talk* (London: New Statesman and Nation, 1934), 4–18

Stalin-Wells Talk: Written Transcript, RGASPI (Russian State Archive of Social and Political History), F. 558, Op. 1, Ed. hr. 3151, List 23

Stepniak-Kravchinskii, S.M., *Collected Works* (Moscow: Khudozhestvennaia litera-
    tura, 1958)

Suvorin, A., *Dnevnik* (Moscow: Novosti, 1992)

Sykes, Christopher, *Nancy: The Life of Lady Astor* (London: Collins, 1972)

Symons, Arthur, 'The Russian Soul', *Saturday Review* (3 May 1902)

Tairov, Aleksandr, Letter to Bernard Shaw, July 1932, RGALI (Russian State Archive
    of Literature and Art), F.1923, Op. 2, Ed. hr. 593

Tchaprazov, Stoyan, 'The Bulgarians of Bernard Shaw's *Arms and the Man*', *SHAW
    The Annual of Bernard Shaw Studies*, 31 (2011), 71–88

Tchaykowsky, N.W., Letter to Bernard Shaw, c. 1911, LSE Archives, F. SHAW/15/3, list 1

'Tolstoi's Views of Art', *Quarterly Review*, 191/382 (1900), 359–72

'Tolstoi's War and Peace', *The Literary World*, 17 (1886), 348–9

Tompkins, Peter, ed., *To a Young Actress. The Letters of Bernard Shaw to Molly Tomp-
    kins* (New York: C.N. Potter, 1960)

'Tribute from London', *The New York Times* (19 June 1936)

Turner, C.E., *Count Tolstoi as Novelist and Thinker* (London: Trübner and Co, 1888)

—— *Studies in Russian Literature* (London: Kessinger Publishing Company, 1882)

'U eksponatov kolkhoznogo muzeia', *Leninets* (21 September 1977)

'Untamed Shaw, 90, Snaps at All Who Stop by "to See the Animal"', *The New York
    Times* (26 July 1946).

'Visitors to USSR', *Moscow News* (18 July 1931)

de Vogué, Eugène, 'Les écrivains russes contemporaines', *Revue des Deux Mondes*,
    59 (1883), 786–821; 64 (1884), 264–301; 67 (1885), 312–56; 72 (1885), 241–79

—— *The Russian Novelists*, Jane Loring Edmands, trans. (Boston: D. Lothrop Com-
    pany, 1887)

'"We Are All Wrong", Says Bernard Shaw', *Moscow News* (8 August 1931)

Weintraub, Stanley, 'GBS and the Despots', *The Times Literary Supplement* (27 July
    2011)

Wells, H.G., *Russia in the Shadows* (New York: George H. Doran Co, 1921)

Whitman, Robert, *Shaw and the Play of Ideas* (Ithaca, NY and London: Cornell
    University Press, 1977)

Whyte, Frederic, *Life of W.T. Stead* (London: Jonathan Cape, 1925)

Wisenthal, J.L., *Bernard Shaw's 'The Quintessence of Ibsenism' and Other Related Writ-
    ings* (Toronto: University of Toronto Press, 1979)

Winsten, Stephen, *Days with Bernard Shaw* (London: Hutchinson and Co., London,
    1949)

Woodcock, G., and Avakumović, I., *The Anarchist Prince* (London, T.V. Boardman
    & Co, 1950)

'The World of the Theatre', *Theatre Arts Monthly*, 14/3 (1930), 183–4

Wright, Patrick, *Iron Curtain* (Oxford: Oxford University Press, 2007)
Zavadskii, Iu., 'O filosofskikh dramakh Shou i sovremennoi teatral'noi estetike', *Voprosy filosofii*, 11 (1966), 93–8
Zhdanov, A.A., *Vstupitel'naia reh' i vystuplenie na soveshchanii deiatelei sovetskoi muzyki v TsK BKP(b)* (Moscow: Gospolitizdat, 1952)

Index

Achurch, Janet 73, 74, 80
Akimov, Nikolai 209
Aleksandrov, Grigorii 207, 208, 209, 211, 212
Alexander II 14, 33
Alexandra Theatre 34
Arcos affair 136
Asquith, Anthony 200
Astor, Nancy 141, 143, 144, 145, 150, 157, 158, 159, 164, 169, 176, 178, 182, 202
Aveling, Edward 9, 13, 20

Bakunin, Mikhail 19, 24, 29
Ballets Russes 4
Balmont, Konstantin 139, 140
Barbusse, Henri 137, 141
Barrie, James 4, 102
Beerbohm Tree, Herbert 2
Bernhardt, Sarah 80
Besant, Annie 4, 12, 20, 44
Blok, Aleksandr 105
Bloody Sunday 32, 111
Brecht, Bertolt 1, 149
Brik, Lilia 207
Bunin, Ivan 139

Campbell, Stella 178, 180, 181, 206, 207, 208, 209, 210, 211
Carlyle, Thomas 15, 26, 27, 37, 38
Catherine the Great 3, 103, 104, 106, 115, 125
Chaliapin, Fedor 99, 165
Chamber Theatre (Kamernyi Teatr) 148, 149, 183

Chamberlain, William 161
Chaplin, Charlie 209, 211
Chekhov, Anton 4, 7, 8, 35, 41, 75, 76, 77, 81, 82, 85, 86, 87, 203
Chertkov (Tchertkoff), Vladimir 45, 54, 55, 56, 58, 61, 62
Chicherin, Georgii 128
Churchill, Winston 138, 169, 203, 204
Cocteau, Jean 206
Crimean War 32
Crosby, Ernest 54, 56
Cunninghame Graham, Robert 13, 32, 105, 122, 123

Darwin, Charles 25, 27, 38, 42
Darwinism 25, 27, 37
Dear Liar (by Jerome Kilty) 206, 207, 210, 211, 212
Devonport, Lord (Hudson Kearley) 89
Diaghilev, Sergei 4
Dinamov, Sergei 77, 184, 185, 191
Dostoevskii, Fedor 4, 35, 45
Dreyfus affair 137
Dukhobors 4, 54
Duse, Eleonora 80

Eisenstein, Sergei 183
Engels, Friedrich 14, 20, 21, 126
Erichsen, Vigilius 106

Fabian Society 4, 23, 28, 62, 137, 162, 195
Feuchtwanger, Lion 137, 141, 147, 166, 171
Five-Year Plan 135, 156, 157, 159, 162
Friends of Russian Freedom 4, 15, 16, 20, 21, 22, 32, 33, 35, 111

Galsworthy, John 77, 102, 142
Garnett, Constance 34, 35, 46
Garnett, Edward 35, 46, 76
George, David Lloyd 130
Gide, André 173
Girdlestone, Edward 25
Gladstone, William 13, 15
Golikov, Vadim 186, 187, 188, 191
Gollancz, Victor 123, 202, 203, 208
Gorky (Gorkii), Maxim 4, 6, 7, 8, 73, 74,
        75, 76, 77, 78, 79, 80, 81, 82, 83,
        84, 85, 86, 87, 88, 91, 92, 93, 94,
        95, 96, 97, 98, 99, 108, 113, 114, 115,
        116, 142, 152, 207, 212
    The Lower Depths 74, 77, 78, 80, 83,
        85, 95
    The Philistines 75, 77
    Summerfolk 8, 75, 82, 83, 84, 85, 86,
        88, 91, 92, 93, 94, 95, 96, 97
Granville Barker, Harley 71, 77, 102

Hardy, Thomas 46, 80, 81
Herzen, Aleksandr 14
Hitler, Adolf 6, 10, 35, 147, 167, 168, 171,
        202, 203
Hyndman, Henry 20, 23

Ibsen, Henrik 1, 49, 51, 69, 72, 73, 98
Illés, Bélla 146

Jackson, Barry 175, 177
James, Henry 1, 2, 12, 27, 43, 44, 51, 74,
        77, 139
Jones, Gareth 159, 161, 162

Kamenev, Lev 129
Kelly, Gerald 106
Kerenskii, Aleksandr 107, 114, 115, 130
Khalatov, Artemii 150, 151
Kilty, Jerome 206, 210, 211
Komissarzhevskii Theatre 84, 200

Korsh Theatre 34
Krassin, Leonid 129
Kropotkin, Peter 6, 9, 14, 17, 20, 28, 29,
        30, 31, 33, 38, 42, 46, 47, 105, 107,
        108, 109, 198
Kropotkin-Lebedev (Kropotkina-Leb-
        edeva), Sasha (Aleksandra) 33,
        105, 106, 107, 108, 109, 198
Krynine, Dmitrii 164
Ktorov, Anatolii 209

Lamarck, Jean-Baptiste 25
Laski, Harold 128, 144
Lebedev (Lebedeff), Boris 33, 34, 107,
        108, 112, 129, 198
Lenin, Vladimir 5, 8, 42, 99, 112, 117, 126,
        127, 128, 129, 131, 132, 133, 135, 141,
        154, 155, 158, 163, 164, 182
Leningrad (St Petersburg) Academic
        Theatre of Comedy 186, 207, 209
Leningrad Drama Theatre 182, 183
Litvinov, Maxim 145, 164, 169
Lothian, Lord (Philip Kerr) 143, 144,
        145, 161, 164, 169
Ludwig, Emil 137, 141
Lunacharskii, Anatolii 129, 138, 145, 146,
        147, 150, 154, 157, 184, 185, 191

MacDonald, Ramsay 167
Maiakovski, Vladimir 207
Maiskii, Ivan 112
Malvern Festival 36, 175, 177, 179, 180,
        197
Maly Theatre 182
Marx, Eleanor 9, 12, 13, 20
Marx, Karl 9, 12, 13, 14, 20, 21, 24, 42, 117,
        126, 166, 184
Masefield, John 205
Maude, Aylmer 4, 49, 50, 62, 63, 64,
        67, 72
Maude, Louise 50, 62

Maugham, W. Somerset 5, 106, 107, 108
Mazzini, Giuseppe 95, 96
McCarthy, Lillah 102, 110
Merezhkovskii, Dmitrii 42, 75
Meyerhold, Vsevolod 99, 183, 192
Mezentsov, Nikolai Vladimirovich 19, 27
Minskii, Nikolai 42
Molotov-Ribbentrop pact 33, 171, 202
Morris, William 12, 13, 17, 19, 20, 23, 55, 72
Moscow Art Theatre 77, 78, 79, 83, 84, 105, 149, 152, 207, 209
Moscow Dramatic Theatre 107
Mossovet Theatre 209, 210, 211
Muggeridge, Malcolm 162
Mussolini, Benito 10, 35, 36, 167, 168
Muzio Gambit 188

Napoleon 55, 70, 119
Nechaev, Sergei 14
Nemirovich-Danchenko, Vladimir 83, 84
New Dramatic Theatre 107
New Economic Policy (NEP) 9, 128, 135
Nicholas II 42, 54, 114
Nietzsche, Friedrich 25, 37, 168
Novikoff, Olga 13, 14, 15

Orlova, Liubov' 207, 208, 209, 210, 211
Orwell, George 10, 203

Pease, Edward 28, 29
Piatnitskii, Konstantin 83, 95, 96
Platonov, Andrei 152, 153
    Fourteen Little Red Huts 152, 153
Pliatt, Rostislav 210, 212
Provisional Government 99, 107, 114, 115, 118, 126
Pushkin, Aleksandr 6, 128, 183

Radek, Karl 145, 147, 150
Ransome, Arthur 5, 132

Reinhardt, Max 4, 36, 78, 79, 83, 94, 95, 181, 190
Remizova, Aleksandra 200
Rolland, Romain 137, 139, 140, 166
Romanov, Mikhail 212
Russell, Bertrand 5, 80

Scholz, August 78, 80, 83
Serebriakov, Esper 14, 22, 23, 28
Shakespeare, William 1, 44, 51, 53, 54, 55, 56, 57, 58, 59, 60, 61, 183
    Coriolanus 53
    Hamlet 58
    Henry IV 53
    King Lear 56, 57, 60
    Macbeth 53, 69
    Othello 58
Shaw (Payne-Townshend), Charlotte 15, 29, 48, 103, 144, 147, 148, 149, 154, 156, 157, 165, 203
Shaw, George Bernard
    Androcles and the Lion 67
    Annajanska, the Bolshevik Empress 8, 33, 101, 103, 104, 112, 116, 117, 119, 121, 122, 123, 124, 127, 130, 197
    The Apple Cart 36, 38, 144, 176, 177, 178, 179, 180, 181, 182, 184, 186, 190
    Arms and the Man 1, 2, 23, 27, 32, 34, 70, 104, 120, 121, 122, 123
    Augustus Does His Bit 68
    Back to Methuselah 8, 67, 71, 132
    Caesar and Cleopatra 71, 103, 107, 149, 183
    Candida 34, 37, 73, 88, 145
    Captain Brassbound's Conversion 123
    The Devil's Disciple 71, 183
    The Doctor's Dilemma 9
    Fanny's First Play 33, 68
    Geneva 5, 19, 36, 176, 192, 195, 202
    Getting Married 31

Great Catherine 3, 82, 101, 103, 124, 125, 182

Heartbreak House 1, 8, 71, 82, 83, 87, 88, 89, 90, 91, 92, 93, 94, 96, 97, 98, 101, 108, 177, 183, 208

Major Barbara 1, 37, 63, 71, 144

Man and Superman 36, 37, 52, 63, 64, 67, 72, 102, 168, 183

The Man of Destiny 70, 119, 204

The Millionairess 5, 195, 197, 198, 199, 200, 201

Misalliance 33, 83

Mrs Warren's Profession 1, 2, 34, 37, 145, 178

On the Rocks 192, 194

The Philanderer 52

Pygmalion 1, 33, 34, 37, 71, 107, 170, 182, 192, 200, 208

Saint Joan 1, 3, 67, 103

The Shewing-up of Blanco Posnet 64, 65, 66

The Simpleton of the Unexpected Isles 196, 198

Too True to Be Good 193, 194, 195, 196, 197, 198

Widowers' Houses 70

You Never Can Tell 68, 192

Shaw, George Bernard – articles and other works

Commonsense About the War 2

Everybody's Political What's What 201

The Intelligent Woman's Guide to Socialism and Capitalism 26

The Intelligent Woman's Guide to Socialism, Capitalism, Sovietism and Fascism 166

More Commonsense about the War 3

Quintessence of Ibsenism 25, 52, 98

The Perfect Wagnerite 50

The Rationalisation of Russia 135, 143

Tolstoy, Tragedian or Comedian 69, 71

Sheridan, Clare 5, 182

Shishko, Leonid 17

Sokolnikoff, Grigorii 166

Stalin, Josef 3, 5, 9, 10, 11, 33, 35, 99, 117, 140, 141, 142, 143, 147, 155, 158, 159, 163, 164, 165, 166, 167, 168, 169, 170, 171, 172, 173, 182, 192, 202, 203, 209

Stanislavskii, Konstantin 84, 150, 152, 212

Stead, William Thomas 13, 15, 48

Stepanova, Angelina 209

Stepniak-Kravchinskii, Sergei 6, 9, 14, 16, 17, 18, 19, 20, 21, 22, 23, 27, 28, 29, 35, 43, 46

Sukhotina (Tolstaia), Tatiana 63

Suvorin, Aleksei 41, 42

Taimanov, Mark 188

Tairov, Aleksandr 149, 183

Tchaikovskii, Nikolai 14, 15, 16, 29, 35

Tolstaia, Sofia 53

Tolstoy (Tolstoi), Leo (Russian: Lev Nikolaevich) 4, 6, 7, 8, 35, 41, 42, 43, 44, 45, 46, 47, 48, 49, 50, 51, 52, 53, 54, 55, 56, 57, 58, 59, 60, 61, 62, 63, 64, 65, 66, 67, 68, 69, 70, 71, 72, 76, 77, 81, 82, 105, 132, 152

Anna Karenina 46

The Death of Ivan Il'ich 69, 70

The Fruits of Enlightenment 67

My Religion 47

Power of Darkness 64, 65, 66, 67, 68

Resurrection 54, 61, 139

Shakespeare on Drama (Tolstoy on Shakespeare) 54

War and Peace 44, 47, 112

What Is Art? 49, 50, 51, 52

What Is to Be Done? 72

Tompkins, Molly 176, 177

Triolet, Elsa 207, 209

Trotskii, Leon 5, 147, 158, 182

Turgenev, Ivan 35, 43, 44

Vakhtangov Theatre 200
Volkhovskii, Felix 16, 35, 46
Voltaire 42, 55, 125
Voynich (Boole), Ethel 35

Webb, Beatrice 1, 3, 9, 24, 25, 129, 130, 131,
        137, 159, 163, 164, 166, 167, 168, 178,
        179, 193, 195, 196, 197, 198, 202, 203
Webb, Sidney 1, 3, 9, 19, 22, 24, 104, 122,
        129, 130, 131, 137, 145, 159, 163, 193,
        195

Wells, Herbert George 5, 7, 81, 99, 115,
        129, 135, 137, 141, 142, 143, 167,
        169, 173
Wilson, Charlotte 15, 113

Zasulich, Vera 19
Zavadskii, Iurii 183, 184
Zhdanov, Andrei 170

www.ingramcontent.com/pod-product-compliance
Lightning Source LLC
Chambersburg PA
CBHW071601110726
47908CB00007B/2200